A2 MEDIA STUDIES
The Essential introduction for WJEC

Developing key topics in depth and introducing students to the notion of independent study, this full-colour, highly illustrated textbook is designed to support students through the transition from AS to A2 and is the perfect guide for the new WJEC A2 Media Studies syllabus. Individual chapters, written by experienced teachers and examiners cover the following key areas:

- introduction: from AS to A2
- key concepts: genre, narrative, representation, audience
- developing textual analysis
- theoretical perspectives
- passing MS4: text, industry and audience
- passing MS3: media investigation and production
- epilogue

Especially designed to be user-friendly, *A2 Media Studies: The Essential Introduction for WJEC* includes activities, key terms, case studies, sample exam questions and over 120 full-colour images.

Antony Bateman is Head of Media and Film Studies at Wardle High School and was previously Creative and Media Diploma Programme Director for Rochdale. He is co-author of *A2 Media Studies: The Essential Introduction for AQA* (2010).

Peter Bennett is Senior Lecturer at the University of Wolverhampton's School of Education. He is the co-author of *A2 Media Studies: The Essential Introduction for AQA* (2010), *AS Communication and Culture: The Essential Introduction* (third edition, 2008), *A2 Communication and Culture: The Essential Introduction* (2009) and *Framework Media: Channels* (2004) as well as co-editor of *Communication Studies: The Essential Resource* (2003) and *Film Studies: the Essential Resource* (2006).

Sarah Casey Benyahia is a teacher and examiner of Film and Media Studies. She is the author of *Teaching Contemporary British Cinema* (2005) and *Teaching TV and Film Documentary* (2008) and co-author of *A2 Media Studies: The Essential Introduction for AQA* (2010), *AS Film Studies: The Essential Introduction* (second edition, 2008) and *A2 Film Studies: The Essential Introduction* (second edition, 2009).

Peter Wall is Chair of Examiners for GCE Media Studies. He is co-author of *A2 Media Studies: The Essential Introduction for AQA* (2010), *AS Media Studies: The Essential Introduction* (third edition, 2008) and *Framework Media: Channels* (2004), co-editor of *Media Studies: The Essential Resource* (2004), *Communication Studies: The Essential Resource* and *Film Studies: The Essential Resource* (2006), and author of *Media Studies for GCSE* (2007).

The *Essentials* Series

This series of textbooks, resource books and revision guides covers everything you need to know about taking exams in Media, Communication or Film Studies. Working together the series offers everything you need to move from AS level through to an undergraduate degree. Written by experts in their subjects, the series is clearly presented to aid understanding with the textbooks updated regularly to keep examples current.

Series Editor: Peter Wall

AS Communication and Culture: The Essential Introduction, Third Edition
Peter Bennett and Jerry Slater

A2 Communication and Culture: The Essential Introduction
Peter Bennett and Jerry Slater

Communication Studies: The Essential Resource
Andrew Beck, Peter Bennett and Peter Wall

AS Film Studies: The Essential Introduction, Second Edition
Sarah Casey Benyahia, Freddie Gaffney and John White

A2 Film Studies: The Essential Introduction, Second Edition
Sarah Casey Benyahia, Freddie Gaffney and John White

Film Studies: The Essential Resource
Peter Bennett, Andrew Hickman and Peter Wall

AS Media Studies: The Essential Introduction for AQA, Third Edition
Philip Rayner and Peter Wall

A2 Media Studies: The Essential Introduction for AQA, Second Edition
Antony Bateman, Peter Bennett, Sarah Casey Benyahia, Jacqui Shirley and Peter Wall

A2 Media Studies: The Essential Introduction for WJEC
Antony Bateman, Peter Bennett, Sarah Casey Benyahia and Peter Wall

AS Media Studies: The Essential Revision Guide for AQA
Jo Barker and Peter Wall

A2 Media Studies: The Essential Revision Guide for AQA
Jo Barker and Peter Wall

Media Studies: The Essential Resource
Philip Rayner, Peter Wall and Stephen Kruger

A2 MEDIA STUDIES:
The Essential Introduction for WJEC

Antony Bateman, Peter Bennett, Sarah Casey Benyahia and Peter Wall

Routledge
Taylor & Francis Group

LONDON AND NEW YORK

First published 2010
by Routledge
2 Park Square, Milton Park, Abingdon, Oxon OX14 4RN

Simultaneously published in the USA and Canada
by Routledge
711 Third Ave, New York, NY 10017

Routledge is an imprint of the Taylor & Francis Group, an informa business

Typeset in Folio and Bauhaus by
Keystroke, Station Road, Codsall, Wolverhampton
Printed and bound by CPI Group (UK) Ltd, Croydon, CR0 4YY

British Library Cataloguing in Publication Data
A catalogue record for this book is available from the British Library

Library of Congress Cataloging-in-Publication Data
A2 media studies: the essential introduction for WJEC / Antony Bateman
. . . [et al.].
p. cm. — (The essentials series)
Includes bibliographical references and index.
1. Mass media. I. Bateman, Antony, 1970–
P90.A225 2010
302.23—dc22   2010024812

ISBN 13: 978-0-415-58659-7 (pbk)
ISBN 13: 978-0-203-83566-1 (ebk)

CONTENTS

ILLUSTRATIONS

ACKNOWLEDGEMENTS

Every attempt has been made to obtain permission to reproduce copyright material. If any proper acknowledgement has not been made, we would invite copyright holders to inform us of the oversight.

Images

0.2   Courtesy of Company © The National Magazine Company Ltd
0.4   © Corbis
0.9a   Courtesy of Grazia © Bauer Media
0.9b   Courtesy of Cosmopolitan © The National Magazine Company
0.9c   Courtesy of She © The National Magazine Company
0.10a   Courtesy of Esquire © The National Magazine Company
0.10b   Men's Fitness © Copyright Dennis Publishing Limited
0.11a   Courtesy of FHM © Bauer Media
0.11b   Courtesy of Zoo © Bauer Media
0.12   GNU Free Documentation License, *Version 1.2*
0.17   © BBC (British Broadcasting Corporation)
1.3   *Dixon of Dock Green* © BBC Picture Archive, *The Bill* © Pearson Television Limited
1.6   © AFP/Getty Images
1.10   © AFP/Getty Images
1.11   © Andrew Williams
1.12   © Tim Graham/Getty Images
1.14   Men's Fitness © Copyright Dennis Publishing Limited
1.15   Men's Fitness © Copyright Dennis Publishing Limited
1.16   © EMAP
1.17   Heat © Bauer Consumer Media Ltd
1.18   Heat © Bauer Consumer Media Ltd
1.20   © Ben Piggot
1.21   © Disney/The Kobal Collection

1.22   *Radio Times* cover 1949 © Radio Times

1.23   The *Wiltshire Times* used with permission

1.24   Maslow's Hierarchy of Needs (from Maslow 1943) Source: *Psychological Review*, 50: 370–96

3.4a   © Getty Images

3.4b   © AFP/Getty Images

3.7   Courtesy of Cosmopolitan © The National Magazine Company Ltd

3.9   Lizzie Miller, as pictured in *Glamour* Magazine © Walter Chin / Marek & Assoc / trunkarchive.com

3.14   © Jerry Slater

3.17a   © Getty Images

3.17b   © AFP/Getty Images

3.19a   © Express Syndication

3.19b   © The Sun/nisyndication.com. Picture by: John Stillwell/PA Wire/ Press Association Images © PA Wire/Press Association Images

4.6a   © Express Syndication

4.6b   'London's Day of Terror' by Ian Mayes, 8 July 2005. Copyright Guardian News & Media Ltd 2005

4.8   'Dirty bomber's plot to hit stations and hotels' by Sean O'Neill and Adam Fresco, 7 November 2006 © The Times, and 7 November 2006/nisyndication.com

5.1   © Saga Publishing Ltd

Text

WJEC examination questions are reproduced by permission of WJEC.

All commentary and advice on tackling papers and questions is the responsibility of the authors of this book and has neither been provided nor approved by WJEC; furthermore the advice given does not necessarily constitute the only possible solution.

'Jordan and her big boobs should just bounce off' by Caitlin Moran, 7 December 2009 © The Times, and 7 December 2009/nisyndication.com

'Man sues over lack of "Lynx effect"', 30 October 2009, Orange News

The team of authors would like to give thanks to the following people who have all contributed to the making of this book: our editor at Routledge, Aileen Storry, our copy editor, Ann King, our production editor, Anna Callander and Jeremy Points for his helpful insight and comments.

HOW TO USE THIS BOOK

There are many reasons why you might be studying media at A2 level. One of these may be simply that you enjoyed the work that you did at AS level and wish to continue further with this study. That is probably one of the best reasons for being where you are. Studying a subject because you enjoy it is always a good way of ensuring you are successful and achieve good results. You may like to bear this in mind when you decide what you are going to do next, especially if it involves further study at university.

In writing this book, we are firmly of the belief that the most important aspect of your A2 study is to ensure that you are as fully engaged with the subject as is possible. You will read later about the importance of your own independence in exploring the media, its products, and the issues and debates that it raises. However, as examiners ourselves, we are not oblivious to the importance of your getting the best possible grade that you can as a result of your hard work on the course. A good grade is often a passport to a good university course or a rewarding job.

It is our belief that your engagement and enjoyment of Media Studies and achieving a good grade at the end of the course go hand in hand. Perhaps just as importantly, we believe that, regardless of whether or not you continue to a higher level, your GCE course will both inform and enhance your media consumption for the rest of your life. As the world becomes more and more media-saturated, an informed understanding of the issues that surround media production and consumption becomes an increasingly important facility in any walk of life.

The structure of our book has been designed with these thoughts in mind. The first part offers you an overview, a fairly broad look at the contemporary media landscape, its output and some of the many issues it raises. The second part is geared more specifically to helping you prepare for the assessment tasks required by the WJEC qualification. We hope you will find that this fairly straightforward distinction will help you get the best out of the book by allowing you to move from the general to the specific in terms of your course of study.

Bear this in mind as you navigate your way through the book. You will probably find that the second part of the book – assessment specifics – will become increasingly significant as you near the coursework deadline and the day of the exam itself.

INTRODUCTION: FROM AS TO A2

What kind of student have you become?

In most occupations, there exists from time to time the necessity to revue your performance. For education professionals this takes place through lesson observations, inspections and performance management. Health professionals are likewise given the once-over every so often in order to assess their work and to ascertain their suitability to continue practising. The purpose of these revue processes can generally be summarised by asking the question: What kind of teacher/doctor/advertising executive/film editor (delete as appropriate) are you? Although you are probably several years from entering a profession in which you need to undertake one of these appraisals, there is as you commence the next phase of your course as a media student the necessity to ask yourself a similar question. So here goes: 'What kind of student are you?'

We divide students into two categories – active and passive. It is often felt that passive students are a real pain to teach because they can be so heavily reliant on their teacher. They expect their teacher to do everything for them, including thinking, and ideally they would quite like their teacher to take the exam for them, providing of course that they managed to get a decent grade. Passive students are as a general rule less likely to do as well as they might expect at AS level because Media Studies is a discipline which seeks to reward students who do not rely on their teacher too heavily. It rewards the student who is prepared to think independently.

These students who think for themselves are called active students and you may be forgiven for forming the impression that teachers of Media Studies like active students. Well, you would be right. Active students are a pleasure to teach (although they can also be a pain, but for different reasons) because they want to know. They have enquiring minds that enjoy finding out about things. In Media Studies this should translate into a desire to seek out media texts and to try applying some of the ideas that have been explored in class to them. Always bear in mind that you are very lucky to be able to study the media. Media texts are nearly always accessible and nearly always enjoyable. These are the raw materials of your programme of study. This is certainly not bad when you can spend an evening watching Ant and Dec or going to the cinema and you can call it homework, provided of course that in this endeavour you are active and not passive!

With any luck, if you started without the level of autonomy that you need to be an active student, you will have developed this to some degree by the time you are studying at A2. If you have not, then here is a serious suggestion: go and do something else. Without the ability to learn independently, you are wasting your time doing A2 Media Studies. The whole of the A2 assessment is geared towards your ability to get up and do things for yourself. Relying wholly on your teacher is a great way to do badly.

Students who are willing to find things out for themselves and develop their skills of inquiry and independent learning are far more likely to thrive in Media Studies than those who rely solely upon what they learn in the classroom.

Figure 0.1 Students researching in the library

So why is this the case? Well, as you will read in the next section, the transition from AS study to A2 study is marked by a shift from textual analysis to an application of wider contexts and theoretical perspectives. Put simply, you are shifting away from textual study in its own right and looking at media texts in a broader way. You will have to look at the context in which media texts are produced and consumed. You will also have to look at some of the theoretical issues that underpin our study of the media at this level. This is a tall order.

Finally, in your AS level you have probably been nursed through your study by a caring teacher prepared to spend time with you when you needed extra help. This may continue over the next year as you embark upon your A2 course but the next stop is university where members of teaching staff are very unlikely to spend extra time with you. It is sink or swim once you get there. Active students make much better swimmers than passive students.

What you learned at AS level

If you are embarking upon a WJEC A2 course in Media Studies, you will have already studied the subject at AS level and possibly at GCSE level before that. In the future, you may well continue studying to degree level and on to a post-graduate level thereafter. As with all subjects, as you progress upward to a higher level it is always good practice to reflect upon your prior learning and remember that it forms a foundation for your current and indeed future learning.

Any A2 course of study is not simply more of the same; there is a significant upward step from the AS level. Although there are similarities between the two levels in terms of content, the WJEC A2 course in Media Studies poses greater challenge and the subject is examined in more depth. This book will help to guide you through the transition and help you meet the challenges of the A2 level course. However, to begin with, let us recap on some AS level learning.

Key concepts

The key concepts of Media Studies are the tools of the subject. In order to produce either a practical production or to analyse a media text or an issue, you need to be able to use the key concepts in much the same way that you need skills with woodworking tools before you can produce a table or a chair. It is knowledge of these key concepts and the ability to apply them which have enabled you to make the progress you have. The concepts and theories found in the study of media act as tools for productions and of analysis, and they help you to understand the media world.

For the course of study you are embarking upon for WJEC in Media Studies, the key concepts can broadly be identified as **language** (including text, genre and narrative), audiences, representation and industry.

Language is the most fundamental concept in Media Studies as it is through the use of language that meaning is attached to texts. Language incorporates all of the ways a text communicates its messages to the consumer. This communication may be both verbal (what is said or what is written) and non-verbal (all other ways of communicating including in the use of colour, font, body language, facial expression, etc.).

How much of the overall meaning of this magazine cover comes from verbal communication and how much comes from non-verbal communication?

The verbal communication is quite literally the words. The masthead tells us what the magazine is called and the use of strap lines at the sides of the cover tells us about the content.

However, the body language and facial expression of the model in the feature article photograph in the image and the use of colour and fonts also play an important part in communicating meaning to the consumer.

Figure 0.2 Hayden Panettiere on the cover of *Company* Magazine, September 2009

Recognition of what is verbal and non-verbal communication is only the first step in using the concept of language to analyse a media text. In order to deconstruct a media text and analyse the constituent elements such as colour, facial expression, use of font, etc., further tools are required and we must look to the study of semiotics for this. Each element of a media text has both a physical part (the signifier) and the meaning which is applied to the physical part (the signified). These two features can be equated to the terms 'denotation' (what is actually there in the text) and 'connotation' (the meaning).

So for the cover of *Company*, we can use semiotics as shown in the following example.

Signifier or denotation	Signified or connotation
The colour pink is used as the main colour.	The primary connotation of pink is femininity. This is the most likely use of the colour here given the nature of the magazine. However, it would be wrong to simply say that pink is used for femininity alone. The darker pink, almost red colour of the model's dress coupled with her confident and sexy stance suggests a much more self-assured and modern connotation of femininity than the more 'girly' pink used in some of the written text. The connotation of a stronger, more confident and sexy femininity offers an interesting juxtaposition to the more sober masthead and background, a simple font in black on plain white.

When analysing texts in this way, it is highly likely that there will among your fellow students be a degree of disagreement over your interpretations. This is perfectly fine, as there are often texts which have more than one possible connotation or meaning. Such a text is called an open text as opposed to a closed text where the meaning is more obvious. There is no doubt that all of the constituent features come together in the *Company* magazine cover to produce a text with little or no ambiguity. Therefore it is a closed text. However, the meanings behind some texts are less obvious and so different interpretations are likely. The important thing when analysing a text and concluding that there is a certain connotation is that you are able to provide evidence or a justification for it. Figure 0.3 will help you through the process of applying meanings to texts.

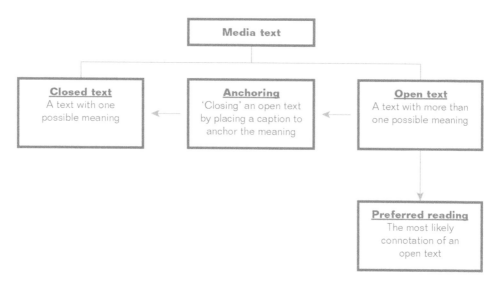

Figure 0.3 Applying meanings to texts

DECONSTRUCTION studying a media text by 'taking it apart' to see its constituent elements and explaining each element.

SEMIOTICS the study of signs and their meanings. First used by Ferdinand De Saussure in his Course in General Linguistics at the University of Geneva (1906–1911), semiotics is an important part of media study as it is a device by which meanings are attached to the signs we see in media texts.

JUXTAPOSITION placing two contrasting elements next to each other in order to increase the impact of each (e.g. darkness seems to be darker when it is placed next to brightness and in a film, or a sudden increase in volume makes the sound seem much louder due to the contrast).

CLOSED AND OPEN TEXTS a text with only one possible meaning is said to be a closed text, whereas a more ambiguous text with more than one possible interpretation is an open text. An open text may also be called **polysemic**, literally meaning 'many signs'.

ANCHORING when a caption is placed in an open text to anchor meaning.

PREFERRED READING the most likely interpretation of an open text.

A further tool of analysis of media texts using the concept of language is to be found in the study of **genre**. At this point in your studies, you will already be aware of the term 'genre' and that a genre consists of a group of media texts with common or shared features. These common features, called the repertoire of generic elements, are referred to as icons or visual signifiers and so the generic elements of a gangster film, for example, would include Trilby hats, pin-stripe suits and Tommy guns, and typical characters such as the 'moll', the 'boss' and the 'soldier'.

While frequently associated with film and TV, the term 'genre' is by no means unique to those media forms. For example, the generic elements associated with the musical genre of rock would include denim and leather, long hair, references to motor bikes, road journeys and love and music which is driven by powerful drums and guitars.

INFORMATION BOX

The generic signifiers of rock include leather, long hair and music with loud guitars.

Figure 0.4 Left to right: Kiss, Iron Maiden, ACDC and Foo Fighters all demonstrate a certain similarity generically

In modern media, there is a tendency for texts to demonstrate the features of more than one genre. If you were to look at a reality TV show such as *Big Brother*, you would find the features of at least three television genres. It is part game show, part documentary and, with its human emotional content, even part soap opera albeit less scripted.

Media texts which include elements from more than one genre are called **hybrids** as they are not truly one genre but have features of many genres.

We tend to think of the term '**narrative**' as referring to the story or the plot of a film. Indeed, one of the most common applications of narrative as a concept is to examine a film text and analyse the structure of its narrative using a theory such as the equilibrium theory of Tvetzan Todorov (1969) or a more recent theory such as the Classic Five-part Narrative theory of Robert McKee (1997). A further analysis of narrative comes when comparing the closed narrative of a film with a tight reading in which the audience expects the plot to unfold gradually, although the time in the film's story is usually compressed into the two-hour duration of the film itself and the plot ultimately ends with a sense of resolution, while the open narrative of a TV soap opera has a much looser reading where time corresponds more to real time and resolution gives way to the need for a cliff-hanger ending.

Todorov's equilibrium narrative structure	Robert McKee's Classic Five-part Narrative structure
Equilibrium (peace)	Inciting incident
Disruption of equilibrium	Progressive complications
Recognition	Crisis
Repair	Climax
Restoration of equilibrium	Resolution

The most common form of narrative is a linear narrative, in which the story unfolds chronologically. However, a number of film texts employ a non-linear narrative whereby the action in the film takes a more random chronology. This is often used to add an extra level of meaning to a narrative and to offer the audience something which differs from the accepted method of telling a story in a film. The director Quentin Tarantino is renowned in his films such as *Pulp Fiction* and the *Kill Bill* films for using non-linear narratives.

However, narrative is not a term which refers exclusively to film or TV texts. An analysis of articles in magazines or newspapers and the construction of news on TV will also reveal that the narratives tend to follow a structure.

Audience as a concept means considerably more than a group of people in a theatre or a cinema. You will already be familiar with the term 'target audience' which refers to the group of people a media text is aimed at in terms of its content. In reality, however, most media texts will be consumed by many more people than those who make up the target audience and not everyone who belongs to a target audience will consume each text. The concept of target audience therefore is of more use when analysing the content of a media text than the consumption of it. Figure 0.6 shows the relationship between the target audience and the wider audience groups of actual and potential audiences.

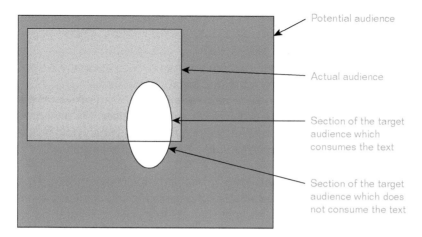

Figure 0.6 Diagram showing the relationship between the target audience and the wider audience groups of actual and potential audiences

POTENTIAL AUDIENCE the group of people who have the capacity to consume a media text.

ACTUAL AUDIENCE those members of the potential audience who do consume a media text.

TARGET AUDIENCE the group of people regarded by the producers as the intended audience for the text. Having a clear idea of this group not only assists in the marketing of a media text, it also provides guidance for the text's production.

Audience is far more than identifying patterns of consumption and marketing media texts to certain audiences. One of the most important elements of the study of audience lies in the effects that media has on those who consume it. These effects are by no means certain but few would argue that an effective advertising campaign can lead to increased sales for a product, and there are critics of violent films and video games which have been the subject of many studies in an attempt to ascertain the effect that consumption of them can have upon an audience.

The concept of **representation** in media deals with how people, either groups or individuals, places or things (a seemingly vague term but one that is needed to cover the array of subjects such as a human emotion, a religion, a building, a charity, etc. which can be shown in a text) are portrayed in the media. It is useful when analysing representations to have a set of questions, rather like a checklist, to refer to as you analyse the subject.

- **What** is being represented?
- **How** is it being represented?
- **Who** is responsible for this representation?
- Is it an **accurate** representation? (Before you can assess accuracy, at least a basic knowledge of the subject in the real sense is required.)
- Does the representation **challenge** or **reinforce** the existing **stereotypes** which exist about the subject? In order to be able to answer this final point, you will of course need to have some knowledge of the commonly held beliefs, the stereotypes, which exist about the subject of the representation.

A representation is a means of **encoding** a message for transmission. Upon receiving the message, the audience **decodes** the message and applies meaning to it. In this respect, representation is closely linked to language insofar as it is concerned with the creation of meaning. It is therefore one of the main devices through which an audience makes sense of the messages within the text. As this decoding is an individual action, the meanings people apply to the representations may vary enormously. This helps to explain how, for example, one person may interpret a certain meaning behind a representation in one way whereas another may interpret the meaning in a totally different way. In short, a representation, through its use of both verbal and non-verbal communication, speaks to the audience and helps the text to have meaning to those who consume it.

As a general term, **industry** has several meanings. In Media Studies, it refers to the organisations which are behind the production, marketing, distribution and regulation of media texts. The producers, marketers and distributors, a group of organisations which might be seen as forming a media industry, work very closely to ensure that the media output is varied, interesting, has the potential to create revenue, is advertised appropriately and that it reaches the correct audiences. Efficiency and value for money are key phrases in the media; an industry renowned for being volatile and unforgiving to those producers whose output fails to be profitable.

Regulatory bodies such as OFCOM, the ASA (Advertising Standards Authority) and the BBFC (British Board of Film Classification) can act as a kind of governing body for the media form they are associated with by establishing codes of conduct. They may also act as a censor and require the removal of items deemed inappropriate or as a point of contact for complaints in the event of a media product causing offence. In this final capacity, the regulatory body may then act as an adjudicator and may force a producer to take remedial action such as issuing an apology or paying damages.

It is perhaps worth mentioning here that you may find yourself studying media texts and recognising that there are many different points of view or influences which have affected the media you are studying. This is because media texts are influenced by many different beliefs or ideologies. An ideology is a set of ideas or beliefs which may be seen to underpin a media text in some way. At its most basic level, a simple media text such as a TV advertisement for a car which is designed to make an audience aware of the car's main features with a view to influencing them to buy one is based upon the capitalist or consumerist ideologies which are part of our society. In this way, most media texts are influenced by or are a product of at least one ideology. In studying ideology, you will no doubt have heard terms like 'capitalism', 'socialism', 'democracy', 'feminism', 'fascism', 'communism', 'postmodernism', 'poststructuralism' and so on, and even 'isms' such as Marxism or Thatcherism which are named after the ideas and beliefs of a person.

It is useful to divide these ideologies into broad categories. Capitalism, socialism, democracy and especially Thatcherism are what might be termed political ideologies, while feminism, postmodernism, poststructuralism and the relatively new queer theory tend to be regarded as social ideologies. There are some ideologies such as communism and fascism which may be regarded as both political and social ideologies. It may be further argued that religious beliefs such as Islam or Christianity form religious ideologies capable of influencing the content of a media text. While not explicitly a concept in the WJEC specification, ideology is a useful tool through which media texts can be analysed.

In the run-up to an election, the main political parties will produce election broadcasts. These are full of either explicit or subtle references to the ideologies which underpin the individual parties' beliefs. These broadcasts as media texts are therefore in themselves full of ideological content.

Figure 0.8 Logos from some of the UK political parties

In the course of your A2 level of study, you will also be required to engage in a synoptic element, and part of this is placing media texts in their contexts when you analyse them. This means accounting for their features based upon the ideologies which influenced them and their historical and geographical origin. This will be looked at in greater detail later in this book.

Production skills

The main function of practical production projects at GCE level is to explore the link between theory and practice, to gain more experience in the planning and decision making which is required when working in the media, and for you to embark upon a part of your study which acts as a counterbalance to the more conventional learning you have done in a classroom.

Now that you are studying this subject at A2 level, it is important that you regard the practical elements not as separate from those done at AS but rather as an opportunity to build upon the experiences you had in the AS practical. At AS level, there is a focus upon research into the topic of the production, the planning and the actual production elements of the project. For practical work to have satisfying outcomes, and this is certainly true of media products made professionally, good planning is essential. This poses a problem for some students, many of whom see the planning or the pre-production stage as the dull part which, when compared to the fun of filming or using computer programs to produce vibrant and creative productions, is a kind of awkward annoyance that stands between you and freedom with a camera, DTP or animation package, and as such needs to be done as quickly as possible.

However, it is important to stress that the planning in an advanced level project is much more than providing evidence that you didn't just make it up as you went along.

Planning is the way you evidence the link between theory and practice and, from an examiner's point of view, the way you demonstrate how you arrived at the decisions which inform your finished product. There are a number of important factors when planning and executing a project:

- Know your target audience.
- Know your target audience. (No, this isn't a misprint. It really is that important).
- Be comfortable in your decision about working alone or as part of a group.
- Engage in both primary and secondary research. Your research will involve an element of audience research in which important questions about the content of the production for your audience are answered as well as research into existing examples of the kind of media text you are hoping to produce.
- Know your limitations in terms of equipment and content. Explosions, car chases, graphic scenes of violence, expensive photo shoots may all show your creativity off in its best light but these are not feasible for this kind of project. Likewise, professional film cameras, editing equipment and blue screen studios are ideal but it is more likely that a home digital video camera and a basic editing package will be all that is available. One of the main things which you need to address is getting the most out of the equipment available to you.
- Concentrate upon the fine detail. For example, the opening sequence to an action film which, if done reflecting the codes and conventions of the action genre, will be gripping and exciting as it sets the tone for the film, may seem an appealing project, but one which is very challenging to see through to fulfilment. However, a simple conversation between two characters within the genre of drama or soap which uses a wide selection of camera shots, especially over-the-shoulder shots which in a two-way conversation should really be done by filming the scene twice from different angles and then editing it together post-production, can, despite the simplicity, score highly if done effectively.

Media Studies in action 1: a case of gender and identity

It is almost certain by now that somewhere in your educational career you will have been given a topic to study in depth. Perhaps this was the effect of an event such as the fall of the Berlin Wall or the assassination of John F. Kennedy, or perhaps you were asked to evaluate the arguments that increasing the use of fossil fuels leads to climate change. In addition, as part of your learning so far in Media Studies, you may have been asked to investigate the point of view that the increase in popularity of reality TV is stifling creativity and leading to a general 'dumbing down' of TV content. The art of analysis, investigation and evaluation are important across a number of subject areas and, in subjects like Media Studies which do not always have a definitive right or wrong answer but which throw up a number of arguments representing different theories and conflicting perspectives, they are especially important.

So having seen the importance of these skills, have you ever actually stopped and asked yourself what you are being asked to do when you are given the task of analysing, evaluating or investigating? Many people seem to confuse this with simply writing about these topics, yet such work is focused; it should be balanced and represent all relevant theories, perspectives and arguments before finally concluding with an assessment which includes comments about the usefulness or value of the topic in question.

In the previous section, there is an example which looks at the cover of a copy of the magazine *Company* using semiotic devices. Such deconstruction of media texts, especially when the text is 'unseen', is a common task at AS level Media Studies which requires you to take the text apart and analyse the meanings of both the text as a whole and the constituent elements, colour, font, verbal communication, etc.

If we examine one of these in more depth, we would soon discover that evaluation is a much more complex skill. Let us stay within the world of magazines and look briefly at how an evaluation of the arguments that representations of women on magazine covers are not an accurate reflection of womanhood and are exploitative.

You could begin by looking at a range of women's magazines.

Figure 0.9 Models on women's magazine covers conform to a conventional idea of beauty

The magazine covers in Figure 0.9 all offer a fairly narrow representation of women. The models on the covers are all young, glamorous, they conform to conventional idea of beauty in that they all have perfect unblemished skin, vibrant and neat hair, and they are dressed and are posing in what could be described as a sexy and confident manner. However, the features on these covers may in some way be explained by the similarity in age, gender and probably aspiration of the target audience. Nevertheless, since the women shown tend to fulfil the narrow stereotype of what society regards as beautiful and attractive, they could be accused of being exploitative and inaccurate since they offer such a narrow representation of womanhood.

Next, look at representations of men in men's magazines to compare.

Figure 0.10 Representations of men in men's magazines

The magazine covers shown in Figure 0.10 also tend to show a narrow representation, this time of men. In an analysis you might comment again upon the representations of men, or more specifically masculinity in these images. Each of the men on the covers conforms again to certain narrow representations concerning age and ethnic group. There is confidence, charm and sex appeal but the men on these covers are generally older than the models seen on the covers of women's magazines. A wider debate about age might be relevant here, as famous men are more likely to be adorning the covers of magazines much later in their lives than their famous female counterparts.

Add another dimension by looking at the representations of women in magazines with male target audiences (Figure 0.11).

Figure 0.11 Representations of women in magazines targeted at men

The representations of women shown in these magazines are similar to the representations on the covers for the women's magazines. The models are again slim, attractive in a conventional sense and pose suggestively, and as such could be seen as narrow and exploitative.

This basic look at three areas of magazine covers could be used to address the issue of representations of women and to form a starting point for an evaluation of the arguments concerning exploitation and narrow representations. The art of evaluation is, however, more complex than simply analysing the covers and arriving at certain conclusions. In order to evaluate the representations of women on magazine covers, you will also need to consider wider theories and perspectives, among them:

- *Feminist theory*. Traditional feminism seeks to challenge the dominant ideologies of the male-dominated or patriarchal society we see in most Western countries. Naturally, a feminist perspective will be critical of the employment of the 'perfect' female form to sell a magazine. In a highly influential work, Janice Winship criticises the way women are represented on the covers of women's magazines as being defined by the patriarchal (male-dominated) society in that they are products.

> **Nevertheless, what I would argue is that the gaze between cover model and women readers marks the complicity between women that we see ourselves in the image which a masculine culture has defined.** ""

(Winship, 1987)

The criticism of the way women are shown on the covers of magazines aimed at men is equally scathing, and Winship advocates that they place even more power into the hands of the males who are targeted by the covers.

> **The woman's image in these latter [men's magazines] is obviously caught up in a provocatively sexual significance. Her partially revealed body speaks the sexuality about which the facial expression often equivocates. Her gaze holds that of the male voyeur; but it is he who has the controlling look: to look or not to bother, to choose to be sexually aroused or not.** ""

(Winship, 1987)

- *Sex-positive feminism*. A completely opposite viewpoint would be offered here, one which centres on the idea that women have their freedom enhanced by sexual liberty. Women being represented as they commonly are in magazines is simply an expression of freedom, and women themselves are exercising a kind of 'free expression' according to the sex-positive feminist perspective.
- *Girl power*. While perhaps not having the history or the clout of feminism, girl power may be seen as a kind of post-feminist response to the traditional feminist theory outlined above. Girl power, a phrase popularised by the 1990s pop group The Spice Girls, encourages women to be in control and to be empowered by their gender. While not being quite as openly supportive of sexual liberation as sex-positive feminism, it adds a wider context and acknowledges that the world in which women's magazines are produced today is quite a different world from when the feminist arguments first arose.

Figure 0.12 The Spice Girls

The Spice girls helped to define the 1990s and introduced the idea of 'girl power'. Their contribution since they formed their group is seen by some not only in musical terms but also by their part in redefining femininity and empowering women.

So to summarise, there are different points of view on the representations of women on the covers of magazines. It has long been the tactic of media producers to attract their audiences through the use of images so, in this respect, the portrayal of women on magazine covers is largely down to the desire of the producers to sell copies. In addition, many of the criticisms concerning narrow representations which can be levied at magazines with women on their covers can also be levied at magazines with men on their covers. Your overall evaluation will need to take all of these points of view into account.

Some autonomy

Advanced studies in subjects like Media Studies are full of theories, analyses and points of views offered by a wide variety of writers and professionals. Some of these contributors are very well known, others less so, but the use of this kind of material often forms the basis for answers in essays, in exams and in research tasks, and since it has been produced by people who are believed either through their experience or through their academic study, or indeed both, to know what they are talking about, it also lends gravitas to the work you produce.

However, what about your own points of view? Well, to put it simply, the more you have progressed over your time as a media student, the more **you** have become worth listening to. Your expertise in the subject is increasing all the time and, through your consumption, analysis and evaluation of media texts as well as your production skills, you will be forming your own valid points of view about a wide range of issues found in the media.

As a student in this position, you are afforded some autonomy; indeed, it is encouraged at all levels at GCE and is essential for the very best marks. Examples of how you might be autonomous include offering a critical evaluation of media products, offering personal responses to a theory, a viewpoint or an analysis offered by a media professional or academic, or providing your own reading or interpretation of the content of a media text.

Media Studies is a conceptual subject, and as such, there is not often a definitive right or wrong answer; disagreements are commonplace, conclusions can con-tradict each other and there are many different ways in which people can read and interpret the messages in media texts. It is important, however, that in your bid to be autonomous you do not simply disagree with another point of view or come out protesting your love for or dislike of a certain media text without any further detail or explanation. You need to ensure that the points you wish to make are valid and are able to withstand a certain degree of scrutiny. Explaining why you have arrived at a certain point of view, revealing your evidence for a criticism or offering the counter-argument which has led you to disagree with a certain theory, is just as important as actually writing your point of view, making your criticism or providing your counter-argument.

Basic research skills

Research in its most basic form means finding something out or acquiring new knowledge. This can mean finding out the answer to a specific problem or question (for example, how Rupert Murdoch rose to become one of the world's most influential media magnates), or it can mean adopting a more exploratory approach to a more open-ended issue such as finding out how the coverage of an event in a certain newspaper affected public opinion.

There are certain techniques with which you should be familiar for conducting research and doubtless you will have employed many of them in your AS studies. In general, Media Studies research usually falls into one of two categories: primary and secondary research. Primary research involves gathering information first-hand. This could be through conducting an interview or a survey or through the direct examination of the text or texts which are the subject of the enquiry or study. As such, primary research is one of the best ways to achieve a level of autonomy, as it requires analysis and evaluation of the actual texts being studied. Secondary research is that which involves using existing material which has been produced by someone else. This includes, for example, books or articles and interviews in magazines or newspapers. Naturally, the more experience the person has or the better their reputation is perceived to be, the more weight the material will have, so an interview with Steven Spielberg on a DVD 'extras' disc will most likely carry more weight than a journalist with no access to Spielberg writing their own thoughts on one of his films in a newspaper, unless of course that writer happens to be someone like Barry Norman or Mark Kermode who have built up something of a reputation as film journalists.

The following is not designed to be an example of preparing to study a specific section of the WJEC A level course or to refer to a specific unit; rather, it is an illustration of how a student may engage in a piece of research through the use of primary and secondary sources. If you were researching a topic, let us say the use of computer-generated images (CGI) in Hollywood films, you could approach your research as follows.

Primary research could involve studying a selection of films which chart the use of CGI for special effects work starting with, for example, *Star Wars* (1977) which had no CGI and in which the special effects were created through extensive use of models, stop-motion photography, costume and make-up. *Tron* (1982) would be a good example of a film which used CGI in a basic form world followed by *Terminator 2: Judgement Day* (1992) with partial use of CGI to create the scenes when the T1000 Terminator character changes shape and appears in his natural liquid metal form. *Star Wars Episode 1* (1999) had the very first completely CGI principal character in Jar Jar Binks, and to bring the research up to date, films such as the *Lord of the Rings* trilogy (2001–2003) and *Avatar* (2009) use CGI not only to create characters but also the worlds they inhabit. The research might look at the greater freedom afforded directors by the progress in CGI and how the films studied use CGI to create the *mise-en-scène* which is in the script.

INFORMATION BOX i

The changing face of computer-generated imagery (CGI) in film would make an interesting research topic. Advances in technology have made what was once unfilmable a regular feature in some of the biggest blockbusters in recent years.

The T1000 from *Terminator 2: Judgement Day* was a major breakthrough in computer-generated image technology, as the character was seen frequently changing appearance and merged with live action. Characters like Jar Jar Binks from *Star Wars Episode 1* (1999) and Gollum from *The Lord of the Rings* Trilogy are principal characters created entirely by CGI.

Figure 0.13 Left to right: a car race from *Tron*; *Terminator 2: Judgement Day*; *Star Wars Episode 1*; *Lord of the Rings*

Secondary research would include interviews with film directors and those who work in the field of CGI together with producers (who finance films) from a range of sources including books, magazines, DVD extras discs and newspapers. You should also be prepared to examine the range of existing research done by film writers, academics, film critics and research done which measures the audiences' response to the films they consume.

It is important to remain focused when researching. The material you use for either primary or secondary research must be relevant and reliable. A judicious choice of sources bearing the need for relevance and reliability in mind should ensure that your research yields results of a high quality and which enhance the quality of your work. In the MS3 module, which is examined in more detail in the next section and in the chapter dedicated to this module (Chapter 5), you are required to undertake a piece of independent research which is based on either narrative, genre or representations. Whichever of these you choose, a good piece of research will engage in both primary and secondary research.

The additional demands of A2

As mentioned at the start of this chapter, the WJEC A2 level represents an upward step in terms of the level of challenge from AS level; it is not simply more of the same. Having identified the main key concepts in the previous section, it is fair to say that at AS level, the concepts of language and representations have been the most prominent, especially in the area of textual analysis. The art of deconstructing a media text by offering an analysis of the constituent parts is very much an AS level skill which, although still important at A2 level, is now complemented by the opportunities to explore these texts in greater depth through looking at the wider contexts in which these texts are produced and consumed. As such, the other concepts of audience, institution, or industry, and ideology become more prominent than they perhaps were at AS level. In addition, the practical work undertaken for A2 level will need to show a greater level of refinement and attention to detail which will separate it from that which has been completed earlier in your career as a student of media. This practical work will also need to have closer links to the key concepts and demonstrate more confidently how the concepts are reflected through practical tasks.

While not entirely a theory-led subject, there are nevertheless numerous theories and perspectives offered in Media Studies by a wealth of writers, academics and media professionals, many of which are at least worthy of consideration if not learning thoroughly in order to enhance your understanding. However, per- haps more so than in many other subjects, theories and perspectives can quickly become outdated as the media world advances relentlessly. It may sound impres- sive to have a list of theories offered by an array of experts, especially if, as highlighted in the previous section, you have kept them relevant and been judicious in your choice of theory. However, an answer laden with theory and bursting with references could potentially show nothing more than that the writer is good at remembering material gleaned from other sources, whereas a good-quality A2 level answer will combine theory, which may be criticised or challenged in its con- tent, with critical autonomy and a debate about the wider contexts of production and consumption.

The focus of the modules at A2 for WJEC

You will have already completed a piece of practical work for your AS level course of study. Hopefully you found this both an enjoyable experience and one from which you learned something about the way media texts are constructed following research and detailed planning. However, the limitations on what you could have done are more likely to have arisen as a consequence of the available resources at your centre than through a lack of imagination on your part, so that in short, within the confines of the context in which you were working, you had a free hand in what you did for your practical project.

Now that you have moved on to A2 level, WJEC are asking you to focus a little more closely upon certain areas of media study in both of the modules which form the A2 course of study. In the first module, MS3, entitled Media Investigation and Production, you again have the opportunity to produce a piece of media, but whereas last time, at AS level, you were allowed to research, plan and produce your own choice of media product, this time you will have to produce a research investigation of between 1400 and 1800 words based upon one of either genre, narrative or representation. This investigation is then followed by a practical production which is informed by the topic of the research. Your production must therefore be linked to the topic of your research investigation. For example, you could choose to research representations of young people in British soap operas for the investigation and then produce the opening three minutes of a new soap in which you demonstrate some of the findings from your research. In addition, your production must be a different media form from the one you did for the AS level practical. This does not mean that if you did a moving image production last time you cannot do one again, but it does mean that if you produced a film trailer previously and wish to produce another moving image, it cannot be a film trailer again.

In the final module, MS4, entitled Media – Text, Industry and Audience, the examining board requires students to answer three essay questions in a two-and-a-half-hour examination. The first essay is from a choice of two on the topic of Text while the other two are from a choice of four on the dual topics of Industry and Audience. For each essay, students must choose a different media type, so TV, radio and magazines could be chosen and, in each answer, students need to refer in detail to three media texts. This means that students need to approach this exam with detailed and thorough knowledge of nine media texts in total, and good answers will refer to numerous secondary texts as further examples or for comparative purposes. Of these three texts for each question, at least one per essay must be British and at least two must be contemporary; that is, no more than five years old. More details about this examination module may be found in Chapter 4 dedicated to MS4.

A more imaginative approach to production work

As previously mentioned, the production work you complete at A2 level needs to be different and it must show progression from that which you completed on the AS course. Does this necessarily mean it has to be better? Well, naturally you should be striving to make the quality as high as you can and, given that you have more experience of practical work than before, it follows that you are probably capable of producing better work, but the focus really ought to be on trying to be more imaginative both in terms of content and in the use of the resources available. Furthermore, your practical production for the WJEC MS3 unit must be linked to the topic chosen for the research investigation, genre, narrative or representation which narrows the confines in which you must work a little more. Hopefully, you were pleased with the finished products which you completed for AS level, so much so in fact that you may find it hard to be more imaginative than you were before. However, you should give some consideration to the following ideas:

- Try animation. Software is now readily available which will allow alternatives to human actors. This software is also not as hard to use as you might imagine.
- Use a more advanced piece of software which will have increased possibilities for editing and desk-top publishing. Manipulation of images is relatively

straightforward and the possibilities are much wider than they have been in the past. Adobe Premiere digital video editing software and Adobe Photoshop offer enormous possibilities for you to allow your imagination to roam freely.

■ Consider the fine detail. When making a video, pay special attention to the sound, which is often overlooked. One way to achieve this is to rerecord certain elements of the video post-production (after it has been filmed) and insert the new soundtrack over your video footage. This is a good way to remove unwanted sound when filming outdoors such as the sound of a siren in the distance or even of a gentle breeze, which can sound like a howling typhoon when you play back your footage. Likewise, make sure that any photography has the correct lighting. You should aim to use lighting creatively. Try lighting your subject from a number of different angles in order to achieve the correct look for the image you are taking.

■ Consider less popular options such as audio work. Radio is so much more than simply playing songs and talking between them. It offers a wealth of opportunity from documentary to comedy, drama to a debate which offers a quite different set of challenges from the conventional video- or print-based task.

■ Do not forget the importance of planning for practical work. It is relatively clear to those with the responsibility of marking work which pieces have been well planned and which have a more made-up feel to them. Planning will focus your mind on the product. It will allow you to envisage it and chart a route towards the fulfilment of the project, and thus it gives greater opportunity to be creative. You may be forgiven for thinking that creative simply means louder, faster, bigger, brighter, higher or more technological. Well, it can mean this, but it may also mean finding a more imaginative way of achieving something that is more conventional. Consider this example. Let us say that you are working with other students and you are producing a short film. Your script requires that a character is pushed and falls from a balcony. Naturally, this is a hard scene to achieve safely, and you should certainly not even consider attempting it for real. In fact, the danger and potential for injury should really lead you to scrap the scene altogether and replace it with a scene which has the same outcome but which is easier to film, say, the perpetrator tripping up the victim. If you sit down with your group to plan and, rather than dismissing the scene, address the question of how the effect of a character falling from a balcony without having to actually film it can be achieved, then your discussion might arrive at the following conclusion. Attach your camera to a piece of string so that the lens points downwards. Twist the string around a few times and then, having started recording, gently lower the camera from the balcony on to the ground below. The twisted string will then make the camera turn around as it is lowered to the ground. When you come to edit the scene, speed it up slightly on your digital editing software and place the footage after a scene of the perpetrator walking towards the victim with intent to push and immediately before a scene of the victim lying motionless on the floor. When edited, the scene will then show the push from our (i.e. the audience's) perspective and will cut to the victim's point-of-view shot of the fall followed by a return to the audience's perspective of the motionless victim.

This is a simple and above all safe way of achieving an effect. Planning gives you a much better chance of overcoming these potential barriers to achieving your practical work.

- You may also find that your creativity flows a little more if you produce a piece of practical work which falls outside your own comfort zone or area of interest. You can find yourself being lulled into a false sense of security by the fact that you consider yourself somewhat knowledgeable about the product you are making. Your decisions will be formulaic and, as a result, the product can be dull and uninspiring. If, however, you begin from square one with an unknown kind of text, you force yourself to be creative since you are learning about the text as you go. On the other hand, you may find that working within your comfort zone is more likely to inspire an imaginative approach, as you have the confidence to take your product in new directions. Whichever of these possibilities is the case for you, thinking outside of the box is a very good way to nurture creativity and imagination.
- When planning to produce a media text, consider the online version. Magazines and newspapers are now supported by websites which you could use as inspiration and which will allow you to produce a text that is interactive and, some may argue, more relevant in the modern world than the printed equivalents.

However, probably the most important element to the A2 piece of practical work and one that you must not lose sight of is that it must be linked to the area of research you studied for Investigative Research. You will no doubt have made important decisions about your practical work for the MS3 unit early on when you started out deciding and planning your critical investigation – literally how the topic in the investigation can be covered in a practical task, or which media types are best suited to the topic of the investigation. One of the criteria upon which you will be marked for in this module is the extent to which your research investigation and the practical production are linked and how the production arises out of or reflects the findings of your research.

There is also a demand at this more challenging level to produce a piece of work which shows a greater degree of sophistication. A piece of work of the same standard which was completed for the AS course will not score the same marks at A2 level due to the more stringent marking scheme applied by examination boards. Sophistication is achieved by making your work as close to professional standards as you possibly can within the confines of availability. As technology improves and people become more adept at using technology, the demands upon students using technology have increased and moderators of practical work have raised their expectations accordingly.

In the real media world, the greatest level of sophistication comes with those texts where the complexities of production are less evident to the general audience. In a professional TV show, we don't tend to notice the editing consciously, or the sound effects in a film. Newspapers and magazines use language so appropriate for their readerships that it simply flows as it is read, and music on a CD sounds smooth and polished and no one instrument drowns out the sound of another, thanks to the work of the sound engineers. In short, at this level more than ever before, you need to try to produce a product which demonstrates the kind of sophistication and quality of finish found in professional products to a greater degree.

Greater autonomy

"You are now worth listening to!" So it says in the earlier recap of AS level study. Well, if that were the case as you drew upon your experience as an AS and as a GCSE student, how much more is this the case now that you have completed the AS level modules and find your way through the A2 course?

While some autonomy is encouraged at AS level, greater autonomy is really an absolute must for all students, especially those with aspirations for the top grades. In fact, this is arguably the largest difference between the two levels and the most notable way in which progression is evidenced. Among the main ways you can achieve greater autonomy are:

- Continuing to offer your own concise, well-thought-out, relevant and incisive points of view about media texts.
- Build up a catalogue of knowledge from your own media consumption and make sure that your examples are not all those which were given in your lessons.
- When media texts are influenced by other texts in terms of content or style, they are said to be **intertextual**. One of the most famous examples of intertexuality is in a scene in a railway station in Brian De Palma's 1987 film *The Untouchables*, where the director plays out a scene reminiscent in part through his use of a baby in a pram in the massacre on the Odessa Steps scene in Sergei Eisenstein's *The Battleship Potemkin* (1925). Any further links which can be made between media texts are evidence of autonomy. Try looking at the video for Queen's 'I Want to Break Free' and *Coronation Street*, or Michael Jackson's 'Thriller' and John Landis' *An American Werewolf In London* or any one of the films from the zombie sub-genre.

INFORMATION BOX *i*

An example of intertextuality. Amid the carnage of the massacre on the Odessa Steps in Sergei Eisenstein's *The Battleship Potemkin* (1925) a baby in a pram makes an unexpected entrance (left). Influenced by this, Brian De Palma used a pram in a similar way in the shootout scene on the steps of the Chicago railway station in *The Untouchables* (1987).

Figure 0.14 Intertextuality – *Battleship Potemkin* (left) and *The Untouchables* (right)

- Being critical of the theories and the perspectives offered by others. This does not simply mean saying that you disagree or even agree with a theory; rather, it means reinforcing or challenging its orthodoxy, highlighting its strengths or weaknesses, which may be many, as theories tend to be frozen in time while media texts are not, and of course giving reasons for your appraisal of the material.

Some students feel uncomfortable with the idea of autonomy, especially if it is at the expense of established theory or perspectives, since this can give the impression that the response is lacking in planning or research and being offered 'off the cuff'. However, this is not the case provided that the autonomy within the response broadly follows the guidance offered above. However, autonomy need not mean this at all. Simply by taking the response in the direction you wish to take it and bringing in the examples you wish to bring in, moving away from a standard and formulaic answer and generally offering your response in a creative and original way, you are also taking steps towards achieving a greater degree of autonomy. This will invariably mean moving away from the texts and issues themselves or the theories and perspectives which underpin them towards the wider contexts which are pertinent to them.

Wider contexts

Over the course of your life it is likely that you will be asked several times to name the piece of music which you think is the greatest ever written. Of course there are several ways to answer this. The most common answer, which is in fact not an answer to this particular question at all, will probably be that you have lots of favourite pieces of music. However, if you were pushed so that you had to pick one, you could answer it by saying, for example, that John Lennon's 'Imagine' was the greatest piece of music owing to the simplicity of the arrangement, the clarity of the vocals and the importance of the message. You could give statistical evidence to support this by the fact that Channel 4 voted it the best number 1 single of all time (see http://www.channel4.com/entertainment/tv/microsites/

G/greatest/singles/results.html for the full list). Since your reasons for this answer relate entirely to the actual text itself, in this case a song, this is a text-based answer.

Consider someone answering the same question by saying that their favourite song was Madonna's 'Crazy for You' because it was the first song they danced to with a boyfriend, or 'The Shock Of The Lightning' by Oasis as it reminds them of the last year they were at school, which was up until that point the best year of that person's life. These responses have little to do with actual text, but they do make reference to the wider contexts.

In Media Studies, a context can refer, as these examples do, to the conditions of consumption, but a context is also defined as the circumstances which exist at the time a text is produced and which can be seen to have influenced it. Since media texts are produced all over the world and at different times throughout history, the main contexts which you will be dealing with are social, political, historical and cultural. In order to be successful at assessing the wider contexts and their significance for the text, it is often necessary to cease consuming the text with your own twenty-first-century experiences in mind and try to place yourself elsewhere; for example, by our modern standards and following the experiences of recent shock-horror films such as *Saw* (2004) and *Hostel* (2005) and their sequels, an early 1930s horror film such as *Dracula* (1931) can seem anything but frightening. However, to the 1930s audience with no experience of colour, prosthetic special effects or digital technology, and whose experiences of film were limited by censorship which seems very strict by modern standards, *Dracula* was at the cutting edge of thrills and chills in the cinema. By this same rationale, the range of computer games, music and films which engage young people today will seem outdated and tame in terms of content and limited technologically in comparison to those available to future generations.

Thus placing texts in their contexts can help to analyse their content more deeply, give further insight into how they are likely to be consumed and can also tell us something about the circumstances which affected their production. Contextualisation is a very valuable tool for comparing media texts, especially when they have been produced in different places or at different times. In the film *The Longest Day* (1962), for example, there are several scenes which show American soldiers landing on the beaches of Normandy on D-Day during the Allied invasion of Europe towards the end of the Second World War. The same event is shown in *Saving Private Ryan* (1997) and, although they both tell of the same event, visually there is a wealth of differences. The death of soldiers in battle as they land on the beach is shown in both films, but there is a visceral, gritty realism in the scenes in *Saving Private Ryan*. Limbs are blown off, wounded soldiers cry out in agony and the use of the handheld camera is highly effective in giving the audience a sense of participation. Overall, the effect is much more shocking and disturbing, and many critics praised the film for giving an accurate portrayal of the horror of war and of that particular event. In one particularly emotive scene, a soldier who has lost one of his arms searches the ground for his lost limb. Upon finding it, he picks it up and continues further on to the beach. For added effect, the scene is played in slow motion and with muffled sound to emphasise the loss of a sense of reality experienced by Tom Hanks' character who witnesses the event. The fighting by contrast in *The Longest Day* seems much more sanitised, with action contrasting vastly to that in *Saving Private Ryan*, most notably when an American general played by Robert Mitchum runs unarmed on to the beach and even has time to smoke his cigar throughout the battle. Fewer soldiers are shown dying, and those who do appear to die do so immediately and apparently in much less pain.

Some of these differences in this example may be attributed to the texts themselves; for example, the Normandy Landings is shown as an opening sequence in *Saving Private Ryan* while it is the climax of *The Longest Day*, but most of the differences are attributed to reasons which become evident upon examining contextualisation. *The Longest Day* was released only 18 years after the events of D-Day. Many of those who had participated in the war and the parents of the soldiers who had died would have been alive and formed part of the potential audience. It would be inappropriate to have shown such appalling and gruesome death to an audience for whom memories of the Second World War and loss would have been so fresh. Furthermore, in 1962, the technology to allow complex special effects had not been developed, nor would the censors have allowed scenes of such violence and suffering. However, by 1997, the Second World War was less fresh in the filmgoing audience's mind, massive advances in special effects allowed for highly realistic scenes of injury and death, and the tolerance for violence and suffering in film from both the audiences and the censors had risen.

Figure 0.15 Scenes from *The Longest Day* (left) and *Saving Private Ryan* (right)

There is, however, a further context in terms of how war itself is represented in these two films. *Saving Private Ryan* was released at a period of time when many Americans had started to question the wisdom of their country's involvement in foreign wars. The overwhelming conclusion on the Vietnam War was that it had been a disaster for the USA, whereas the outcome of the Second World War owes much to American involvement. To most commentators America came out of the Second World War somewhat more positively than it did from Vietnam and, following that campaign, war itself had become the enemy, and the madness and futility of war is one of the key areas explored in *Saving Private Ryan*. In *The Longest Day*, war was represented much more positively. The soldiers go into battle more willingly, while war is shown as glorious and as a necessary means to achieve an end.

In addition to looking at the features of a media product which are shaped by historical contexts, as we have done with the previous example, the study of wider contexts can embrace the same period of time and look at how a product can impact upon other media types. Garnering much critical acclaim for its gritty and realistic representations of war, *Saving Private Ryan* seemed to reinvigorate the war genre and to lay the foundations for further film releases such as *The Thin Red Line* (1998) and *Black Hawk Down* (2001), and also for the genre to embark upon a journey which would embrace a number of different media platforms. In a further collaboration between the film's director and star, Steven Spielberg and Tom Hanks joined forces to bring both *Band of Brothers* (2001) and *The Pacific* (2010) to TV screens. According to Spielberg, the medium of television removed the two- to three-hour time constraint that film imposed and allowed for much more story development. Widening the context of the war genre even further, technological improvements in the world of computer gaming has led to the same level of gritty realism in recent computer role-play games like the Modern Warfare series in which players can interact with the war environment, make decisions with life-and-death consequences and experience the role of combat soldier from the safety of their own home. At the end of the first decade of the twenty-first century, with Britain and the USA engaged in war in Iraq and Afghanistan, the wider contexts which inform the war genre across a range of media types are still an important factor in their continued popularity.

INFORMATION BOX – NEW MEDIA IN ACTION

Call of Duty 4: Modern Warfare, the computer game shares features and is intertextual with films and TV shows which, traditionally at least, are perhaps more associated with the war genre.

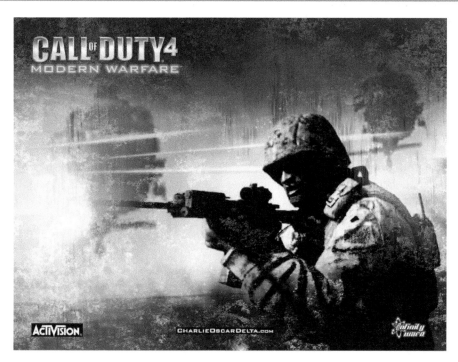

Figure 0.16 *Call of Duty 4: Modern Warfare*

Theoretical perspectives

The word 'theory' is used often enough to either send shivers down the spine of students or to instil in them a sense of boredom and tedium which does little but detract from the hands-on parts of the subject. To the modern student, theories in all subjects seem to fall into one of two categories. They have the reputation of appearing either blindingly obvious on the one hand or so complex that, rather than providing elucidation, they muddy the water and make the topic about which the theory has been written even less easy to come to grips with.

The irony is that both of these points of views are equally valid. On the surface, some theories are fairly obvious, while others are undeniably complex. Helpfully, or perhaps not, many of the theoretical perspectives relevant to Media Studies are found in other subjects, and so a GCE student of Media and, say, Sociology, Film Studies or English will find some cross-curricular links. One thing which is very much the case is that the discerning A2 level student will probably treat the wealth of theoretical perspectives in Media Studies with respect and disdain in equal measure. Once again, as we saw in the section on autonomy, there are opportunities for theories to be both praised and criticised so long as you can justify your stance within the relevant context of your area of study.

Whatever your own opinion of theory, there can be little doubt that the challenges which are posed in the final year of an A level course require you to have not only the knowledge of some key theoretical perspectives but to have the ability to use them appropriately and with relevance in your work. It is useful to think of these perspectives as forming part of a toolkit into which you delve to take out the required tool when it is needed. When you are studying a certain medium, say, newspapers, then it is not enough to simply write about the content, to comment upon the use of language, the political ideology implicit in the articles or to identify the fact that there seems to be a large amount of American news without pulling out the required theoretical perspectives from your toolkit and linking them to the points you are making. It is these theories which will give your work a sense of substance. However, before looking more closely at these theoretical perspectives, it is worth noting at this point that the overuse of theories, especially when it appears to be simply for the sake of it, is to be avoided, not least because without the knowledge and the correct application, your work can appear at least naive if not simply incorrect.

Although frequently used as much the same thing, there is a difference between a theory and a theoretical perspective. A theory refers to a suggestion usually, but not always formulated by academics or professionals in a study of a certain topic. Much of the content covered earlier in this chapter is based upon a theory. Semiotics, for example, is a theory that is usually traced back to Ferdinand de Saussure (1857–1913) and which relates to how a media text is made up of many different signs that combine to give meaning to a text. In a further example, upon studying the content of newspapers, Galtung and Ruge (1965) formulated their theory on what makes an event newsworthy. This has become known as the theory of news values!

However, a theoretical perspective refers to the encapsulating tradition or wider viewpoint from which a theory comes. Consequently, theoretical perspectives are fewer in number than theories. For example, the theory of hegemony, developed by the Italian Philosopher Antonio Gramsci, tells how there is a tendency for a small but powerful group of people to exert a disproportionate amount of influence over a much larger but less powerful majority. This theory may be used together with studies of globalisation to explain the power and influence of American culture over the rest of the world, and in Britain it describes the power held by the ruling elite over the rest of the general population. This theory is important to Media Studies as it is argued that this situation is reinforced and legitimised through the content of the Mass Media. Perhaps this theory rings true for you; after all, few would argue that our news media has much more coverage of American news than of just about any other nation except our own. A visit to your local cinema or even glancing at the TV schedule will reveal a plethora of American culture, and most of the frequently advertised and therefore some of the most notorious brands in the world such as Coca-Cola, Disney, Time Warner, McDonald's or Starbucks are American companies.

The theory of hegemony can, however, trace its routes back to the Marxist theoretical perspective which is generally critical of the power held by the few over the many, and which seeks to redress the balance to achieve a more equitable and egalitarian society.

HEGEMONY a theory from the Marxist tradition which refers to the winning of consent by a powerful, though usually small and elite group of people over a weaker group. In Media Studies, we are particularly concerned with cultural hegemony in which the ruling elite are seen to legitimise and maintain their privileged and powerful place through the content of media texts.

There are many theoretical perspectives and, to be honest, there is unlikely to be a time when you will know all of them, since they have a tendency to emerge and evolve as time passes. Nevertheless, there are a number of key theoretical perspectives which A2 level students should be aware of and have at their disposal in their toolbox to draw upon while working at this level. The main theoretical perspectives which you will find the most relevant to your study of media are discussed more fully later in this book, but for now, what follows is a brief introduction to these perspectives.

- *Structuralism*. As the name implies it refers to structure, and in the media sense it is the idea that the structures which govern communication are a kind of structure which pre-exist any one individual. This perspective allows us to see how genre on the one hand or less complex communication such as the speech we hear on the other are the way they are owing to the pre-existing structures in which media producers operate. If a TV producer wants to make a soap opera, there exists a repertoire of generic elements – a structure – which help to define the programme as a soap opera.
- *Poststructuralism*. Rather than being a continuation of the structuralist perspective, poststructuralism takes an opposing point of view. The search for a larger meaning is pointless and the underlying structure hypothesis is disregarded. Instead, poststructuralism is concerned much more with individual interpretation of the messages which exist in a media text and which may change over time rather than with the text's production or any definitive meaning within.
- *Postmodernism*. Our society, according to the postmodernist perspective, is fragmented and diverse. Consequently, any theory which tries to deal in a universal truth is wrong. Postmodernist arguments are of great appeal to media students since it seems to give grounds for dismissing all other theories which seek to apply a universal principle. Among the chief considerations of postmodernism is the belief that all media texts are equal and that concepts of high- and low-value culture are irrelevant; all media texts from the most 'highbrow' to the most populist are worthy of equal consideration. In a

Figure 0.17 Scene from *EastEnders*

The structuralist perspective on soap operas such as *EastEnders* argues that the structure of a soap existed before the programme was first made. The show simply fits into the structure of being a soap opera by demonstrating the features of a soap opera.

The poststructuralist perspective is more concerned with the messages within the show and how these might change over time than with any underlying structure.

postmodern text, ambivalence and ambiguity are features of the narrative and genre, neither of which tends to follow the conventional patterns found in the mainstream. A further key feature of the postmodernist perspective is the relationship between media representations and reality, an area which was of interest to Jean Baudrillard. He argued that there was a changing relationship and that, at best, media can ever only be a reflection of reality but that the relationship between representations and reality can become ever more distorted over time until finally the relationship between the representation and reality breaks down and there is a state of hyperreality. The representation has become a simulacrum.

One of the main attractions with the postmodern perspective is its rejection of the distinction between high and low culture. To most, the only link between Federico Fellini's *8½* (1963) and Peter Segal's *Fifty First Dates* (2004) would be the presence of a number in the title and the vague similarity in the romantic content, but to the postmodernist they are of equal critical interest and relevance as media texts.

Figure 0.18 Posters for the films *8½* and *Fifty First Dates*

- *Feminism*. As the name implies, the feminist perspective generally takes the view that, historically, the patriarchal nature of society, of which media is an integral part, and which is both male dominated and male centred, has advanced the interests of men over women. As we have seen in the earlier section looking at women's magazines, there are several different perspectives within the feminist ideology but all may be summarised as seeking to rectify this imbalance and remove inequality through action ranging from the subtle to the more radical.
- *Postcolonialism*. Great Britain, along with most other countries in Western Europe, through military dominance was once able to establish empires throughout the world. Britain entered developing countries and established rule over other countries as well as setting up colonies. At one point, Britain ruled half the world but, over time, these colonies gained independence.

Among countries which were formerly British colonies are the USA, India, South Africa, Australia and Canada. However, the influence of British rule and culture may still be seen in many of these countries. Indeed, Canada and Australia are among those which not only have English as the most widely spoken language, but also still retain the Queen as their Head of State. Generally, the postcolonial perspective is one which recognises that there may not be an actual empire any more, but there is a cultural imperialism which pervades media from non-Western cultures. In other words, non-Western media texts, when they are the subject of examination and analysis, are studied largely through Western eyes with Western values and Western beliefs. This may help to explain why many of the norms and values that exist in media texts which relate to other cultures seem rather alien and unusual to the Western audience.

INFORMATION BOX

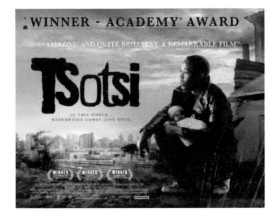

Figure 0.19
Film poster for *Tsotsi*

The film *Tsotsi* (2005), which was set in South Africa and featured an entirely South African cast, may at first appear to be an entirely South African film, but from the postcolonial perspective the film may be seen as being influenced by Western values. The narrative and characters conform to those found in Hollywood and, as this film poster shows, its critical success, which is used as a marketing tool, is measured not by its 'South African-ness' but by the Western awards it has won in Los Angeles, Toronto and Edinburgh, and, of course, the Academy Award it won for Best Foreign Language Film of the Year.

- *Marxism*. Few theoretical perspectives have the distinction of taking their name from the person who first formulated the ideas central to their philosophy. Marxism is, however, one such case, as it refers to the ideas regarding the nature of the distribution of power and wealth as proposed chiefly, although not exclusively, by Karl Marx. Earlier in this chapter, we saw an example using hegemony, a theory which although first proposed by Antonio Gramsci is very much at home in the Marxist ideology. Marxism criticises the capitalist nature of industrialised and modern societies in which the power is held by a ruling class that exerts its influence over the working masses who are relatively powerless to fight against this. The relationship between the ruling class, which Marx termed the bourgeoisie, and the workers, who he termed the proletariat is one of conflict. Once again, this perspective is important to Media Studies, as Marxists argue that the media is one of the main channels through which the ruling class maintains their influence over the workers, not least because the overwhelming majority of the individuals who own and control the media itself form part of this ruling class.
- *Liberal pluralism*. Acting as an opposing viewpoint to that held by Marxists, liberal pluralism is a theoretical perspective which is not critical of the nature of capitalist society; rather, it embraces the freedom (liberal) which modern democratic societies allow and acknowledges the fact that many different seats of power and the numerous ideological and political perspectives (pluralism) within them exist. Whereas Marxists see the media as a tool through which the inequalities between the powerful and the rest, the wealthy and the relatively poor are both facilitated and legitimised, liberal pluralists see the media, especially a free media with a varied output, as having a largely beneficial role in a society, one which inspires debate, discussion and disagreement, and which entertains, educates and informs all people.

References

McKee, R. (1997) Classic Five-part Narrative, taken from McKee's story seminar at Northern Alberta Institute of Technology.
Todorov, T. (1969) *Grammaire du Décameron*. Mouton.
Winship, J. (1987) *Inside Women's Magazines*. Pandora.

part 1

MEDIA THEORIES, CONCEPTS AND ISSUES

1 KEY CONCEPTS: GENRE, NARRATIVE, REPRESENTATION, AUDIENCE

2 DEVELOPING TEXTUAL ANALYSIS

3 THEORETICAL PERSPECTIVES

KEY CONCEPTS: GENRE, NARRATIVE, REPRESENTATION, AUDIENCE

1

In this chapter we will look at:

- The role and function of the key concepts in A2 study
- Genre
- Narrative
- Representation
- Audience

If you think back to your Media Studies course at AS, you should realise just how important the key concepts proved to be in guiding you through your understanding of how media products are constructed as well as how they are used and interpreted. In this chapter we revisit some of these concepts in order that you can continue to apply them in your study. The difference between AS and A2 in relation to these concepts is a subtle but important one. At AS your main focus is the interpretation of media products in order to understand how they work and what they do. At A2, as we have suggested, 'why' becomes a much more important question than 'how' or 'what'. So through careful application of the key concepts, not only to analysis of texts but also to issues and debates, you should be able to explore in a meaningful way just why media products are the way they are. What are the pressures and protocols that determine their nature? How far is genre or format a factor? Do narrative structures play an influential role in deciding what a media product looks like or sounds like? How far are issues of representation and ultimately ideology seminal in determining the nature of products? To what degree do audiences have an impact on the shape and nature of a product? In this chapter we hope you will find some of the answers to these questions.

Genre

In this section we:

- Consider and explain the concept of genre.
- Look at the function of genre in relation to audiences and producers of media texts.
- Consider the role of genre as a critical tool in the analysis of media texts.

Figure 1.1 Scene from *44 Inch Chest*

What clues are present in this still as to the genre of the film? Try the activity below to help you.

Look at the image in Figure 1.1. Try to identify the type of film this image is taken from.

- Can you work out what sort of storyline the film is likely to have?
- Can you determine who the villain may be?
- Can you make any suggestions as to the actors or directors that might appear in this type of film?
- What else can you deduce about the film?

The function of genre

In working out the answers to the questions above, you will have used your knowledge of genre. Genre is the term used for the classification of media texts into groups with similar characteristics. The concept of genre is useful in looking at the ways in which media texts are organised, categorised and consumed. It is applied to television, print and radio texts as well as to film. The concept of genre suggests that there are certain types of media material, often story types, that are recognised through common elements, such as style, narrative and structure, that are used again and again to make up that particular type of media genre.

Genre is a formula that, if successful, is often repeated again and again and may be used over a long period of time. For instance, in a gangster film, such as the one in Figure 1.1, we expect to see some, or all, of the following elements, which will also probably have been in a gangster film from the 1930s:

> Car chases
> Urban settings
> Guns
> Heroes
> Corrupt police/politicians
> Villains
> Beautiful women
> Violence
> Italians (Well, because ours is a British gangster film these are Cockneys!)

An important element in identifying a genre is the look or iconography of the text. Iconography refers to those particular signs that we associate with particular genres, such as the physical attributes and dress of the actors, the settings and the 'tools of the trade' (for example, cars, guns), and constitutes a pattern of visual imagery that remains common to a genre over a period of time. In the above example of gangster movies, the urban settings, guns, car chases and perhaps a plate of spaghetti with meatballs (or in the British version a steak meal!) all contribute to the iconography which signifies to the audience the genre of the film they are viewing.

There are also certain actors whom we may associate with this genre of films (James Cagney in the 1930s, Robert De Niro in the 1980s or currently Ray Winstone) as well as certain directors (Martin Scorsese and Guy Ritchie).

ICONOGRAPHY

ACTIVITY

Reading the media

Look at a selection of films that are currently being shown in your area and try to categorise them into different genres.

continued

- What types of stories do the films tell?
- Where are the films set?
- What types of characters appear in the films?
- What particular actors and/or directors are associated with the films? Have they been involved with similar types of films before?
- What is the 'look' or iconography of the film?
- What music is used?
- Suggest reasons why the particular genres you have identified might be popular.

Take two examples of films of the same genre from different eras that interest you, for instance, *The Day The Earth Stood Still* (2008 and 1951), or *Inglourious Basterds* (2009) and *The Dirty Dozen* (1967), and identify their similarities and differences. Suggest reasons for these similarities and differences.

Figure 1.2 Scenes from the 1951 and 2008 versions of *The Day The Earth Stood Still*

Genre and audiences

Audiences are said to like the concept of genre (although we may not identify it by that name) because of its reassuring and familiar promise of patterns of repetition and variation.

The concept of genre is important in arousing the expectations of an audience and how they judge and select texts. Placing a text within a specific genre plays an important role in signalling to an audience the type of text they are being invited to consume. Audiences become familiar with the codes and conventions of specific genres. Familiarity through repetition is therefore one of the key elements in the way audiences understand and relate to media texts.

Not only do audiences come to expect certain common codes and conventions but these can also provide a short cut that saves the audience (and the producers) time in developing a new set of conventions each time they consume a new text in that particular genre. This can be seen where two existing genres have been brought together to create a new one; for example, television docu-soaps, which combine elements of documentary and soap opera. These rely on an audience's understanding of and ability to read each specific genre – they understand how documentaries work and they understand how soap operas work; therefore docu-soaps are able to satisfy their expectations of both.

In this way it may be argued that genre functions as a means of directing an audience to respond in certain ways to a particular text based on the expectations that they bring to it. The pleasures that an audience finds in the text will be to some extent dependent upon it fitting within certain patterns determined by the genre, based on what they have grown to expect from their previous experiences of texts within the genre.

In a similar way it may be argued that the consumption of genre texts is to a significant degree gendered. By this we mean that certain genres will have an appeal to women while others will be more popular with men. Soap operas are generally seen as a genre that has a specific appeal to a female audience. One reason for this is the emphasis placed upon female characters within the genre. These are often strong characters able to exert control over their own lives rather than being seen as subservient to a prevailing patriarchy. Unlike, say, action films, a popular genre with men, soaps do not rely for their impact upon a fast-moving narrative but rather dwell on the complexity of human relationships. Similarly, the resolution of the narrative within an action film has a greater appeal to a male audience, just as might the climactic end to a sporting event. The narrative outcomes of soap operas are generally much less conclusive. Indeed, the cliff-hanger at the end of each episode deliberately seeks to withhold the narrative outcome to ensure the audience returns for the next episode.

David Morley in *Family Television* (1986) found that men often disapproved of watching fiction on the grounds that it was not 'real life' or sufficiently serious. He also found that men tended to define their own preferences (sport, current affairs) as more important and more 'serious'. Morley suggests that men do in fact enjoy more 'feminine' genres but are perhaps not prepared to admit it.

ACTIVITY

How far do you think Morley's assertions are about gendered consumption?

Here is an activity you can try to test it out.

continued

First, you need to identify two groups, one of males and another of females, from a range of different age groups.

Second, you need to design a brief questionnaire for them to complete. Remember: you need to get some details of their age and background as well as their gender. Use the questionnaire to explore their likes and dislikes in terms of particular genres across any medium. Try to get a reasonable size sample of say 10 to 20 from each group.

Once the questionnaires are completed you will need to do some analysis of the results. It is a good idea to try to represent your findings graphically, for example, in the form of a pie chart. Now consider your results and try to establish whether consumption of genre in the media is gender-specific.

ACTIVITY

Look at the promotional material that is used to market either a new radio, television or cinema product.

- Identify those elements that are recognisable as belonging to a particular genre by the audience.
- Are there any elements that distinguish it from other established products of the same genre?

Often the promotion and marketing for new texts invite the audience to identify similarities between a text and predecessors in the same genre. The audience can then take comfort in the fact that what they are being offered is something that they have previously enjoyed and the producers hope that they will enjoy it again.

It has been suggested that proficiency in reading texts within a genre can also lead to the audience's pleasure being heightened as they recognise particular character types or storylines.

On a more sophisticated level, audiences can also find pleasure in the way in which genre conventions are subverted. A comedy series such as *Outnumbered* delights in subverting the conventions of situation comedy by offering something which feels more improvised than contrived and moves the focus from the situation to the mode of address. This creates a productive friction between dramatic and almost documentary elements which also represents the differences between children and adults (and their worlds). A director like Quentin Tarantino plays with the notion of genre in many of his films by juxtaposing different genres within a single movie.

Genre and producers

Producers are said to like the concept of genre because they can exploit a winning formula and minimise taking risks. The concept of genre also helps institutions budget and plan their finances more accurately and helps them to promote new products.

One of the main functions of most of the mainstream media is to make a profit. Just as a high street retailer has to sell goods that the customers will want to buy, so a media producer has to create texts that audiences will want to consume.

One way to do this is to find what audiences already enjoy and to offer something similar. Genre is an easy way of doing this. Where a formula has been proved popular with audiences, it makes sense for the producer to use that formula again and to create a new product that contains similar recognisable features which it is hoped will have an immediate appeal to an established audience.

ACTIVITY

How might the use of a proven formula apply to the popular music industry? Is this also the case when listening to radio music stations? Imagine you were interested in investing in a rising music star: what qualities, in the current climate, would you be looking for? Solo singer or group? Image? Musical genre?

It is for this reason that certain genres seem to be continually popular, such as hospital dramas on television. Some genres, such as wildlife programmes, although popular for many years, have changed over time as technology has changed, although the codes and conventions or the presenter may have stayed the same. Indeed, genre is such a useful tool that it is now the case that small niche audiences are targeted by themed cable and satellite channels carrying programmes of just one genre. These niche audiences are groups of people with specific media interests, such as holiday, history or 'adult' programmes. This has the very real advantage of delivering a ready-made audience to advertisers marketing specific products. For example, a channel dedicated to travel programmes will clearly attract an audience in the market to buy holidays. For example, recent popular genres include moving house such as *Location, Location, Location* or 'around Britain' programmes such as *Best and Worst Places to Live in the UK*.

ACTIVITY

Look at programmes in these genres and try to identify similarities or differences between them. Consider who the target audience is and why the programme is popular.

Other changes in genres over a period of time may be the result of changes in society itself. Consider, for example, the police series on television. The representation of police officers in programmes like *Dixon of Dock Green* (Figure 1.3a), broadcast in the early 1950s, is quite a long way removed from the way they are represented in some more contemporary programmes such as *CSI: Crime Scene Investigation* or *The Wire*, although some might argue that there are still many similarities between *Dixon of Dock Green* and *The Bill* (Figures 1.3b and 1.3c).

The dominance of genre, coupled with the caution of many media producers, can mean that some new texts are marginalised because they do not fit into the generic conventions that audiences recognise and accept. However, there are always new combinations of programmes being produced that can be difficult to fit into a particular genre yet are successful. For instance, where do series such as *Glee* and *24* fit?

Figure 1.3 Genres change over time. Consider, for example, the representation of the police in the series *Dixon of Dock Green* (top) and its contemporary counterpart *The Bill* (bottom left and right).

New genres or new takes on existing genres are often created by taking the conventions of existing genres and mixing these together to create a new 'hybrid'. This process is called hybridisation. It is often difficult to tell whether *The Bill* is a crime series programme or an example of a soap opera set in a police station. This ability of genres to transmute into other forms can obviously, in the eyes of many theorists, limit the value of genre as a tool in analysing texts. You might like to consider, for example, the way in which the horror movie has developed the capacity for self-reference to the point that some texts have deliberate comic elements about them. It is hard to argue the value of genre as an organising principle of the construction and consumption of texts when they can alter their shape in this way.

Indeed, some would argue that the most successful of media texts are those that do not readily fit into established genres. However, a counter-argument might rest on the vast majority of media output conforming reasonably well to established genre conventions. For example, programmes such as *Casualty* and *Holby City*, even *House* and *Bones*, all fit reasonably comfortably into the genre of medical dramas.

ACTIVITY

Look at the stills from television cop shows broadcast around 50 years apart (Figure 1.3). What can you learn by looking at these stills about the way in which the genre has changed over that period of time?

Interestingly, the term 'genre' is one you are unlikely to encounter in the media industries themselves. Television, for example, prefers to use the word 'format' to describe shows that have specific qualities that they share with others. Format television has become an increasingly important element in broadcasting in this country and across the world. Even a publicly-funded television producer such as the BBC is under a commercial imperative to raise additional revenue by selling programmes and ideas globally. *Strictly Come Dancing* is a prime example of the way in which a home-grown format has been exported worldwide.

Variants of the show are broadcast in 40 countries, each with its own individual local cultural identity, but all using the basic formula established in the British format. In the USA, for example, in show is called *Dancing with the Stars*, but the judges include Len Goodman and Bruno Tonioli, who also feature in the British series. The UK has become so successful in recent years in developing and exporting formats that it is said that over 50 per cent of all formats originate in this country.

ACTIVITY

Make a list of shows that you think might form part of a global format. Try some research on the web to find out about the exported versions of these shows. For example, *Who Wants To Be a Millionnaire* is called *Qui veut gagner des millions*? What do you think is the attraction of these programmes for audiences worldwide?

Genre as a critical tool

The idea of genre has been used for some time. For example, Literary Studies categorises texts into such genres as sonnets, tragedies and picaresque novels. It was the film theorists of the 1960s and 1970s who recognised the importance of genre to Film and Media Studies. They saw genre as important because media texts are the product of an industrial process, rather than the creation of an individual, as typified by the Hollywood studio system, or indeed Bollywood today.

Much of the early work of theorists such as Steve Neale and Tom Ryall was concerned with defining the nature of genre and considering how the concept of genre influenced both the way in which texts were created and the ways in which audiences consumed them. This relationship is often depicted as a triangle in which the dynamics between audience, producer and text each occupy the three points of the triangle (Figure 1.4).

Grouping texts according to type makes studying them more convenient, recognises the industrial constraints upon producers of media texts and also allows these texts to be looked at in terms of trends within popular culture (e.g. the western or sci-fi in 1950s and 1960s). Genre theory acknowledges that while an individual text may not be worthy of detailed study, a group of texts of the same genre can reveal a great deal, especially in terms of audience appeal (e.g. Hammer films).

This grouping can, however, seem at times quite arbitrary. Often texts are grouped into a genre because of the themes that they deal with. Situation comedy has for

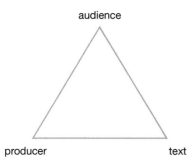

Figure 1.4 The audience/producer/text triangle

its theme humorous events that take place within situations such as family life. There are of course arguments that other characteristics within might be used to link them together. For example, geography might be considered a common factor in linking together different texts. Those that deal with or are set in London, it could be argued, should share generic conventions, in which case *The Bill*, *EastEnders* and *Only Fools and Horses* might form a genre category of their own rather than being crime series, soap opera and sitcom. You might like to consider the way in which a social networking site creates genres by hyperlinking similar search content to the specific content you are viewing in the same way that online retail sites such as Amazon often offer links to DVDs or CDs of a similar genre when you search for a specific title.

ACTIVITY

- Select a range of texts from different media platforms, including the web, that are focused on London.
- Identify which genres these texts would normally be associated with.
- Consider, if there were to be a genre called 'texts about London', how well these texts might form a group.

Limitations of genre

As you will see from the above activity, although genre is a useful means of grouping together texts so that we can consider them as a unit, the assumptions we make about how best to group them are at times quite arbitrary and even flawed.

1. The concept of genre can clearly have limitations when applied to a range of media texts because of the variety and the need for constant updating of texts that are being produced. Many texts may look similar but are too different to be grouped together.
2. Sometimes the category becomes too generalised to be helpful. For instance, soap opera could be described as a genre because there are many common characteristics (domestic settings, continuing storylines, cliff-hanger endings, familiar characters and so on) but how helpful is it to say that *Doctors* and *EastEnders* belong to the same genre? We need to be able to distinguish between sub-genres within a genre, for example, American 'fantasy' soap operas and British 'realism' soap operas. How would you describe Australian soap operas such as *Neighbours* or *Home and Away*?
3. Although we have used the concept of genre for all types of media text, it has been argued that genre is most useful for film and television and is of limited use when applied to newspapers, magazines or radio.

4. The value concept of genre is further tested by how technology has presented us with both new ways of consuming media texts and the platforms used for their consumption and delivery. An innovation such as *E20*, where an internet-only spin-off from the prime-time soap *EastEnders* offers linked but not dependent content, is an example of a small step that symbolically might be a giant leap. While extending marketing, this 'naughty little brother or sister to the main show' is also repositioning us with regard to changing expectations. While it is possible, for example, to group websites into 'genres' according to their themes, such as news websites or even pornographic websites, it may be difficult to see the precise value of doing this. News is probably better considered in its cross-platform role by considering how the technologies of print, moving image, sound and the web shape the nature of the product which we call 'news'.

ACTIVITY

Carry out a survey of the television schedules and try to categorise the main genres that appear. In addition, look at satellite, cable and digital channels.

- What are the most common genres that occur on the main terrestrial and freeview channels? How many of them are established genres and how many do you think are more recent or hybrid genres? How would you account for the popularity of two or three of the most popular genres in the schedules?
- Do you think that certain genres are especially appealing to different audiences? Consider, for example, when specific programmes are scheduled and what sort of audience is likely to be viewing at that time.
- Do you think genre plays an important role in determining the way in which schedules are created?
- Consider how the concept of genre is used by digital and satellite channels. Look, for example, at the way in which Sky Movies breaks are segmented into different channels. How do these channels use genre as a way of organising the scheduling of films? Are other channels themed in this way? Look at the way in which factual programmes are scheduled.

Narrative

In this section we:

- Consider the significance of narrative in both fiction and non-fiction texts.
- Look at narrative construction and mode of address.
- Examine the relationship between narrative and genre.

Narrative construction

Narrative is the way in which a story is told in both fictional and non-fictional media texts. From our earliest days narrative is an important part of our lives. For many people, their earliest recollections relate to bedtime stories or stories told by their teacher in primary school. Another reason why narrative is so important to us is that it acts as an organising principle that helps us make sense of the world. To a child the world is a mass of unconnected and incomprehensible events, some pleasurable, some frightening, none of which makes a great deal of sense. Narrative, or storytelling, performs the important function of interpreting the world and shaping it into a comprehensible and comfortable form that allows us to see the forces of light and dark, and good and evil, battle against each other. Usually we are rewarded with the comforting outcome of the triumph of good and the reassurance of an equilibrium in which all will live 'happily ever after'.

As we grow up, narrative remains an important source of reassurance in a hostile universe, in much the same way as it did when we were children. Indeed, satisfying our need for narrative can in itself become associated with reward or punishment. Bad behaviour at school or at home may be punished with the denial of an end-of-day or bedtime story. Good behaviour, on the other hand, is rewarded with a narrative.

Narrative, therefore, plays an important role in our growing up and consequently in forming our social values.

> **Indeed so commonplace and natural does story-telling appear that it may seem invisible to study. Yet story-telling is a complex process with important implications.**

(Tilley, 1991)

·

Watch a children's/family television programme that involves some element of storytelling such as *Doctor Who*. Paying particular attention to the narrative, consider how conflict within the narrative is developed. What devices are used to indicate to the audience where their sympathies are expected to lie between the characters?

Figure 1.5 A scene from *Doctor Who*, a family programme

Clearly narrative is a powerful force not only to help us make sense of our world, but also with the potential to influence our behaviour. Similarly, for the media producers, narrative is an important tool for organising seemingly random and incoherent events into a coherent and logical form that an audience can assimilate. Consider, for example, a news story that has occurred in some remote part of the world. It may be a disaster, such as an earthquake or a famine that has damaged the lives of many thousands of people in a terrifying way. A journalist writing a newspaper story has to explain what has happened in a few hundred words and, perhaps, a couple of photographs. Often the journalist will do this by focusing on specific detail about the impact of the disaster on the lives of individual people or families. In this way members of the audience have a clear point of reference with which to make a comparison with themselves or their own families. The scale of the disaster, too vast to comprehend, is understood in terms of the individual human being, with whom we, the audience, can empathise.

Narrative may be used as a potent means of influencing the responses of an audience to a particular event. This is often determined by the way in which the information is presented. Certainly when we are being told about a conflict, in a western or gangster movie, for example, the narrative often unfolds in such a way as to make us 'take sides' in support of one party or the other. The narrative may thus be used to position an audience in such a way as to limit the range of readings available to them from the text.

It is important to note that although the term 'narrative' is associated, through its literary origins, with fictional texts such as films and novels, it also plays an important part in non-fiction texts such as newspaper stories. Consider how the news photograph (Figure 1.6) exploits the moment of conflict between the police and the protesters to achieve its effect.

We have seen that narrative is a means by which media producers shape and control the flow of information to an audience. At a basic level, narrative may be seen as the sequencing of information about events into a logical and cohesive structure in time and space. Indeed, it has been argued that the underlying structure of all narratives is basically the same, with variation taking place only in terms of character and setting. The Bulgarian theorist Tzvetan Todorov reduced the concept of narrative to a simple recurring formula:

equilibrium → disequilibrium → new equilibrium

A narrative starts with a state of equilibrium or harmony, for example, a peaceful community getting on with and enjoying life. A firm sense of social order is established. Into this world of stability comes a force of disequilibrium or disruption, an evil outsider, intent on destroying the sense of well-being. By some mechanism such as the intervention of another outside agency, such as a lone gunfighter, the force of evil is overcome and order and harmony, in the form of a new equilibrium, are restored.

ACTIVITY

A photograph can be read as a frozen moment in an ongoing narrative. What do you think were the events leading up to the moment in this photograph? What do you think happened afterwards?

Figure 1.6 Protestors in Iran, December 2009

Figure 1.7 A scene from *Zombieland* (Ruben Fleischer, 2009)

The horror movie is another example of a film genre in which external forces disturb the equilibrium of a community.

Clearly you will see the plot of many Hollywood movie genres (e.g. western, sci-fi or even musical) fitting into this structure. Less obviously, the plot of the television news follows a similar pattern. The opening shot introduces us to the harmony of the studio as the news programme opens. The tragic events of the world news, reports of wars, famines, social unrest and political intrigue, invade our living space and disrupt the harmony. Finally we are offered a light and comic story to provide relief from this narrative of world disorder and disaster before we are returned to the newsreader shuffling papers and calmly saying good night. The equilibrium of the familiar world – our living-room – is re-established, disrupted only briefly by the tragic events of the world at large. Similarly, in a programme such as *Crimewatch*, despite depicting the nightmare deeds of the criminal community, the narrative closes in the security of the studio with a familiar and friendly presenter reassuring us that we are unlikely to become victims ourselves. We may have experienced the dangers of the world, but we are told that we can still sleep soundly in our beds.

In their book *Film Art: An Introduction* (2006), Bordwell and Thompson offer a technique for looking at film narrative in segments or sequences. These are called scenes, or distinct phases of the action occurring within relatively unified space and time. The segmentation allows us to see major divisions within the plot and how scenes are organised within them. This is a useful device that may be applied to a number of different narratives in order to reveal the way in which they are constructed. To some degree these divisions may be viewed on the chapter menu of any DVD of any film. Taking time out to look at the scene sequences offered by your favourite films on DVD will perhaps give you a feeling for the conventional nature of film narratives, which are generally linear sequences progressing from a fixed point in time forward to a second point.

ACTIVITY

Use the chapter menus of a couple of films with which you are familiar to address the following issues:

- The extent to which (where appropriate) chapter titles contribute to your understanding/appreciation of the overall narrative.
- Identifying those chapters that move the narrative forward (and to what degree they do this).
- Identifying those chapters that 'step aside' to provide descriptive detail (to 'thicken' the narrative rather than extend it).
- Identifying those chapters that in some way resist or counter the forward momentum.

Given the overwhelming popularity of linear narrative it is not surprising that few films risk the breakdown of this narrative convention to any significant degree. Techniques like flashback may be used to break up the monotony of the chronological sequence but these elements are contained within a recognisible convention as an organising principle for the narrative. Even in the recent *The Curious Case of Benjamin Button* where the central character lives his life in reverse, the innovation is the 'high concept' of the film's pitch rather than a challenge to chronological structure.

Of course, ruptured narratives are common outside of the mainstream, for example, among the surrealists from Bunuel to Lynch, but mainstream cinema rarely takes risks without semantic intent. What this means is that those who challenge the linear structure are, in so doing, challenging its power as a structure of meaning, one which imposes certain kinds of certainty on an unwitting audience. Thus a film like *Jumanji* offers a narrative shaped by the roll of a couple of dice as a direct challenge to the order imposed across the family film (whose function it is to show a return to the kind of order that will defend a structure like the family). Similarly, Tarantino's mixed-up sequences in *Pulp Fiction* are more than playful: they call everything that Tarantino is both showing and referencing into question. In both of these examples the argument is enacted in the non-linear structure.

Similarly, and in a genre not known for its formal experimentation, the 'offbeat' romantic comedy *(500) Days of Summer* attempts to do exactly what the title (impossibly?) implies: present an experience rather than a sequence. As the tagline proclaimed: "This is not a love story. It is a story about love." Hence, while some have reconstructed a linear version of the plot (see www.Imdb.com), this is not the narrative of the film, which is in fact constituted from the numbered days suggested by the title. By opening with Day 483 and a couple on a bench holding hands (the girl is wearing a ring), the film not only offers us a job of reconstructive work to do but also confronts us with issues of sequence which add an extra dimension to the film's discourse on love and its meanings, even its provenance. Time, in fact, is brought to the fore since, whatever the label, this scene is also the first, number one. This is all playful and allows the transition from summer to autumn (Tom's next object of desire) to be both arch and gentle.

ACTIVITY

Select a film or fictional television programme you have watched recently which you feel has made attempts to play with narrative sequencing and produce your own model of its narrative segmentation. A comedy film or situation comedy might make an interesting example. You should try to

continued

identify the way in which different strands within a narrative might work in relation to one another. In a situation comedy, for example, there are often narrative strands that run in parallel with one another, such as the activities the next-door neighbours are undertaking. Here the narrative function might be to invite comparison and contrast between two sets of characters and their narrative functions. What have you learned about the structure of the text from breaking it down into segments?

This activity should help you to understand that even seemingly simple and straightforward programmes often reveal quite complex narrative structures. It also serves to suggest how narrative works across a range of texts, some of which are non-fictional. Consider, for example, how in a confessional programme like *Trisha* a narrative unfolds in each part as each of the characters adds to the conflict that is the mainspring of the show. This provides a good example of narrative flow whereby the unfolding of the narrative is carefully controlled by the production team. Real-life characters designed to provide further opportunities for conflict are unleashed and duly move the narrative forward to its climax. Similarly the results of a lie detector or DNA test may be used to heighten or even resolve conflict.

Character is an important aspect of narrative, particularly in fictional texts such as films, TV and radio drama. In soap operas, for example, certain character types consistently recur to the point where they become almost stereotypes. For example, grumpy old people and angst-ridden teenagers are to be found as stock characters across the range of television soap operas. Grouping people into different categories like this is called character typology, and it should be clear that this principle can be extended across a range of genres, such as the police series or the gangster movie.

ACTIVITY

Take a close look at two episodes of different prime-time soaps. Try to make a list of recurring character typologies using characters from each of the soaps. Now consider the extent to which you feel the characters are stereotyped to fit these typologies. Do any of the characters transcend the stereotype that has been created? You should consider how far the writing and the acting reinforce or challenge the stereotype.

Vladimir Propp, a Russian structuralist, studied fairy stories and established a number of character types and events associated with them. He called these events 'functions' and suggested that their number was limited to 31 functions. His work has been related to Film and Media Studies, and it is possible, for example, to use Propp's theory to fit the character types in a range of texts, especially feature films.

Typical Proppian characters and their functions would include:

- the hero
- the villain
- the donor (offers gift with magical properties)
- the dispatcher (sends hero on mission)
- the helper (aids hero)
- the princess (hero's reward).

Using the above list, identify these characters in any Bond or similar action/adventure film. How well can these characters be related to any other film or television programme that you have watched?

An important influence which character has on narrative is that of causality, which is concerned with the idea of cause and effect. Characters usually act out of motives. When different characters are introduced to us, we usually get to know what their motives are, for example, what goals they have. These motives are likely to be the cause of events that unfold around this particular character. At the beginning of a film or drama we will find out about a character's goal; it may be to get a partner, rob a bank, control the world, murder a spouse, or perhaps all of these. These motives will drive the character and become the cause of action within the text. Clearly this is likely to bring the character into conflict with other characters who may be acting out of different motives and are intent on achieving different goals. Conflict is central to the functioning of narrative not least because it is conflict that invites us, the audience, to take sides.

ACTIVITY

As we have indicated, narrative is an important concept in non-fiction as well as in fictional texts. Consider how conflict is used as a basis for telling stories in any of the following non-fiction texts:

- Newspaper articles. Consider how a range of different types of stories are presented. You should look at political stories, sports

continued

stories as well as foreign news and celebrity stories. Identify the two sides represented in the conflict and see if you think there is a bias in the story towards one side or another.

■ Factual television programmes. You should include current affairs programmes and documentaries in your survey. One useful means of exploring conflict is through wildlife programmes, especially those that feature predatory animals. The heroes and villains of these programmes are likely to change according to which ones have 'star billing'.

Mode of address

Mode of address is the way in which a particular text will address or speak to its audience and is an important concept in narrative study. It refers to the way in which a media text may be said to 'talk to' its audience. As such, it also has important implications for the way in which the audience responds to the text. For example, the use of a voice-over, an off-screen narrator who talks directly to the audience, is often seen as an authoritative mode of address, providing the audience with information that is incontrovertible. The authority of this voice is often further reinforced by the use of a well-known actor with a particularly distinctive voice.

The use of voice-over is a feature of news, current affairs programmes and some documentaries, in which this commentary holds the narrative together and develops it. Similarly, voice-over is used as a narrative device in cinema. It is a distinctive feature of the genre *film noir*, for example, in Josh Hartnett's commentary on the action in Brian de Palma's *Black Dahlia* (2006) where the film begins with Officer Dwight 'Bucky' Bleichert's *voice-over*:

> " Mr. Fire versus Mr. Ice. For everything people were making it out to be, you'd think it was our first fight. It wasn't. And it wouldn't be our last. "

Similarly, who can forget the voice-over that sets up David Fincher's masterpiece *Fight Club* or this near-death experience from *Kick Ass:*

> " Even with my metal plates and my fucked up nerve endings, I gotta tell you, that hurt! But not half as much as the idea of leaving everything behind. Katie, my dad, Todd and Marty . . . and all the things I'd never do. Like

learn to drive or see what me and Katie's kids would look like or find out what happened on *Lost*. And if you're reassuring yourself that I'm going to make it through this since I'm talking to you now, quit being such a smart-ass! Hell dude, you never seen *Sin City*? *Sunset Boulevard*? *American Beauty*? **"**

(Dave aka Kick Ass)

Such a voice-over is an off-screen (asynchronous) voice that directly addresses and confides in the audience. One effect of using this device is to make the audience a party to information that may not be shared by the rest of the characters on screen. It therefore offers us, the audience, privileged information about what is going on. We are positioned to accept, often without question, the information being communicated by this off-screen voice. On occasions the off-screen voice may also make us wary of trusting the character, for example, in the opening scene of *Taxi Driver* (1976), in which Travis Bickle reveals his conflicted personality in a tirade against humanity.

ACTIVITY

Make a recording of a documentary that deals with complex medical or scientific issues about which you are likely to know very little.

- What methods does the commentary use to help the audience understand the complex information being conveyed? Is there a sense of conflict engendered in the programme? If so, how is this set up? resolved?
- How about an activity analysing a film such as *Bowling for Columbine* in terms of the narratives that it sets up? In what different ways could an image like the one in Figure 1.8 be read if the voice-over gave different information about the scene? Try adding your own voice-over to a film with a definite ideological slant and see how the words change the way the scene is read by the audience. To what extent are the audience members guided in their understanding through your voice-over? In what ways do they resist the reading your voice-over presents?

continued

Figure 1.8 Michael Moore in *Bowling for Columbine*

The issue of audience positioning is a complex one and is dealt with more fully in the section on media audiences. An important effect of narrative, however, is the way in which it may be used to place or position an audience in relation to the text. In the example of *Taxi Driver*, the device is used to provide the audience with the opportunity to be party to information not shared by other characters in the film. This was an important device used in *film noir*. Not only does it provide the audience with information that assists in the development of the narrative, but it also gives access to the innermost thoughts of the main character, thus providing the audience with an insight into motivation and psychological make-up.

Roland Barthes explored the concept of narrative as part of his work on structuralism. He argued that narrative works through a series of codes that are used to control the way in which information is conveyed to the audience. Two of these codes are particularly important for our understanding of how narrative functions in media texts. The first is called the enigma code. An enigma is a riddle or puzzle, and some types of narrative make extensive use of this code. An obvious example is a detective story, in which we, the audience, are invited to solve the puzzle of 'whodunit' by interpreting the clues and pitting our wits against those of the fictional detective whose job it is to find the perpetrator of the crime. Enigma is a narrative device that teases the audience by presenting a puzzle or riddle to be solved.

This is an obvious use of enigma as a narrative device. However, there are many other, less obvious ways in which these enigmas are used. One example is the use of trails for programmes to be broadcast later on television or radio. These often rely on teasing the audience with information that can only be fully understood by tuning in to the programme itself. Similarly, a non-fiction text such as the news begins with headlines, which provide cryptic details of the stories that are to follow, ensuring that the audience stays with the programme to find out the full story behind the headlines. Print media uses similar devices, with newspaper headlines or magazine front covers offering brief information to invite the reader to purchase the product and consume the larger narrative within (e.g. "POP STAR IN DRUGS TRAGEDY"). Similarly, advertisers often use billboards to tease us with little clues about a product, such as a feature film, to be launched on to the market.

One of the pleasures an audience receives from consuming a media text is that of predicting the outcome to a particular narrative. Clearly this is much of the appeal of crime-based texts, in which the audience is positioned alongside the detective in trying to solve the crime or mystery.

Another code that Barthes writes about is the action code. This is a narrative device by which a resolution is produced through action (e.g. a shoot-out).

This code suggests how narratives can be resolved through action, often on the part of the protagonist or hero. Typically a resolution is achieved through an act of violence, such as a gun battle. The action code is, therefore, often considered to be a male genre, with problems being resolved through action such as physical violence or a car chase.

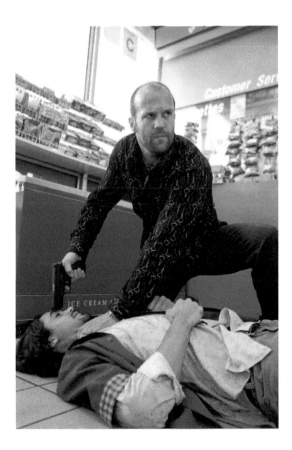

Figure 1.9 A scene from *Crank*

Figure 1.9 shows a scene from *Crank* (2006). Barthes (1997) argues that the action code sees problems resolved through action such as violence or gunplay as in this shot. Can you suggest other similar examples?

Of course, narrative is a highly manipulative device in the hands, for example, of film and television producers. It may be used to control to some degree the responses of audiences and persuade them to occupy a certain position in relation to what they are viewing. In a format such as presenting news, this is a powerful position to occupy and can ultimately shape people's attitudes, both socially and politically. However, digital technology has created many more opportunities for audiences to respond directly to the narratives that the media brings into their lives. Feedback is just one of these, as television viewers or radio listeners can react immediately to programme materials through a range of communication devices, such as email and text, to get their own views aired and potentially shape the narrative that is unfolding. Much reality television relies on audiences voting on issues such as the continued participation of characters within a drama, thus giving each of us potentially the power to determine the narrative outcome.

ACTIVITY

Make a list of programmes to which audiences can directly respond and influence how the narrative unfolds. What do you think are the advantages to media producers of encouraging audiences to interact with their output?

Relationship between narrative and genre

A study of different genres in film and television will suggest that the formula requires the narrative to be closed in a different way for each different genre. For example, a soap opera will usually end with a cliff-hanger – a narrative device designed to create suspense for the audience and ensure that they tune in to the next episode.

Narrative is also often recognised for the different devices it employs to engage the audience with the text. Alfred Hitchcock spoke of a device that he called 'the bomb under the table'. Here suspense is built for the audience by making them party to information not shared by the characters on screen – in this case, a bomb under the table ready to explode but about which the on-screen characters are wholly unaware.

Most narratives will move in a straight line, following the basic chronology of a story unfolding. This is often called a linear narrative because it involves a plot that moves forward in a straight line without flashbacks or digressions. However, in controlling the flow of information, a number of devices may be employed to realign the narrative. An obvious example is flashback, whereby the narrative allows a character to remember events that have happened in the past, usually to shed light on events 'currently' taking place within the narrative. Similarly, a complex narrative may allow events taking place in two different locations at the same time to be shown alongside each other. This is called parallel action in which two scenes are observed as happening at the same time by cutting between them, and provides the audience with a privileged view. An extreme form of this is the use of split-screen techniques, whereby two narratives can literally be shown simultaneously on screen.

Some media texts play on the need of the audience to find logical sequencing in narratives by denying this. For example, if we are watching a film and a character we know to have been killed suddenly and inexplicably reappears, we find it hard to make sense of this event. Indeed, the contract that we, the audience, agreed to whereby we suspend our disbelief is clearly threatened by this. *Pulp Fiction* is an example of a film that uses this device, confounding the audience by the reappearance of a character whose death we had witnessed earlier.

This method of deliberately disrupting narrative flow in order to achieve a particular effect, such as the repetition of images or the disruption of a chronological sequence of events, is called anti-narrative because it works in contrast to the accepted chronological cause-and-effect patterns of a narrative. One reason that filmmakers and producers of television programmes are able to do this is the fact that audiences have become extremely sophisticated in the way in which they read complex moving image texts.

Narrative and digital technology

NARRATIVE AND NEW MEDIA PLATFORMS

As you will have seen, narrative is a particularly useful tool for exploring the way in which media texts are constructed and the ways in which they can be consumed or read by audiences. As one of the prime concerns of narrative study is to explore the way in which the flow of information is controlled with a text, it also has useful applications in looking at more recent media forms. If you consider the structure and organisation of a website, you should be able to see how narrative is a key element in the way in which an audience will engage with such a text.

Websites are generally constructed to have a home page or landing page which is the first page to be accessed either via a search engine or from a list of bookmarks. The home page fulfils a similar function to a newspaper front page or magazine cover in that it reassures readers that they have arrived at the right place and that what they see grabs their attention sufficiently to keep them viewing.

The home page is also the link or conduit through which the rest of the website may be accessed. A good home page will not only engage in its own right but will also offer a pathway to other areas of the site. The use of hyperlinks and menus is critical in this process of signposting the way to further information and detail within the site. Notice how a good website will always provide a link from whatever pages you are on back to the home page so that if you become lost in the narrative, there is a readily available escape route back to where you started.

Of course the paths through the web can be labyrinthine simply because of the temptation that afflicts all surfers to click on links either in the hope of finding what they are looking for or more likely for the sheer pleasure of doing so. Web browsers are, however, designed with this random surfing in mind. Such functions as the back button, the bookmark facility and the history menu provide ways of sign-posting the narrative so that it is always possible to pick up the trail and set off in a more productive direction.

What is especially interesting about the narratives of the web is the extent to which we, the audience, are empowered to drive the narrative forward. In a tradi-tionally constructed text, it is the producer who determines how the information flows. To a large extent we have little control over what information we receive and the order in which we receive it. Web narratives are quite different. They permit us to link together many separate elements of the web in the order which we choose, be it logical or not. In this way narrativity on the web has become highly participative. The individual surfer is able to create a unique narrative through the association of the sites he or she visits in the order in which he or she has chosen to visit them. In effect they link together disparate elements from the web and create their own personal narrative by the associations they create between sites. Part of the pleasure of these narratives is their random nature. Hence the 'I feel lucky' option in the Google search engine.

ACTIVITY

Other media forms such as the blog and the podcast clearly have narratives. Some of these relate closely to the narratives of established media forms. For example, the podcast shares many narrative con-ventions with a traditional radio broadcast.

Look at a couple of sites which offer blogs and podcasts and identify how the narrative devices they use are similar to and different from more established media forms. You may like to consider, for example, that in a blog the chronology means that the most recent entry is generally the first to be accessed.

If you get stuck, try looking at the following:

http://www.stephenfry.com/blog/
http://www.britblog.com/
http://dilbertblog.typepad.com/
http://podcast.com/
http://www.bbc.co.uk/radio/podcasts/directory/

ACTIVITY

How might narrative theories be applied to a medium such as Twitter? Think about the way in which people are updated via Twitter and the way in which we can use Twitter to follow the progress of celebrities through their daily lives.

Representation

Case study 1.1
REPRESENTATION

When you switch on your TV, the images are largely iconic; they look like the images that you see when you look through your window at the world outside. Indeed, TV is often described as 'a window on the world', which suggests that what we see on our screens is in fact the world outside. However, television is not a 'window', nor could it ever be. Every televised image is the product of many decisions about how reality should be transformed. For this reason, television cannot simply show reality; it can only offer versions of reality influenced by the decision-making processes of media producers and the technical constraints of the medium. This is what we mean by the construction of reality by the media. Because all media messages are constructed in this sense, everything contained within them

continued

is a representation. Of course, representation does not just concern pictures; it concerns every aspect of communication. Newspaper journalists, for example, may talk about 'telling it like it really is' or 'transparent reporting'. The implication is that they convey 'reality' exactly as it is to their readers.

Much of the nature of the construction of television programmes and films is designed to make them appear as natural and as realistic as possible. Continuity editing, for example, creates the illusion that programmes have a natural flow, that they are put together without seams. With television's technical ability to produce slow-motion action replays and use multiple camera angles, a sporting event viewed on TV has a reality beyond that of spectating at a live event. In a sense, the television experience becomes 'more real than real'. Inherent in this are obvious consequences for the individual. The postmodernist commentator Jean Baudrillard talks of distinctions between the real and the unreal collapsing, so that TV no longer *represents* the world, it *is* the world. We are overloaded with information and images to such an extent that we no longer differentiate between the real world and media constructions of the world: a condition which Baudrillard describes as hyperreality.

Mediation as a process

When a medium (such as radio or film) carries a message it is mediating it, simply carrying it from one place to another. Mediation is the act of 'going between', in this case between 'an audience' and 'the world', but this simple process has some very complex implications. Inevitably, the relationship between the world and the audience is changed by the process of mediation. When you sit down and think about it you might come to the conclusion that most of what you know and most of your experiences are 'merely' mediated, since the encounters have been second- rather than first-hand. Think of what you really know about Africa or GM foods, let alone the war in Iraq or al-Qaeda, then subtract all you received on the subjects from 'mediators'. What is left? At best, perhaps, your holiday in Tunisia or the Gambia.

ACTIVITY

Think of some of the ways in which mediation could be described as an 'interested activity'. Bear in mind that mediation does not necessarily imply deliberate distortion or cynical manipulation of audiences (though both of these may occur). Try this 'investigation':

Figure 1.10 Barack Obama features frequently in the news

Compile two lists.

- *List 1*. What I know about Obama (if your answer is 'nothing' at least respond to the following prompts: his politics, his age, his ethnicity, his social background, his family).
- *List 2*. What I was able to find out about Obama in 30 minutes with internet access (if your answer is 'everything', prioritise).
- *Supplementary*. Does this exercise prove that (a) we know very little about Obama, *or* (b) we don't need to know about Obama as long as when we do we know where to look? And for Obama you might substitute anyone or anything.

continued

The media rarely 'sees' by accident and never without interest, although it is often at pains to 'cover its tracks' by allowing reportage and 'realism' to be casually confused with reality. Writing specifically about television realism, Abercrombie (1996, p. 27) identified three aspects of realism (which affects a particular kind of mediation).

- Realism offers a 'window on the world'; an apparently unmediated experience.
- Realism employs a narrative which has rationally ordered connections between events and characters.
- Realism attempts to conceal the production process.

The paradox here is that so much that appears natural, from the live outside broadcast to the painstakingly researched film drama, is in fact the result of a complex industrial process. What is 'real' is defined in terms of what is realistic. Neil Postman (1985) has claimed that "TV reality is *the* reality", suggesting that the mediated world has become a blueprint for the unmediated version. This is the hyperreality, this world of simulations, that the postmodernists see as central to the way we live now. Baudrillard argues that we now live in economies based on the production of images and information where once we produced 'things' (material products). The danger is that we lose a sense of context, particularly in a historical sense, that the endless mash-up of 'contemporary' and 'vintage' means that nothing is truly over or securely real. In this context, Baudrillard argues, we are open to a sentimentalised version of the past: "When the real is no longer what it used to be, nostalgia assumes its full meaning." In simple terms in the age of the trans-media narrative the interplay of media representations becomes more important than the relationship between those representations and their subject reality.

ACTIVITY

A major television event of 2010 was the Spielberg/Hanks production *The Pacific*, the latest offshoot of the Private Ryan/ Band of Brothers family. Watch the trails for this series along with the introduction to any of the first-person shooter WW2 computer games (preferably *Medal of Honour* or *Call of Duty* with *Medal of Honour: Pacific Assault* offering the clearest comparison). What similarities do you notice between the two sets of representations?

Given that both consciously offer 'realism', how do you respond to them in the light of the aspects of this process offered by Abercrombie:

- That realism offers a 'window on the world'.
- That realism employs a narrative which has rationally ordered connections between events and characters.
- That realism attempts to conceal the production process.

Stereotypes and minorities

Reality TV offers us 'real people' in 'real situations'. Magazines help us to deal with 'real problems' and the popular press deals with the 'real lives' of 'ordinary people' (as well as celebrities, of course). Soap operas give us an opportunity to share the lives of 'realistic characters' in lifelike settings. But is any of this reality-obsessed entertainment actually real? Of course not. As we have already seen, these fictional and non-fictional texts have no alternative but to provide mediated versions of the world. Some commentators have argued, though, that we, as audience members, may be organising and understanding our own lives in the terms provided by this mediated version of reality. In other words, there is a link between media representations and the identities of audience members. Representations of 'people like us' suggest to us who we are, what we can become and how we should evaluate ourselves. As Woodward puts it:

> **Discourses and systems of representation construct places from which individuals can position themselves and from which they can speak. . . . The media can be seen as providing us with the information which tells us what it feels like to occupy a particular subject-position – the streetwise teenager, the upwardly mobile worker or the caring parent.**

(Woodward 1997, p. 14)

continued

Logically, the impact on identity is felt particularly strongly by members of groups which are negatively represented in the mainstream media. In a study of black minority television viewers, Karen Ross found that most of her respondents were critical of British television's representations of ethnic groups and the relations between them. In the following extract, Ross makes it clear that the representation of places as well as groups can have an important impact upon feelings about identity and self-worth.

> **The lack of positive role models and the way in which black minority characters are routinely stereotyped contribute to feelings of low self-esteem and failure, especially among black minority children. . . . Because most black minority children in Britain were born in the country, their knowledge of 'home' is very limited, gleaned from what their relatives tell them and, of course, from television. Viewers reported sadness at the reactions of their children to their homelands of Africa, India or Pakistan which, because the media's slant on the developing world tends to be negative, is one of shame at the 'backwardness' of their country of origin.**

(Ross, 2000, p. 145)

ACTIVITY

What are the significant details that define the following as 'realistic'?

- *EastEnders*
- *Britain's Got Talent*
- *Twilight*
- *Family Guy*
- *The Hills*

Representation, the construction of versions of reality to stand in for reality, does indeed take place at all levels of the (technical and creative) media process: in the writing, direction, camera work and action. However, as

Abercrombie points out, it is one of the abiding characteristics of realism that "the illusion of transparency is preserved": he goes on to clarify this when he writes, "The form conspires to convince us that we are not viewing something that has been constructed."

The representation, for example, of minority groups often founders at a simple level. We fall for the one about the neutrality of the media, the plausibility of 'the camera never lies', and we confuse 'resembles' with 'represents'. The former is an implication, the latter an active process. If we wish to represent a multicultural society or one in which women are challenging the traditional roles allocated to them, we must do so. It is disingenuous of media professionals to act as if the ideological meanings of a text are a mystery, unknown even to its makers and even beyond its makers' influence. Although it may be true that ideology operates at the level of the unconscious, this is not to say that ideological issues are invisible.

ACTIVITY

Imagine that the next two days of your life are being filmed as an innovative 'total drama' project, with the working title *Yet Another 48 Hours*. For 48 hours, cameras will unobtrusively track your every move and interactive viewers will be able to monitor your 'actions'.

You are called in at the end of the project to discuss the production of an edited 90-minute version. You are asked for your opinion on two issues.

1. What would be the differences between a film of your life for two days and a conventional film or television 'drama'?
2. What principles would you suggest on which to model a 90-minute version of the recording?

The representation of minority groups often amounts to a failure to be proactive, as any amount of content research will prove. People with disabilities, for example, seem to have dropped 'beyond the frame' of the mediated world as if they were always just out of shot. This is what Barthes (1977) called 'absent presence', the fact that the very invisibility of some

continued

groups becomes an almost palpable issue. If we consider the representation of minority ethnic groups in the British media, the world of television situation comedy or game shows will furnish fruitful examples of absent presence. Conversely, a consideration of human interest stories and accompanying photographs in local or national newspapers might be relevant.

It would be easy to see 'absent presence' in mainstream soap operas like *Coronation Street* and even *EastEnders* as a pressure that has progressively made programme makers address this issue. However, we must not succumb to a crude oversimplification of the issue and merely see the problem in terms of a journey from 'none of them' to 'more of them', whomsoever 'they' may be. This is not a numbers but a meanings game: it is not about quotas but about questions.

Stereotypes are moulds into which reality can be poured, or at least part of it. A stereotype is a shorthand form and as such is a reduction of the complexity of the reality represented. Stereotypes do not normally try to open debates about, for example, gender representations; they actually paper over them or 'skirt' around them.

The idea of stereotyping is often used with negative connotations, as if the removal of all stereotypes would make media representations fair and unbiased. However, a brief examination of the concept reveals that stereotypes are a necessary component of all mediated communication. There is never the time or space to do justice to the complexity of human beings. The variety of our environments and the sheer diversity of individuals make it inevitable that short cuts are taken in the telling of stories and the reporting of events. Furthermore, in an influential essay on stereotypes, Tessa Perkins (1997) made the point that we tend to form assumptions about stereotypes which may in themselves be misleading. For example, we sometimes assume that stereotypes are always wrong and always negative; but this is not necessarily the case. Nor is it necessarily true that stereotypes always concern minority or oppressed groups, or that they are simple and unchanging. On the other hand, it is possible for contradictory stereotypes to be held of the same group (see Perkins 1997, p. 75).

Perkins goes on to reinforce the point that stereotypes are essentially *ideological* because they are predominantly evaluative beliefs expressed about groups and by groups. As with any ideological effect, the repetition of stereotypes and the absence of plausible alternatives means that the values wrapped up in the stereotype come to appear as 'common sense'. The stereotype does more than simply *describe* characteristics assigned to a particular group, it also carries value judgements. Andy Medhurst illustrates this principle in relation to stereotypes of gay men:

> **[T]he image of the screaming queen does not just mean 'all gay men are like that', it means 'all gay men are like that and aren't they awful', which in turn means 'and they are awful because they are not like us'.**

(Medhurst, 1998, p. 285)

In terms of the representations of minority groups, stereotyping is often a double handicap as even the range of stereotypes is often limited.

ACTIVITY

Consider the following groups. Bearing in mind Tessa Perkins' points, examine the prevalent stereotypes and explain how they are delivered either in the popular press or on television.

- fathers
- the police
- terrorists
- the French
- bankers

What are the particular issues for us as media students in each case?

Stereotypes are clearly useful in the sense that any shorthand is: they allow us to take a quick look and know what we're being given since we only need the 'gist', for example, that he's French, she's a bimbo and he's Irish. However, what we are also doing is undermining the integrity of the world we are 'viewing', unless we are also given the chance to address or challenge these crude assumptions.

Alternative representations

As noted above, the ideological effect of stereotyping is most pronounced when stereotypes are reinforced by repetition and an absence of alternatives. However, it would be a mistake to see all media representation

continued

working in this way. There are many justifiable concerns about negativity and bias in media representation, but it is worth bearing in mind some of the following.

- There are alternatives to the mainstream media.
- The mainstream media often provides space for alternative representations.
- Many groups have intervened successfully to take more control over representation.
- 'Dominant' representations can change with great speed.
- The media provides many positive role models.
- Campaigns against biased and negative stereotypes have succeeded in changing industry practices, voluntary codes of conduct and statutory controls (laws).
- Media-literate audiences have a sophisticated understanding of the techniques and devices used to 're-present' reality.

An excellent case study for the alternative take on representation is provided by Matt Groening's *The Simpsons*, which has been inhabiting its own heightened reality since 1989 in the most conservative TV environment in the world. Here the cartoon form is used to animate all kinds of debates about how the world is and how it can be. The show targets cant and hypocrisy wherever it finds it, from the exploitative manipulation of mass advertising to the crusading mock respect of political correctness. In one episode, Apu, the Hindu manager of the 'Kwik-e-Mart' (a large corner shop!), reveals to Homer his shrine to Ganesha, the elephant-headed god. Homer is certainly challenging in his response: 'Wow. You must have been out having a wazz when they were giving out the gods.'

On the other hand, if you want a summary of dominant stereotypes of gender, ethnicity or social class, where better to go than to the films of the Farrelly Brothers or that dubious British classic 'brand', the *Carry On . . .* series of films? Here the stereotypes are so crudely humorous that they unconsciously provide a platform for their discussion or at least an exposure of their limitations. The same may be true of *Footballers' Wives* or *Sunday Sport* or rap music videos, or even *Hello!* magazine.

Types of realism

Ideology is about the relationship between representation and power, which is why representations of the powerless are always more significant than representations of the powerful. We are surely right to be more concerned with negative representations of ethnic minorities and women than with those of middle-aged white men merely because the dominant ideology is, according to Fiske (1989), 'white, patriarchal capitalism'.

Ideology is forever raising the stakes and leading us into the temptation of ready-made ideas: stereotypes which draw the personal always in the direction of the general and, with a little luck, the universal.

In a society bombarded with images of women in high heels and lingerie or both, we are constantly challenged by the assumption, 'this is what women are like'. We are also provided with a set of reasons why this should be so, which at their most persuasive are described as 'common sense' (perhaps the most powerful form of ideological communication). This is the battleground of what Gramsci calls hegemony, the aggressive negotiation of meaning in which the dominant ideology must engage to keep itself 'healthy' and perpetuate itself. In simple terms ideology has become an active ingredient in society, embedding itself within social institutions such as education and the media. We find social values everywhere, disguised yet actively persuading us in every aspect of our lives (work and leisure) that society's dominant opinions are indisputable.

Take a look at the picture of Graham Norton in Figure 1.11 and see how easy it is to employ the anchor 'this is what gays are like' and how it is almost impossible to imagine 'this is what men are like'. In fact Norton's preferred word would probably be 'queer', a classic piece of appropriation by the gay community of a favourite form of homophobic abuse. The TV drama *Queer as Folk* took this to the limits and still stands as a byword for courageous and controversial programming. It is deliberately provocative to the 'straight' community which may have settled for the rather more coy representations of 'gay'. In the same way that rap group NWA helped to reclaim the word 'nigger' to the discomfort of liberal whites in particular, so 'queer' is a mite more powerful than

continued

the limp-wrist 'salute'. Graham Norton is a flamboyant role model and pioneer, but he is also 'professionally gay'. What we see is a persona, performance and a great deal of staging: something constructed inside and outside the terms of his sexuality.

Figure 1.11
Graham Norton

ACTIVITY

Identify the elements that make up the Graham Norton 'phenomenon' as presented in Figure 1.11. Which of these elements are also components of his perceived sexuality?

Introduction to case studies

The case studies that follow investigate some of the issues that are involved in our creation of and participation in a mediated reality. At the same time they hope to remind all of us that representation is the broadest and most significant media issue. In considering the representation of 'place' we are trying to dispel the impression that something as multidimensional and organic as a site of human settlement, a village, a town, even a country, might be semantically neutral. The fact that we don't think too much about the meaning of our towns, cities, even our country, is an issue in itself. Places are significantly represented across the media in both casual and detailed ways, from the offhand things that people write and say to the fully fledged 're-creations' that are modern British soap operas.

Case study 1.2
'SLUGS AND SNAILS AND PUPPY DOGS' TAILS': THE MEANINGS OF MEN

'Straightforward' and 'unproblematic' are not words used often to address issues of gender representation. Gender is an issue embodied by most representations of the human form in any context. Gender is usually to some degree expressed as a binary opposition where being male (for example) is partly understood in terms of not being female.

In her 1990 book *Gender Trouble*, Judith Butler argued that certain cultural configurations of gender have gained a 'hegemonic' hold. These are those that stress gender as a binary opposition, either one thing or the other. This necessarily disallows views of gender that are more fluid. This division, which tends to leave men powerful, has ironically only been confirmed by feminism, which has unwittingly reinforced the dichotomy. In other words, the issues of gender are never reached because we are too concerned with the particular problems of inequality. Butler claims that the whole issue of gender and sexuality is ideologically manipulated in a context where sex (male, female) is seen to cause gender (masculine, feminine) which is seen to cause desire (heterosexuality). In other words, the assumption of much of what we receive from the media is that gender is somehow fixed. Thus boys will endlessly be stereotypically boys and girls girls, and masculine men will forever consort with feminine women.

This would appear to be the agenda for the new generation of so-called lads' mags which began by claiming that they were underlining the progress

continued

that gender equality had made by being ironically retro about it. Suddenly 'dolly birds' were back, albeit in the context of Austin Powers movies and the popular 1990s programme *TFI Friday*, and 1960s chic became the trend. Men took their lead from *The Italian Job* (1969) and Andy Williams rereleased 'Music to Watch Girls By'. Even those magazines that appeal more directly to the new willingness of men to take themselves seriously as (though always rugged) 'things of beauty' such as *Men's Health* and *Men's Fitness* rely on the old dispensation. For fear that they might descend into a perilous self-love/vanity/anxiety, these magazines regularly provide a plausible reason for all this posing, such as to 'get the girl'.

ACTIVITY

Consider the roles of men and women in one or more of the following media contexts:

- MTV or an equivalent music channel
- TV news and current affairs programmes
- a mainstream magazine for men or women.

To what extent are the roles (and meanings) of women predicated upon/related to the roles (and meanings) of men?

In the representation of men in the mass media, the primary question 'Who is he?' tends to amount to 'What does he do?' (What role has he achieved?) If the same process is followed for the representation of women the questions tend to be very different. In this case, 'Who is she?' tends to mean 'Who is she related to?', 'Who is she doing that for?' or even 'Whose is she?' This even happens at a metalingual level, at the level of the media code, where men are still much more likely to be the focus of media texts, the central characters. As a result females and female characters are much more likely to find their roles ascribed. For example, in the most ideologically regressive medium of all, mainstream Hollywood cinema, it is highly likely that at least one of the functions of any female character is to be the wife, partner, mother, sister or 'love interest' to at least one more significant male character. Try this out next time you visit your local multiplex cinema or watch a film on television at home. Women are more often than not defined by their relationships with men. Even when there is good reason to do so, we do not conventionally read men this way.

Figure 1.12 The Royal Family

Figure 1.13 *Gavin and Stacey*

Look at Figures 1.12 and 1.13 and think of the ways in which these publicity photographs present male and female characters. What are the significant paradigms?

continued

This is, of course, central to Laura Mulvey's arguments in her influential essay 'Visual Pleasure and Narrative Cinema' [1975] (2003), which reinforce the idea that women understand what it is to be looked at, to be an object of what she usefully labelled the 'male gaze'. 'Male gaze' is, it seems, the dominant perspective of the mass media: what else could explain the predominance of certain kinds of images of certain kinds of women? Not only is this a patriarchal perspective but it is supported by a hegemonic alliance of common sense and prejudice which suggest that this boys-watching-girls stuff only works one way. Men look at women in a particular way because of how they're wired, it is argued; women, on the other hand, don't particularly like looking at men in this way.

John Berger perhaps summed this up best in his seminal study *Ways of Seeing* (1972): "[M]en look at women. Women watch themselves being looked at. This determines not only most relations between men and women but also the relation of women to themselves."

In an age of Botox injections and cosmetic surgery this issue is hardly being addressed; 'because you're worth it' too easily translates for many women into 'because it's all you're worth'. Writing in the *Observer* of 2 May 2004 in a piece with the tagline 'Women who buy into the illusion of youth delude themselves if they think it is an act of emancipation', journalist Yvonne Roberts attacked the ways in which women in particular are persuaded to look younger. She questioned the ways in which women are sold cosmetic improvements as something for themselves. Roberts uncovers the 'social, political and economic inequality' that is the basis of this issue, suggesting that 'females have always been strongly conditioned to believe that beauty is a large part of a woman's worth'. She is most scathing on the beauty industry, revealing 'the most vital of beauty secrets: cash conquers all', but also on what she calls 'the female physical elite' who end up with 'the face of a child, the body of a boy and the neck of a woman heading towards old age'. She also, almost mournfully, quotes sociologist Wendy Chapkis who has pointed out that 'we end up robbing each other of authentic reflections'. In other words, we've lost our perspective on what it is to age.

A new twist was applied by an article in *Zoo* magazine on Swedish uberbabe Victoria Silvstedt in February 2004 which had the provocative tagline: 'I hope your readers like my boobs.' This is interesting because what the article revealed was that these 'boobs' were, as it were, 'new' (for new read 'enhanced') so there was an even more real sense of their existence as extrapersonal objects. It is as if the process of disempowerment has become even more profound or desperate. Where the traditional pin-up would once say (in effect), 'Look at my lovely boobs which I am lucky enough to have', they are now saying, 'Look at my lovely boobs which I have been clever/wealthy/desperate enough to buy'. Despite the significant increase in the popularity of plastic surgery, there are just no semantic equivalents.

Men remain representationally largely free to be what they are (if not what they want to be) and even at times to be who they are. Our tendency in the representation of men is to allocate meaning specifically, to take them one by one. Women are more readily allocated to predetermined 'role' groups wherein their meanings are long established. Once identified, this is a relatively easy process to challenge and there are plenty of examples in all media forms of work that set out to establish interesting and problematic female characters, who require us to apprehend them as individuals rather than as types. However, it remains true that part of the power of these progressive pieces is an acknowledgement that the norm is still one that offers us endless variations on the mother/virgin/bitch/whore paradigm.

Moreover, it remains overwhelmingly the case that women are largely excluded from whole swathes of media output by the very nature of this limited range of representations. For example, in a media sense women are not funny (the exceptions prove the rule), perhaps because comedy lives on imperfection and an ugliness that women are not really allowed to have. This is an acid test, where the proof of the pudding lies very much in the eating: ask yourself if this is true (not if it should be). Then ask yourself why, despite the plethora of pretty-girl exploitation shots in Media Studies text-books, it is also true that representations of men are significantly more interesting than representations of women. The ideology here is multilayered in a world that is flooded with images of a few sorts of women, yet it is much more telling in its representation in far fewer images of a more significant range of men. Even when the focus is as narrow as 'fitness'.

ACTIVITY

What do we learn about men from these two 'advertisements' (Figures 1.14 and 1.15)? In what ways are the meanings directed by significant anchors?

Interestingly the focus here is rather more impersonal that in the average pretty-girl pic. It's the six-pack that offers in both cases a dominant focus, a grid of muscles that can be worked irrespective of the rest of you and to a degree independent of your natural (or God-given) endowment.

continued

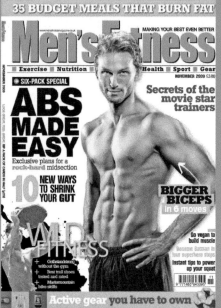

Figure 1.14 *Men's Fitness* advert

Figure 1.15 The cover of *Men's Fitness* Magazine, November 2009

Although this takes work, it doesn't define you, and anyway everybody knows (in other words, it is common to the representations we see of the world) that men of all shapes and sizes get women of the right shape and size.

Man sues over lack of 'Lynx effect'

A luckless Indian romeo is suing Lynx after he failed to land a single girlfriend during seven years of using their products.

Vaibhav Bedi, 26, is seeking £26,000 from parent company Unilever for the "depression and psychological damage" caused by the lack of any Lynx effect.

Court officials in New Delhi have agreed to order forensic laboratory tests on dozens of his half-used Lynx body washes, shampoos, anti-perspirants and hair gels.

Lynx – marketed as Axe in India – is famous for its saucy ads showing barely-clothed women throwing themselves at men.

But Bedi says in his court petition: "The company cheated me because in its advertisements, it says women will be attracted to you if you use Axe.

"I used it for seven years but no girl came to me."

When contacted Unilever declined to comment on the case.

But India's leading compensation litigator Ram Jethmalani warned: "There is no data to substantiate the supposition that unattractive and unintelligent men don't attract women.

"In fact some of the best looking women have been known to marry and date absolutely ghoulish guys. I'd suggest that the company settles this issue out of court."

http://web.orange.co.uk/article/quirkies/man_sues_over_lack_of_lynx_effect?sid=393db7306793

ACTIVITY

What messages are there in this story about the different ways in which men and women are represented and understood? Are these messages substantially different for male and female readers?

Reality TV: the heights and depths of hyperconsciousness

No exploration of the issues of representation can ignore the impact on a study of realism that has been made by reality TV. For postmodernists the very idea that you would need to use the 'R' word is perfect proof that the whole project of realism, the feasible representation of reality, is in crisis. If 'What Katie did Next' is 'reality' then what about all the other things Katie does on TV, including promoting what she's doing next? There can be no going back to an old dichotomy of 'reality' and 'representation' once you inhabit a hyperreality which itself comprises versions of versions of reality. Baudrillard called these 'simulacra'.

A more positive take might suggest that 'Reality TV' evidences a more subtle understanding on the part of audiences and producers, who appreciate the ironies involved, who have a hyperconsciousness to greet their hyperreality. One significant television moment was the collision of airliners into the World Trade Center on 11 September 2001. In the midst of countless horrors and widespread disbelief was a double seed of doubt, not only that we might not be being told the truth but also that the pictures themselves were failing to convince. This was a wake-up call. In registering the unpalatable fact that representations (live recordings) of a genuine disaster were unconvincing by the standards we expect from, for example, feature films, we learned something about representation, and hopefully, reality.

ACTIVITY

Suggest reasons why we might find live television reportage of the plane collisions less convincing than those we would subsequently see in a film like *World Trade Center* (2006)?

Television has always 'employed' reality as a component in its output. We are well used to discriminating between realistic drama, of the sort that *EastEnders* or *Casualty* serve up, and the representations which are going on whenever a celebrity appears on TV, 'playing themselves', you might say. In short, television has always shown us 'real' people being themselves, often using their own names. They populate a sliding scale which runs from so-called 'stars' to television journalists and weather girls (or, as they're now called, 'the cast' of *I'm a Celebrity, Get Me Out of Here!*).

From *BB* to *Celebrity Big Brother*: pride comes before a fall

What happened with *Big Brother One*, and the formalising of reality TV (largely by Endemol) is that this age-old hierarchy was first disrupted and then in time reconfigured. Acting on a hunch that 'ordinary' people were at least more interesting than B-list and C-list celebrities, Channel 4 unleashed *Big Brother* and suddenly we were all stars or versions of stars. The show had been a massive hit in Holland, demolishing the argument that 'it could only happen here', and it took Britain by storm. *BB1* was presented as a social psychological experiment but there were questions to ask even from the start. While the 'reality' was a focus for marketing the show, ironically the real focus of the show was the contrivance: the house and the 'game' – a prize of £70,000 if you can convince us you're a genuine human being.

BB was an extension of the fly-on-the-wall documentary with more cameras and more control over the environment in which the observation would take place. It was a technique common in natural history programming. Where a subject could not be adequately filmed in its own habitat, a faithful reproduction of that habitat would be built into which camera positions would be mounted.

ACTIVITY

What differences, if any, do you see between:

- Photographing the yellow-bellied sapsucker in a faithfully reproduced version of its natural habitat?
- Recording the antics of contestants in the Big Brother House?

Anyway, whatever the differences, for a short period there was a spate of shows that gave ordinary people chances of a number of lifetimes. What were being peddled, and being sought if not engineered by programme makers, were 'rags-to-riches' narratives. For a while social psychology was replaced by social work as Jamie Oliver offered 'n'er-do-wells' the chance to be chefs in *Jamie's Kitchen* while in the background various manifestations of a talent show massed their melancholy armies. *Jamie's Kitchen* was a fairly standard and effective 'warts-and-all' documentary which offered insights into the problems associated with so-called problem children. It also and probably more compellingly told us quite a lot more about celebrity chef Jamie Oliver.

The rest of the story is interesting since it represents the almost total transformation of the apparent focus of reality TV from 'ordinary people' to 'celebrities', in representational terms a complete role reversal. This is partly because the first unforeseen implication of shows like *BB* was that it created instant celebrities, even out of those, like the late Jade Goody, who finished fourth. But it was also the fact that, on reflection, the lives of B- and C-list celebrities proved more interesting, particularly if we the public were allowed to goad them. What many commentators have missed is that reality TV was driven not by humankind's desire for more reality but rather by technology, by conditions being right for a new kind of interactivity and transmedia experience. The involvement offered was not with reality but with the shows and an experiment in a limited form of management of programme outcomes by audience vote.

ACTIVITY

List the different ways in which you were offered participation in the last series of *The X Factor*.

One 'platform' that has embraced the public vote is our ailing popular press and a raft of rudely healthy celebrity magazines. As ordinary people have given way to celebrities (or become them), so the 'character' of the 'franchise' has changed. Led by the hugely successful Ant-and-Dec-fronted *I'm a Celebrity, Get Me Out of Here!*, this new wave delights not in exploring 'reality' but rather by giving vaguely undeserving celebrities a taste of it. It is interesting to speculate whether this 'Celebrities Uncovered' theme is part of a long-term reconfiguration of the popular press in particular followed by the fallout from the accusations of intrusive reporting which resulted from Princess Diana's death in 1997. At the time the public seemed to feel that things had gone too far. In the celebrity-behind-the-scenes gig our intrusiveness is endorsed. There are many issues here, since aren't celebrities by definition those people we are prepared to pay to see appear as themselves?

ACTIVITY

You just haven't earned it yet baby

Privacy is very much a hot media topic with celebrities using laws brought in to address media excesses to iron out their little misdemeanours and media organisation wailing about public interest.

Make a list of celebrities who, in your opinion, deserve to have their privacy protected and any who don't. What are your criteria for *excluding* people from this protection?

At the end of the day our narratives of the everyday have become celebrity narratives (and transmedia narratives at that) and reality TV has folded itself back into the 'play of illusions and phantasms' that is 'celebrity'. 'Celebrity' may, in fact, be even more than Disneyland, in the postmodernist Baudrillard's terms "the perfect model of all the entangled orders of simulation". Queen of the reality TV side of things is Katie Price (aka Jordan) whose stock rises and falls on a series-by-series basis. She has been lately undermined by the failure of her marriage to the hapless hunk Peter Andre and subsequent quickie remarriage to an orange-faced, transvestite cage fighter.

ACTIVITY

Strangers in a fight

On the celebrity hustings, words fly thick and fast and nothing remains unlabelled. What are your initial impressions (today) of these characters who will feature in our next story?

- Katie Price
- Peter Andre
- Alex the cage fighter
- Cheryl Cole
- Ashley Cole

On what are these impressions based?

Like an old tale still. . . . The myths of modern celebrity

Baudrillard famously wrote that "when the real is no longer what it used to be, nostalgia assumes its full meaning" and much of what is done representationally to celebrities seems to be harking back to days of clearer values. The stories we are told of Katie and Peter and Cheryl and Ashley are no more or less than contemporary myths, stories particular to our 'tribe' which allow us to articulate our concerns about our culture.

Ellis Cashmore's extensive work on David Beckham's celebrity proposes Becks as a blueprint for modern celebrity. Beckham has been turned into a product in an unprecedented way but can seemingly do no wrong, escaping infidelity and pink nail varnish with comparative ease. Cashmore suggests that central to this identity is having a good story, which is a traditional one: "The Beckham fairytale – which like all fairytales embodies ideas about ourselves." The 'ourselves' here is as much collective and cultural as it is personal and psychological.

The contemporary celebrity fairytale is very much a traditional structure with tabloid and magazine editors and cable TV producers vying with each other to unfold the developing narrative from love at first sight to taking sides in the messy divorce. One theme that seems to reassure us is that despite their money, talent, looks and status these celebrities cannot find happiness. If this can be rubbed in with a bit of moralising about good old-fashioned family values, all the better. If you're prepared to prostitute your marriage to the highest bidder as a spectator sport, what can you expect? However, this is a popular media, remember, who brought us the reality show *Jodie Marsh: Who'll Take Her Up the Aisle*?

When 'Dosh and Pecs' (aka Peter and Katie) hooked up on a reality TV show it seemed a marriage made in TV tabloid heaven. As Britain's most famous glamour model and Australia's most famous six-pack, their 'affair' seemed both expedient and doomed. Six years, and marriage and divorce later, they are still inextricably linked. Moreover, they have become properly established within the frames of reference of even those who take little interest in celebrity gossip. In addition, people will take sides in their affairs on the basis of strongly formed opinions of their characters as human beings. This phenomenon was created out of an extended reality TV franchise which directed our attention to the similarities between their stories and the essential lives we all lead as boys and girls, husbands and wives, sons and daughters, moms and dads, with a bit of glamour and sexual electricity thrown in for good measure.

The relationship as media narrative was officially launched in March 2004 with a WORLD EXCLUSIVE (was the world listening?) in *OK!* Magazine.

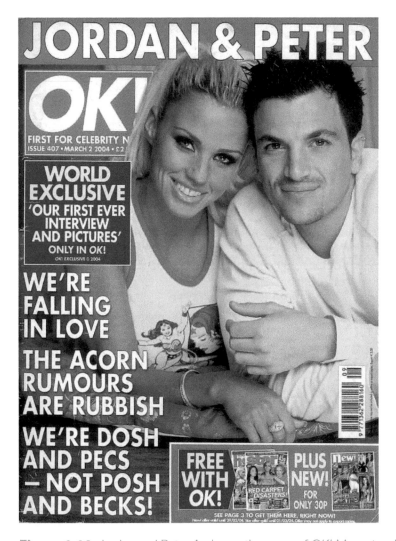

Figure 1.16 Jordan and Peter Andre on the cover of *OK!* Magazine, March 2004

Looking back at 'where it all began', what strikes you about this cover? Who has fared best since this shot was taken in terms of enhancement of their meanings? The evocation of 'Posh and Becks' is interesting: how do 'Dosh and Pecs' compare?

The journey from then to now can be told in a set of titles, including one abortive foray into the late-night chatshow format:

When Jordan Met Peter
Jordan and Peter: Laid Bare
Jordan and Peter: Marriage and Mayhem
Jordan and Peter: The Baby Diaries
Katie and Peter: The Next Chapter
Katie and Peter: Unleashed (chatshow)
Katie and Peter: Stateside
What Katie Did Next
Peter Andre: The Next Chapter

What do you have to say about the grand narrative built by Katie, Peter and Jordan here?

This journey has made Katie and Peter two of the most recognisable celebrities in Britain and has generated millions of column inches across not only newspapers and magazines but also in celebrity comment on TV and radio. At the serious end of this have been concerns about both the corroding influence of 'pure' celebrity (defined in terms of people who are famous for being famous) and the poor role models that are being offered to their young fans. Katie, as ever, has attracted the most criticism, particularly among some feminists, fearing that she is taken as some sort of post-feminist icon by some young women. Caitlin Moran in *The Times* spells it out.

continued

All over the world, humans are fizzing and buzzing and thinking. They are knocking off the entries on humanity's billion-year-long To Do list – which has slowly raised us from protozoa and germs into two-legs with iPhones and trilbies.

And, in the midst of all this, like some impossibly contrarian parlour game, there are people who will argue that Katie Price is a feminist role model for young women. "She's strong, she's clever, she's Celebrity Mum of The Year, she's making it in a man's world," they say. "She's a modern businesswoman."

OK – I want to go through these. Following what seems to be a media obligation, this week *Hello!* refers yet again to Price's intelligence – calling her "as smart as paint". Aside from noting that, as yet, not a single country in the world has yet to employ a 2-litre tin of Dulux Non-Drip Emulsion as Chancellor of the Exchequer, over the years I have devised a very simple IQ test for public figures. It is to ask: "Who around here has been forced to eat a kangaroo's anus by Ant & Dec in the last two weeks?" If you raise your hand, you're probably not leaving through the door marked Mensa. Stephen Hawking has never chowed down on roo-bum.

"She's strong." No, she's not strong. She's incredibly weak. At the tail end of 10,000 years of patriarchy, there's nothing strong about being a woman with gigantic silicone tits and a face full of filler, who's into ponies and the colour pink, and goes on about blow jobs a lot. She's scarcely a black lesbian physicist wearing slacks in Alabama in 1932.

Also, strong people tend not to go quacking to the press every week about how they're "feeling" and how unfairly everyone's treating them, and what an arse their ex-husband's been. As Blanche in *Corrie* said: "In my day, when something bad happened, you'd stay at home, get drunk and bite on a shoe." Price could learn much from this. This idea that Price is "strong" has come solely from the fact that she keeps saying "I'm strong", while doing really weak things. There's a similar bit of neurolinguistic programming going on with her being a "great parent", and being voted Celebrity Mum of The Year.

"I take care of my kids," she says. Well, to quote the comedian Chris Rock: "You're SUPPOSED to look after your kids! What do you want – a cookie?"

Thing is, I don't really mind anyone misguidedly thinking that Price is like some cross between Einstein, Nelson Mandela and Ma Walton. It's a busy, mixed-up world and we've all got to pick our fights.

But what I find absolutely intolerable is people who claim that she's a feminist role model – simply because she has earned a lot of money.

The reasoning is this: men still have all the power and money. But men have a weak spot – sexy women. So if what it takes to become rich and powerful is to sex-up the blokes, then so be it. That's business, baby. You might be on all fours with your arse hanging out in "glamour" calendars – but at least you're making the rent on your enormous pink mansion.

Well, there's a phrase for that kind of behaviour. It is, to quote Jamie, the spin doctor in *The Thick of It*, being a "mimsy bastard quisling f***".

Women who, in a sexist world, pander to sexism to make their fortune are Vichy France with tits. Are you 32GG, waxed to within an inch of your life and faking orgasm? You're doing business with a decadent and corrupt regime. Calling that a feminist icon is like giving an arms dealer the Nobel Peace Prize.

I once spent a week with Price for a feature. Do you know the worst thing? She couldn't hold a conversation to save her life. As she has to turn out an "exclusive" about her life pretty much every week, it means everything she thinks or says has a price. Even politely asking "What did you do last night?" involved her calculating whether what had happened was an anecdote she could "give" to me, as part of "the package" – or sell to another magazine for a bit more.

I dunno. Maybe I've got my priorities wrong. But if I were worth £30 million, yet were getting my management to ring a journalist the morning after an interview to say: "Could you not print Katie's bra

continued

size? I know she mentioned it to you – but we want to sell it to *OK!*",
I would think my life was going a bit wrong. I think I'd get on my pink
pony and gallop away for a couple of years.

http://www.timesonline.co.uk/tol/comment/columnists/caitlin_moran/ar
ticle6944843.ece

ACTIVITY

What is the substance of Caitlin Moran's argument? Imagine you have
been charged with briefing Katie Price for a 'right to reply'. What are the
counter-arguments?

While the upmarket rags pick around the absurdity of super-inflated people being
interesting to us, and worry about a world that is obsessed with surfaces, the
popular media sticks with the traditional stories of the 'natural' relationships
between perhaps men and women. If on the one hand it's difficult to be a feminist
if your cup size is larger than D, it's also impossible to be a 'real' woman if you
are seen, repeatedly, to hold the whip hand in your relationship (particularly a
relationship with a patently 'real' man like Peter Andre). In the trial by television
Peter proved (convinced us) that he was a 'good father' but without cynicism, you
must admit that the standards for fathers and children are hardly stratospheric.
Any father who finds any 'quality time' with his brood on a regular basis has by
these standards climbed into the top half of the parenting 'markscheme'. Mothers,
on the other hand, must always put their children first and no career will trump
this 'natural' responsibility.

These issues were further highlighted in the last years of the noughties by the
juxtaposition of 'Dosh and Pecs' with [C]ashley and Cheryl Cole following news
of their (seemingly inevitable) breakup. Again the extent to which traditional
representational models were dominant is at least concerning. Despite the
attempts of our football-obsessed culture to suggest that footballers are not
'empty' celebrities because they have 'talent', it is clear that both Cheryl Tweedy
and Ashley Cole are products of fame academies and that objectively such
relationships are likely to come under particular strain. However, without the kind
of 'permission' that might have been implied by *Jordan and Peter: Marriage and*

Mayhem, the Cole marriage too has become a site on which the popular media has reworked some well-worn themes. In this narrative Cheryl is Superwoman: managing her immaculate appearance, looking after her old mum and representing timeless working-class Geordie 'lassishness'. [C]ashley, on the other hand, is a feckless, libidinous, immature and arrogant 'arsewipe' who prefers phone sex with unspecified slappers to love with "the world's most eligible lady". Here is a set of representations which are carrying an awful lot of value and values.

ACTIVITY

What do the stories of Cheryl and Ashley Cole tell us about attitudes towards:

■ Social class
■ Regionality
■ Ethnicity
■ Gender
■ Marriage
■ Material success?

The article from *Heat* Magazine might provide some prompts.

DIGNIFIED CHERYL:

"I NEED TO BE ALONE"

SHE KNEW IT WAS OVER AS EARLY AS LAST JUNE

A RELIEVED NATION PUNCHED the air last week when Cheryl Cole finally announced that she was leaving her cheating husband Ashley. But *heat* can now reveal that the dignified silence she is keeping masks her secret heartache – their marriage was over some months ago, with pals close to the couple claiming they haven't had sex for months.

While Cheryl put every ounce of her energy into saving their relationship, cocky Ashley repeatedly refused to accept that his infidelity was the cause, instead blaming those she loved most – including her mum Joan Callaghan (who has shared their marital home for two years), Girls Aloud bandmates, rapper will.i.am and even her dogs. The love rat is still bragging to friends, "She'll be back."

Now, as she finally walks away with her head held high, *heat* gives you the truth proud Cheryl hid from the world about her ruined marriage.

THEY STOPPED HAVING SEX

The passion in their marriage dwindled to virtually nothing over recent months. In the evenings, Cheryl and her mum would stay up watching television together while Ashley either played video games with friends, including fellow Chelsea sex-cheat John Terry, in six-hour stints, or went to bed.

"Their relationship took a hammering two years ago after Aimee Walton went into great detail about their alleged night together," a source close to the star tells *heat*. "Things couldn't just go back to the way they were after something like that and in a way, Ashley should have to pay for his crimes. It's hard to go back to the way things were when you know he has been with someone else. As hard as Cheryl tried to make it work, in the bedroom was a different situation all together." Ashley refuses to take any responsibility for the breakdown of this important part of their relationship, instead blaming everyone but himself, including her mum and her dogs. He once complained that the latter – two Chihuahuas named Coco and Buster that she allowed to sleep in the bedroom – "got in the way of marital intimacy". Asked recently if she was pregnant, Cheryl replied, "No. Chance would be a fine thing."

THREE PEOPLE IN THE RELATIONSHIP

Cheryl's mum Joan has lived with the couple for almost the entire length of their marriage and in both of their marital homes, not just since Ashley's infidelity as has been reported. Joan doesn't trust Ashley and he insists her living there is the reason for his and Cheryl's sex life almost vanishing.

"He blames a lot of their problems on Joan being there all the time and killing the passion," our sources says. If Ashley was doing his favourite thing, playing his PlayStation, Joan would simply walk in and unplug it, saying it was immature and that he should be making more effort with his wife.

A pal of the footballer told us, "It's no secret that Cheryl's mum living with them didn't go down very well with Ashley and he often felt as though he was living at her house rather than the other way around. He would moan to Cheryl that he couldn't do what he wanted to in his own house and that Joan was cramping his style, but Cheryl was insistent that her

mum should be there – she wanted her there. He tried telling her that he wasn't happy with the living arrangements, and it was the source of a few rows. He felt they couldn't be spontaneous with their relationship with the mother-in-law there all the time. It was suffocating." Rather than join his wife in trying to save their marriage, Ashley chose to have sex with other women, resulting in the revelations that would ultimately see her ditch him.

SHE TRIED TO SAVE THEIR MARRIAGE

Despite suffering the humiliation of seeing Ashley's affairs revealed so publicly, Cheryl masked her private heartache and tried to rebuild the marriage. Ashley, driven to jealousy by the massive increase in the public's admiration for her and seeing his own reputation was left in tatters, made little effort to help.

"Cheryl did her best to make that marriage work. Ashley complained about not being involved and that he felt left out because her career took over and she was away a lot, but she would always invite him down to *The X Factor*. Often he couldn't make it because of games, but that's not her fault and when he did come down he'd be backstage in the dressing room. Cheryl wanted to involve him and unlike a lot of the judges after the show would return home rather than going out until late. She took her marriage seriously. She always made sure that Ashley was a part of the party and if you look at pictures of them on nights out, she is always with him holding his hand in a very public display of affection. Particularly since the allegations of an affair with Aimee Walton – she wanted people to see that she was putting the past behind her and that other people should too. Of course, there was a lot of repairing that had to be done – but it needed to be both sides that were working on it. It's easy to say the word sorry, but his actions, she has since found out, clearly indicate that he didn't mean a word of it."

SHE IS LOSING WEIGHT AND BECOMING DEPRESSED

Though Cheryl appears as glamorous as she always has to the outside world, her friends fear that she is going to collapse from not eating and that she could end up depressed. She has accepted visits from best pals Nicola and Kimberley, but has even told them that she needs some space. Her friend told us, "Cheryl isn't eating at all. She seems so utterly miserable all she can do is mope around the place, which is understandable. She isn't taking care of her diet and we are all so worried that she is going to overdo this and get ill. She needs to keep up her energy, but it seems she just doesn't have the will or desire to eat or do anything at the

moment."After Ashley's first affair, Cheryl dropped to 6st. Now she has lost five pounds in the last three weeks alone, the anguish she feels over his betrayal allowing her to stomach little more than peppermint tea.

DESPITE EVERYTHING SHE REMAINS PROUD AND DIGNIFIED

Cheryl was further rocked by claims she had entered into a relationship with dancer Derek Hough when she escaped to LA after the latest round of revelations about Ashley emerged. Despite all that her cheating husband has done to her, she's still doing his best to respect his feelings.

"Her relationship with Derek was purely professional," her friend told us. "She was upset that she was accused of seeing him and being close to him and she thought it cheapened what she had with Ashley, suggesting she would go off with the first bloke she clapped eyes on."

HAPPY ENDING

Now that Cheryl has ditched the dead weight of Ashley, she is finally free to focus entirely on her career. We hope she also eventually finds a decent man who will give her the love and respect she derserves. One thing's for sure, she won't be short of offers.

Figure 1.17 Dignified Cheryl: "I need to be alone." Text from an article in *Heat* Magazine, 6–12 March 2010

This article tells the whole story through sub-headings. Think about how this might be illustrated as a display or podcast:

They stopped having sex

Three people in the relationship

She tried to save their marriage

She is losing weight and becoming depressed yet despite everything she remains proud and dignified

Happy ending

Meanwhile as Cheryl's bright star rises so Katie, now Jordan, glowers in the penumbra, playing the 'bully' to Cheryl's dignified spouse, Tramp to her Lady. And so we return to the simplest issues of representation; what is there between THE LADY and THE TRAMP?

Figure 1.18 The Lady and the Tramp. Cover of *Heat* Magazine, 6–12 March 2010

ACTIVITY

Make a detailed list of the components of these two images of young women. What do they share? How is such a difference in meaning achieved?

Case study 1.3
THE REPRESENTATION OF PLACES

Places are represented to us in the same way as people and ideas, with various degrees of approval, malice and indifference. In doing their work these representations create for us a sort of semiotic map of both Britain and the world that for most of us resembles those maps made by early cartographers and explorers. The general shape is there but the detail is largely provided by accident: either you've been there or it was featured in that series on the telly. You may have only really heard of 'West Bromwich' for its 'Albion', Sale for its 'Sharks' or Hamilton for its 'Academicals'. If asked for an opinion on places such as these you will instinctively reach for any associations which have tended to surround them as a result of others' representations, which may be equally uninformed. If there are enough of these you may even have a stereotype on which to draw.

ACTIVITY

Land down under

Your task is to illustrate/support the word *Australia* by selecting five images and five words or phrases. You should try to express what this area of the world means to you as straightforwardly as you can.

You may or may not have chosen boomerangs and kangaroos but it is very unlikely that either failed to skim/hop across your mind. Equally a set of more specifically media images may have reared their heads, perhaps *Neighbours* or one of those Minogue girls (perhaps your parents would mention Rolf Harris). For the blunter of you the words may have included 'convicts', for others 'cricket' or 'Aborigines'. The very fact that some of you will have been relatively careful about what you chose for fear you might be being given some kind of test of your values or might reveal something about yourself tells us that these matters are interesting, even with a fairly remote idea like 'Australia'.

What you have made is a crude map of meaning which can be read as such and will likely tell us something about how we see Australia. You will likely be nodding along with this but read that last sentence back slowly.

ACTIVITY

'How we see Australia': map readings

(This works best if you have more than one map)

Simply identify the themes in your map(s) of Australia.

■ How do you see Australia according to your 'summaries?
■ How much have you 'seen'?

Perhaps a more pertinent question for most of us is 'In what sense do you see Australia?', since most of us will never have been there. To some degree we are sharing in a collective process of meaning making and for most of us this collective significantly includes a range of media sources from *Crocodile Dundee* to *Skippy the Bush Kangaroo*. Our Australia is a set of myths, though it may feel more substantial.

continued

It's hardly profound to say so but the world we think we know is prompted by the partial coverage provided by our national media. Even with multiple news sources you would need tireless energy to sight some versions on the Western news agenda.

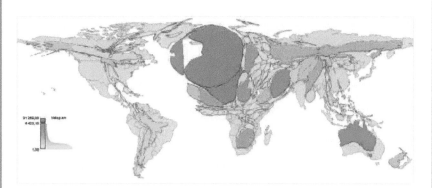

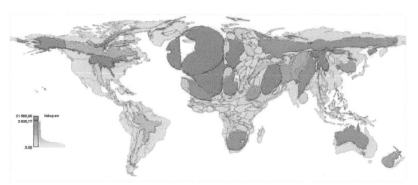

Figure 1.19 The world according to the *Daily Mail* (top) and the world according to the *Guardian* (bottom)

Much of this is perfectly understandable: we would expect Portuguese affairs to feature massively on Portuguese news, though on our map Portugal is barely an unpicked spot (called Cristiano Ronaldo). More interesting are our own semiotic maps of Britain's hotspots and not-spots. As suggested before, to many of us we're talking about the Mappa Mundi.

continued

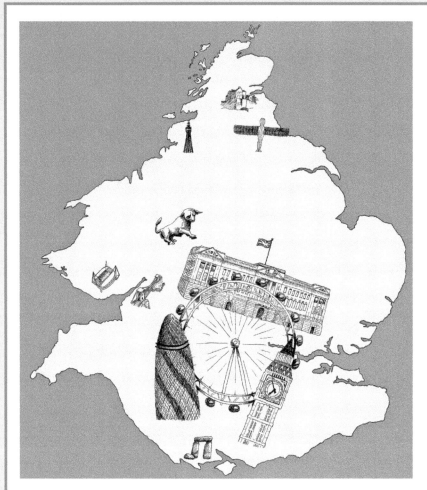

Figure 1.20 Distorted Mappa Mundi-style map of perceptions of Britain

Explore the map of Britain (Figure 1.20) and discuss the different codes of representation which are operating as you travel around the map. Add your own significant locations. You may wish to consider, for example, the following:

- Regionality (Why is North versus South stronger than East versus West?)
- Nationality
- History
- Social class
- Culture
- Personality/character of inhabitants.

You may also say where you would most/least like to live, and the extent to which your meanings will or will not accompany real experience of the places you are 'understanding'. Which is the best British town you have visited? And the worst? What are your reasons?

When Middlesborough, a town on the river Tees in the North East, was voted the worst town in Britain, Sky Sports anchorman Jeff Stelling, himself from nearby Hartlepool, blew a fuse on live television. Stelling leapt into a now famous rant against the nature of these polls which adds much to our ongoing discussion in an entertaining fashion. You can assess "Jeff Stelling loses it" (the rant crosses a commercial break and is only interrupted by Everton scoring a goal) on YouTube at http://www.youtube.com/watch?v=XxrJqtf0RJI.

ACTIVITY

North versus South: Jeff's telling

> The people who compile this tosh, no disrespect, are the type who only go north of Rickmansworth when they're going to the Edinburgh Festival and think that people in the North live in Coronation Street-style terraces.

Stelling's broadside is both tongue-in-cheek and genuinely felt. What oppositions does he set up between North and South, to what extent are these representations identifiable and what useful purpose, if any, do they serve?

continued

Obviously, for some to come from Britain's worst town would be a veritable badge of honour. A durable media narrative is the 'girl/boy from nowhere' story and if nobody's heard of Tanworth-in-Arden or Little Rock or even Althorp before you came on the scene the better 'somewhere' seems. Humdrum towns it seems are often the spur to creative types, if only to leave them. John Cleese regularly gives Weston-super-Mare and his desire never to return as a reason for his success. When Ricky Gervais decided it was time to do something with his life, his father apparently replied, "But you haven't seen all of Reading yet." Perhaps our own places always seem lesser, more mundane because they are more situated. American names have far greater force, romance, scope. The writer Julie Burchill makes this point about the epithet 'American' in a review of Charles R. Cross's Kurt Cobain biography *Heavier than Heaven*.

> **American downfalls always seem bigger and sadder than other types – attain instant gravitas – because we seem to hear the lonesome wind of the American dream, the settling and the savagery and the submission of all else, howling through one simple life. (That's why, say, American Beauty and American Gigolo sound like such profound titles compared with Belgian Beauty and German Gigolo).**

It's often said that if Shakespeare were alive today he'd be writing *The Sopranos*/working in Hollywood. Shakespeare's place names are chosen to add drama and intrigue and are most often Italian, due to that region's hot (and dirty) reputation. Julie Burchill is arguing that for the modern European imagination America does a similar job, so that *The Merchant of Manhattan* is infinitely better than *The Merchant of Mansfield* and *Timon of Alabama* trumps *Timon of Aldershot*.

The American city with its spectacular play of light and shade is a model for both modern and futuristic metropolises everywhere: comic, computer games, feature films (though these often blur).

ACTIVITY

Vice City. Liberty stories?

Consider the meanings of the locations of one of the following:

- The Vice City locations of the GTA franchise.
- The significant locations of a major Hollywood film with a fictional setting.
- The imaginary world created by an American-produced comic.
- The significant locations from a fictional US TV series.
- The significant locations of an American-style theme park.

Subsidiary (1)

Baudrillard said that "everywhere in Disneyland the objective profile of America . . . is drawn". To what extent is this true of your locations?

Subsidiary (2)

Imagine a computer game whose Vice City was based on photo-fit British cities. How would it differ?

Subsidiary (3)

To what extent is there a historical dimension to these representations?

ACTIVITY

Five formats in search of a setting

Suggest interesting and predictable British settings for the following:

- Drama about clever successful types.
- Soap set in a close-knit community.
- Film about teenage hopelessness.
- Gentle comedy about generation differences.
- Docu-drama following a minority ethnic family.

You get the picture. Representation is an interested activity which matters to people, since beyond all else it is a personal way in which we make sense of the world.

Audiences

In this section we look at:

- How audiences are made up and how our engagement with media forms is patterned and determined.
- Ways in which audiences are becoming increasingly segmented.
- Terms such as 'hypodermic needle theory', 'uses and gratifications', 'mode of address' and 'situated culture'.
- Some of the issues around the 'effects' debate.
- 'Passive' and 'active' views of the audience and how audience participation is increasing.

Different types of audience

In one sense everyone is part of the audience in that we are all, to some degree or another, exposed to media texts. However, it can sometimes be difficult to stand back and think about the different ways in which our daily lives interact with the media. It is well worth considering the extent to which, in an average day, we will be part of many different audiences for a wide range of media. This may include being part of a radio audience in the morning as we get ready for college, school or work, watching breakfast television or reading the newspaper, listening to music on an MP3 player, logging on to read our emails and surf the web, sharing photos or texting friends on our mobile phones, or glimpsing advertising hoardings as we travel to school, college or work.

Throughout the day we will be, either consciously or unconsciously, exposed to different media products – becoming part of many different types of audience. As we mentioned in the introduction, it may be as part of an audience of over nine million people all watching the same episode of *EastEnders* at the same time. It may be as part of an audience sitting alone in our cars listening to the same radio show, or as one of 300 people watching a film together in a cinema. It may also be through the more personal and private consumption of MP3 players, newspapers, either local or national, or magazines, or through the one-to-one communication of texts or email. We may work in an environment in which a radio is on in the background, or somewhere – for example, a hospital or a shop – that has its own radio station. We may also have access to a computer at work or while studying where we can listen to a radio station (according to the Radio Advertising Bureau (RAB), at any given time 20 per cent of internet users are listening to radio – see http://www.rab.co.uk/rab2006/showContent.aspx?id=1425) or receive up-to-date RSS news feeds from newspapers or news agencies.

Why are audiences important?

There are several reasons why audiences are important. The first is perhaps the most obvious.

- Without an audience, why would anyone create a media text? What is the point of a film that no one sees?
- Audience size and reaction are often seen as a way of measuring the success (or otherwise) of a media product. One of the reasons why we say that the *Sun* newspaper is successful is because it sells over three million copies a day and is read by nearly 12 million people.
- Audiences who buy media texts are providing income for the media companies which produce them.
- Much of the media available to us, however, is free or subsidised; it is financed by advertising, and the advertisers want to know that they are getting value for money. In other words, they want to know how many and what types of people are seeing their advertisements.
- As the media become more central to our lives, so many people want to know how we use the media, what we understand of what we consume, and the effects that the media has on our lives.

How have audiences changed?

Concerns about the size and impact of the media on audiences, the 'effectiveness' of advertising and how audiences interrelate with the media have been with us since the development of a 'mass' audience at the beginning of the twentieth century.

We know that the media is constantly changing, and this means that audiences, too, must be changing, partly as a result of the changes in media technology but also because of the changes in the way we live our lives and because we as individuals change. Cinema audiences in the 1950s wore special glasses to watch such films as *It Came from Outer Space* (1953) and *Creatures From the Black Lagoon* (1954), which were made with special 3D effects that made the monsters seem to come out of the screen to attack the audience. Although this was seen as a gimmick in the 1950s and the films quickly disappeared, there has been a reappearance of 3D effects in recent years, especially through the growth of IMAX cinemas, where, once again, audiences wearing special glasses can see characters and objects appearing to fly around in space in front of them. Access to 3D television programmes is now available.

The word 'broadcasting' implies a 'few-to-many' model where a small number of broadcasters transmit programmes to a 'mass' audience of perhaps more than 30 million people all watching or listening to the same event, at the same time, participating in the same experience. The 1966 World Cup final attracted a television audience of 32 million viewers, while the wedding of Prince Charles and Lady Diana in 1981 attracted 39 million. It is estimated that over two billion people

Figure 1.21 Children watching a 3D film

tuned in to watch artists and concerts from Live Earth in July 2007 while an estimated 3.8 billion people globally tuned into the Beijing 2008 Paralympic Games.

Today we have a very wide range of broadcasting and press services available to us. Radio and television, in particular, have moved away from the original ideas of addressing a large 'mass' audience. Today the concept is one of narrowcasting, where programmes are aimed at specific, specialist audiences in a way that is similar to the range and variety of magazines available in a newsagent. There is now a wide range of specialist channels and stations aimed at small and specific markets that might be defined on the grounds of age (Classic FM, Disney, or Angel Radio in Havant, where they refuse to play any music recorded after 1959), gender (the digital television channels Dave or NUTS), interests (most obviously sports channels, but also television channels such as National Geographic, UK History, Sky Arts or Teachers TV) or ethnicity (radio stations such as Sunrise in London and Bradford or television channels such as PCNE Chinese, Bangla TV or Channel East, aimed at Chinese or other Asian audiences). All these television and radio stations, magazines and newspapers (both local and national) are now supplemented by websites that offer a more specialist range of services for consumers (see e.g. http://angelradio.moonfruit.com/ 'Snap . . . Crackle . . . but no pop').

This change from 'broadcasting' to 'narrowcasting' results partly from the development of new digital technologies that are increasingly becoming part of our ordinary domestic lives. These include products such as DVD players and recorders, computers (both at home and at school, college or work) and cheap satellite and cable television receivers. For instance, once upon a time it was the norm for a household to have only one television set, often placed in the living-room and usually with the furniture organised around it. Before that it was not unusual for households to have just one radio (or wireless) set that again would have been placed in the living-room and the furniture arranged around it. The illustration on the cover of the *Radio Times* (Figure 1.22) represents a view of how families were thought to consume radio in the 1930s and 1940s.

As you will have discovered, today most households have several radios and televisions spread around the house, perhaps in bedrooms as well as in the living-room, maybe in the kitchen and, in the case of radios, in cars and as part of hi-fi systems or MP3 players. Many homes will also be able to receive radio and television programmes through their personal computers. Part of the reason for this growth in hardware is that personal computers, television sets and radios have become increasingly cheaper to buy, more compact in size, and can offer an increasing range of functions and services. When colour television sets first came on to the market they cost the equivalent of several weeks' wages, whereas today they represent less than one week's wages. Radio receivers, television screens and MP3 players are becoming increasingly smaller and can now be incorporated into other technology such as mobile phones. As more and more of our lives become linked with media consumption and as more and more of our peers have several radio and television sets, so there can be a pressure on us as consumers to buy more and more of these products – especially when we are told that each new piece of technology is better than the previous one. Again in the introduction we asked you to consider how quickly the media hardware in your household has changed and what has happened to hardware such as cassette decks, record players or CRT televisions. Increasingly advertisers try to persuade us that up-to-date hardware is an important part of who we are and our 'modern' lifestyle.

ACTIVITY

Compare the cover of the *Radio Times* in Figure 1.22 with the covers of current listings magazines to see what types of images are used today (see also section on media ideology, pp. 13–14). In what ways are the images in today's listing magazines different to those from the *Radio Times* in 1949? What assumptions do the images in the listings magazine make about audiences today and how they consume television?

continued

Figure 1.22 *Radio Times* cover, 1949

Some of the changes you may have identified in the ways in which we consume media products will have come about owing to the increase in services available to us. When television first started it was broadcast for only a few hours a day, mostly in the evenings, and the BBC had something called 'the toddlers' truce', when television closed down at teatime, after children's television, to allow parents to put their children to bed. On Sundays broadcasting was very limited because it was assumed that most people would be going to church services or wanting religious programmes.

Now we have several hundred television channels that broadcast 24 hours a day. Part of the reason for this is that television companies now recognise that there are many different groups of audiences who watch television at different times of the day and want different types of programmes.

'Martini media'

Today the rate of change is becoming faster and it is difficult to predict what our domestic media will look like in ten years' time. Mark Thompson, the current Director General of the BBC, when launching the BBC's plans for a digital future talked of the new world of 'martini media' where viewers and listeners want to pick 'n' mix their programmes "anytime, anyplace, anywhere" (see www.bbc.co.uk/pressoffice/speeches/stories/highfield_ft). 'We', the audience, are increasingly becoming members of various communities who, probably for some of the time, will watch or listen to BBC programmes but not necessarily when they are transmitted. Today we can relisten to radio broadcasts or rewatch television programmes over the internet, we can time-shift with DVD and hard-drive recorders and tomorrow we will have access to 'TV on demand', possibly through our mobile-phone-cum-MP3 players. It is increasingly difficult in an age of electronic programme guides (EPGs) and online broadcasting to know exactly when, how or why members of audiences may consume a particular television programme. This not only raises questions for public service providers like the BBC but also for the more traditional, terrestrial providers who have largely survived financially on the basis of delivering large cohorts of audiences to advertisers.

The 'free' audience for programmes such as *The Premiership* or *Match of the Day* is likely to decline as more and more football clubs offer their own subscription channels (e.g. Manchester United's MUTV) or because of the growth of 'interactive' digital channels such as the *Sky Sport* channels that offer the viewer a choice of camera angles, instant replays and additional information about players and teams. It is also possible to select your own 'news story' on digital news channels, and travel channels offer the opportunity to book holidays as well as giving weather details from around the world.

Increasingly we are relying upon the mobile phone instead of Radio 1's *Chart Show* to give us the latest record charts (which today also include sales of music 'downloads' as well as the number of actual records sold), and we will be able to download and play the latest releases and order tickets for concerts at the same time. When the Chemical Brothers' album *Push the Button* was released, over 275,000 people sampled the tracks by pressing the red button on their television remote controls during advertisements for the album that were broadcast during shows such as *The Simpsons* and *Soccer AM* (see http://www.thinkbox.tv/server/show/ConCaseStudy.10).

However, there are some observers who are concerned that those who are less affluent may end up with an inferior and limited, but 'free', choice. The popularity of the BBC Freeview digital service suggests that there are a large number of people who want access to digital services but do not want the range that is on offer via the subscription packages. BBC's Freeview may also be seen as an attempt to 'marry' new digital services with the BBC's public service broadcasting remit. Freesat offers the same service but for those who are unable to use their rooftop aerial.

Part of the change that has occurred over the years results from the way in which the technology that produces media texts has changed. The introduction of such innovations as the 'Steadicam' or high-definition portable digital video cameras has made news, documentaries and 'live' programming much more 'action-packed' and attractive to viewers. There was a vogue a few years ago for investigative programmes that used small hidden cameras to expose various malpractices. Consider, for example, the technology required to produce a programme such as Channel Four's *Big Brother*, or the way in which video phones are used in the reporting of the Iraqi and Afghan wars.

Another example of how our patterns of consumption have changed is cinema attendance in this country.

How is audience consumption patterned and determined?

We have already mentioned how we, as audiences, use different media at different times of the day. It is worth spending a little more time exploring the relationship between our patterns of media consumption and the routines of our daily lives. One of the measurements of the extent to which we now live in a media-saturated society is the degree to which our routine daily activities are interlinked with the media.

Many of us wake up in the morning to the sounds of a radio rather than an alarm clock. We may possibly have gone to sleep with the same radio playing and set to its 'sleep' function. Many televisions also have the same feature, although it may be harder to imagine drifting off to sleep part-way through a television programme or a film (intentionally at least!). We have also already mentioned breakfast television, which many of us now take for granted as a way of getting the latest news over our breakfast or while getting ready for school, college or work. We may also check our emails or texts before setting off to work, school or college.

The programmes we watch and/or listen to in the morning often have regular features or segments that are broadcast at the same time each day. In this way we are able to measure our progress each morning by their regular appearance, for example, the news headlines, reviews of the day's newspapers or spoof 'wake-up' calls made to unsuspecting members of the public.

It is interesting to reverse the equation and consider to what extent the media *organises* our daily routines rather than just fitting in around them. Some people will refuse to go out in the evening or answer the telephone or speak to visitors until their favourite programme has ended. Mid-morning television shows encourage housewives to sit down with a cup of coffee and relax after getting the family off to work and/or school. Increasingly television programmes ask us to phone or text in during certain times to win prizes, join in a vote or offer our opinion.

Of course, one of the impacts of digital technology is the opportunity to watch our favourite programmes, either broadcast as repeats or downloaded using such technology as BBC iPlayer.

ACTIVITY

- Consider your own daily/weekly routine and the manner in which the media interweaves with it.
- Consider the extent to which your consumption of the media fits around your schedule or whether your schedule is to some extent shaped by your media consumption; do you, for example, sometimes plan your activities around particular media output?
- How often do you make use of the opportunity to access programmes using iPlayer?

If you look at the radio or television schedules, you will notice that particular categories of audiences are addressed and particular genres of programmes are featured at particular times. We are all familiar with the notion of 'peak viewing time', but it is perhaps more interesting to look at the schedules outside this period to see what types of audience are being addressed, say, between 9 a.m. and lunchtime on a weekday on the different channels or on a Saturday or Sunday morning. One of the 'battlegrounds' between mainstream television channels such as BBC2, ITV1 and C4 is the early evening slot between 5 p.m. and 7 p.m. There has been fierce competition between programmes such as *Weakest Link, Deal or No Deal, Golden Balls*, etc.

ACTIVITY

Popular media such as television and the press try to make the most of special occasions such as royal or sporting events. They attempt to turn these occasions into rituals in which the media plays a central part. The idea of a typical Christmas Day that centres around the television is one example – it is assumed that the family cannot fully celebrate Christmas without watching the Queen's Speech, film premieres and special editions of popular programmes.

Sporting events such as the World Cup or the Olympics are other occasions on which we, the audience, are encouraged to celebrate the success (or otherwise) of our teams through our participation in a 'television event' that often has special theme tunes ('Nessun Dorma' for the 1990 World Cup is perhaps one of the best-known examples) and a special presentation studio for links and interviews. The normal schedules may be changed to highlight the importance and uniqueness of the occasion. There will probably also be special 'souvenir' editions of television listings magazines or newspaper supplements from which we can get background information and keep a record of the progress of the events.

One of the reasons that media companies like to turn these occasions into rituals is that by packaging them in this way they hope to attract larger audiences than normal. These packages can then be sold on to advertisers. Another reason is that, as pay-per-view becomes increasingly available, it is a way of making these broadcasts look 'special' and worth paying extra money for. This is increasingly the case with sporting events such as world championships in, for example, cricket, rugby, boxing or golf.

ACTIVITY

Who is the audience?

Many commentators suggest that in any text there is an implied audience, that the producers of media texts have a 'typical' audience member in mind when they start to create a text. (Look at the section on production skills (chapter 5) – you are asked to do the same thing in terms of your target audience.)

Ien Ang, in *Desperately Seeking the Audience* (1991), discusses the manner in which media producers and institutions view audiences as an 'imaginary entity', as a mass rather than as a set of individuals. They will, however, often have a 'typical' audience member in mind when they produce their texts.

In the 1980s trainee ILR (independent local radio) presenters were supposed to have had an imaginary person, 'Doreen', whom they were told to consider as the 'typical listener'. Presenters were told about her age, her likes and dislikes, her habits, her household and her husband. They were told that Doreen is 'typical'. She is educated and intelligent but may only listen to the radio with half an ear and does not necessarily understand long words or complicated discussions. They were told that this does not mean that Doreen is stupid and should be talked down to, but that they should make sure that she understands and is engaged with what is happening on the radio. They were encouraged to address Doreen and her husband personally, as if they knew them.

Academic research, however, has produced another version of this 'imaginary entity'. In *Understanding News* (1982), Hartley identified seven types of what he called 'subjectivities' that are used by media producers to help define the social position of the individual audience member and to engage with him or her:

- self-image
- gender
- age group
- family
- class
- nation
- ethnicity.

Fiske, in *Television Culture* (1987), added four more:

- education
- religion
- politics
- location (geographical and local).

However, Hartley acknowledged that sometimes these categories can get mixed up or can conflict with each other; for instance, some notions of nationhood and some types of ethnicity (Hartley, 1982, p. 69). It is also not clear to what extent these subjectivities are equal or whether in particular circumstances some may be more influential than others.

These categories are useful in identifying the way in which individual members of mass audiences are identified both by themselves and by media producers and advertisers. Fiske, talking about television, says that it "tries to construct an ideal subject position which it invites us to occupy, and, if we do, rewards us with . . . the pleasure of recognition" (Fiske, 1987, p. 51).

ACTIVITY

Using the subjectivities above, try to construct a profile of an 'ideal viewer/reader' for a particular programme or publication. Consider what clues to this type of person there are in programmes such as *Newsround* or *The Bill*, or in a newspaper like the *Daily Express*. Apart from the categories already listed, consider also the likes and dislikes the 'typical' members of these audiences might have, their interests, their taste in clothes and music, the types of books and/or magazines that they consume.

■ Give your 'typical' viewer a name and a place to live.
■ Compare your profile with those produced by others. Discuss and account for similarities and/or differences.

"Television doesn't make programmes, it creates audiences" (Jean-Luc Godard)

Advertising is important to a whole range of media products because these products are financed by advertising revenue or subsidised by the revenue that advertising brings in. The media therefore spends a lot of time and money looking at the circulation and ratings of their products.

Even if you pay for some media products, the advertising may still have subsidised the price and made the product cheaper for you to buy. Take a local weekly newspaper such as the *Wiltshire Times*, which costs 60p a copy and is probably considered a good buy for that price. It will have lots of local information, stories and photographs. However, if we look through the *Wiltshire Times*, we see that nearly 40 per cent of it is made up of advertisements, either for such products as cars, computers or shop goods, or for job vacancies, private car sales and other

Figure 1.23 The *Wiltshire Times*

services (classified ads). One of the reasons why people buy this newspaper is to obtain the information contained in the advertisements. If we want to buy a new car, find somewhere local to live, or see what is on at the cinema, we can look through the advertisements in our local paper and see what is available.

The cover price of the *Wiltshire Times*, 60p, probably represents about 15 or 20 per cent of the true cost of printing an edition of the newspaper. Without the advertising the reader might have to pay about £3 a copy, and at that price it is unlikely that the *Wiltshire Times* would sell many copies. A few years ago there was an enormous growth of free local newspapers that were financed purely through their advertising revenue. The *Wiltshire Times* has a circulation of about 19,000, but the company that publishes it also publishes several other local newspapers, both free and paid for, whose circulation varies between 20,000 and 50,000. It also has a website (http://www.wiltshiretimes.co.uk/news/).

Similarly, if you buy magazines, you are certainly not paying the full cost of producing those magazines. The advertising revenue is probably paying up to three-quarters of the production costs.

The attraction for the advertiser is that these media outlets provide an opportunity to advertise their products to particular social groups of people. In relation to the *Wiltshire Times*, it is a group of people defined by the particular area in which they live. The newspaper will probably have a lot more additional information about its readers in terms of demographics – age, social class, gender, income – similar to the 'subjectivities' that Hartley and Fiske identified. The newspaper will have spent a lot of time and money trying to identify and categorise its readers so that it can then 'sell' these readers to its advertisers.

You may think that this does not apply to the BBC because it does not take advertising. Certainly it is true that at present on its main channels the BBC does not have 'paid for' advertising, but it is moving into other types of services and many BBC programmes are available on digital channels via subscription, and many of its magazines (e.g. *Top Gear* and *Gardeners' World*) carry commercial advertising.

The BBC is also in competition with the commercial channels in an attempt to prove its popularity and to justify the licence fee. If the BBC's audience share falls below a certain level, the criticisms of its licence fee increase (see section on public service broadcasting (PSB), p. 247).

ACTIVITY

List all the different media texts that you have consumed in the last week. Divide your list into those texts that you had to pay for individually (cinema, newspapers, magazines, books and so on) and those that were available to you free of charge (e.g. television channels and radio stations). Are the services provided by the BBC free?

Being able to identify both the size and type of their audience is very important for both the BBC and commercial media. There are various organisations which carry out this research and whose findings are sold to media companies. Currently BARB measures the audiences for the five terrestrial channels and all the digital channels. According to BARB, its ratings are based on the use of 5,100 panel homes, representing about 11,500 viewers. As the way we consume television is changing with the introduction of many more digital channels, 'narrowcasting', 'time-shifting' (recording programmes and watching them later) and the 'shuffling' of programmes (when they are repeated several times a day or over several days), television companies and BARB will need to develop ways of measuring much smaller but more specialised audiences. (There is more information regarding viewing figures and statistics at http://www.bfi.org.uk/filmtvinfo/gateway/categories/statistics/.)

Both NRS (National Readership Survey) and ABC (Audit Bureau of Circulation) carry out a similar function for the newspaper and magazine industry, producing circulation figures but using different methods. ABC measures the sales of newspapers and magazines, while NRS interviews a sample of approximately 40,000 people about their reading habits. RAJAR (Radio Joint Audience Research) also uses the sample method and compiles both BBC and commercial radio listening figures. All these organisations have websites that contain up-to-date figures as well as explaining how they carry out their research (http://www.nrs.co.uk; http://www.abc.org.uk; http://www.rajar.co.uk).

Another industry-based organisation that offers detailed information regarding newspaper circulation and readership is JICREG – the Joint Industry Committee for Regional Press Research (http://www.jicreg.co.uk/about/index.cfm).

According to the Radio Advertising Bureau all commercial radio stations have a clearly defined core target audience – those who are at the centre of its market and who, it is hoped, will become station 'loyalists'. Around this core are other, secondary, listeners.

All these organisations use the same categories for classifying audiences. These are based on the National Readership Survey's social grades used in advertising and market research. This divides the adult population of Britain into six grades and identifies the types of occupation that each grade represents and (as at 2005) the percentage of the population that fits into that particular grade:

A. Higher managerial, administrative or professional (3.8%)
B. Intermediate managerial, administrative or professional (22.1%)
C1. Supervisory or clerical, junior managerial, administrative or professional (28.9%)
C2. Skilled manual workers (20.6%)
D. Semi-skilled and unskilled manual workers (16.2%)
E. Casual labourers, unemployed, state pensioners (8.4%).

Sex, age and ethnicity are also important. Age is generally divided into the following categories:

- < 15
- 15–24
- 24–35

- 35–55
- 55 >

For more detailed information on how the National Readership Survey categorises the British public, see its website (http://www.nrs.co.uk/open_access/open_ methadology/index.cfm).

Research within ethnic minority groups published by Ofcom in June 2007 found that

> **consumers from ethnic minority groups are among the most enthusiastic and technology aware consumers of communications services in the UK . . . [however] they watch less TV – especially the biggest traditional channels and those with internet are more likely to have broadband and to use and depend on a mobile phone than the rest of the population.**

(http://www.ofcom.org.uk/media/news/2007/06/nr_20070621)

The statistical information provided by organisations such as BARB and RAJAR is then supplemented by more detailed and qualitative data about audiences. This is often carried out by advertising or marketing companies for particular broadcasters and media companies, and focuses on the audience's lifestyle, habits, opinions, and sets of values and attitudes. Advertising companies claim that they can segment audiences on the basis of 'socio-economic values' such as:

- **Survivors** Those who want security and like routine.
- **Social climbers** Those who have a strong materialistic drive and like status symbols.
- **Care givers** Those who believe in 'caring and sharing'.
- **Explorers** Those for whom personal growth and influencing social change are important.

Thinkbox is the television marketing body for many of the main UK commercial broadcasters and aims to help advertisers get the best out of television. It offers clients profiles of various audience types such as "Stylish singletons (independent, single, career-minded women in their 30s); Technophiles (enthusiastic pioneers of new technology) and Tweenies (brand conscious 10–12 year olds). . . . Flourishing Fifties, Wise Guys and Yummy Mummies" (although you have to register, you can obtain more detailed information about these groups at http://www.thinkbox.tv/ server/show/nav.00100d00a).

These socio-economic groups may have various names (see e.g. the Insight Social Value Groups at http://www.businessballs.com/demographicsclassifications.htm), but they are all based on the work of the American psychologist Abraham Maslow and his idea of a 'Hierarchy of Needs' (see Figure 1.24). Maslow suggested that we all have different 'layers' of needs and that we need to satisfy one before we can move on to the next. In other words, we all start at the bottom of Maslow's hierarchy, having basic *physiological* needs such as food and shelter for our survival. We can then move up the hierarchy to the level of *safety* needs, probably to do with having a regular income, from a job, for example, that guarantees us a regular source of food and shelter – perhaps being able to pay the rent or mortgage. The next level is to do with belonging to a *social* group, whether it be our family, work colleagues or peer group. In fact most of us belong to a variety of different social groups, for example, as students, family members, social groups, work groups and so on. Our *esteem* needs are to do with wanting to gain the respect and admiration of others, perhaps through the display of status symbols such as expensive consumer goods. Maslow argues that many people stop at particular levels and only a very few reach 'self-actualisation' at the top of the hierarchy. These are the people who are considered to be in control of their lives and to have achieved all their goals.

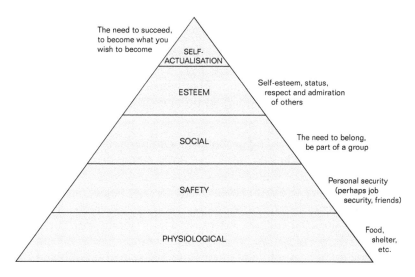

Figure 1.24 Maslow's 'Hierarchy of Needs'

Advertisers are increasingly using ideas such as Maslow's and are combining both demographics and lifestyle categories in an attempt to be more effective and efficient in the way they target particular groups of people. They are trying to sell their products in a way that meets the target audience's perceived needs (there is more information on Maslow's Hierarchy of Needs at http://www.businessballs.com/maslow.htm).

> **We must get away from the habit of thinking in terms of what the media do to people and substitute for it the idea of what people do with the media.**

(Halloran, 1971)

The history of audience research is a story of the shift from the view of the audience as passive to one that views the audience as active in its relationship with media texts.

THE HYPODERMIC NEEDLE THEORY

The Hypodermic Needle theory suggests that the media 'injects' ideas into a passive audience, like giving a patient a drug.

Some of the earliest academic studies of media audiences appeared in the 1920s and 1930s and looked at what we understand as the 'mass media' – cinema, radio, popular magazines and newspapers – as they became increasingly available to the majority of people in Europe and America. In these early studies the audience itself was seen as a 'mass' audience – a mass of people, all together, consuming the same product and receiving the same 'mass' message. This seemed to be particularly effective when the Nazis in Germany and the Communists in the Soviet Union used the media as a propaganda tool. They appeared to be successful in making their ideas dominant and 'injecting' large numbers of people with their messages.

The Frankfurt School was made up of German Marxists who, in the 1930s, saw the success of Nazi propaganda and later, in 1950s America, of commercial television. They believed that the media was a force for pacifying the population and restricting and controlling public and cultural life by injecting a 'mass culture' that functioned as a distraction from the mundanity of ordinary daily life. Members of the Frankfurt School, including Theodor Adorno and Max Horkheimer, suggested that the American culture industries, in particular commercial television and popular cinema, moulded people into a standardised, passive state of being that allowed them to be easily manipulated.

Although in America most of this manipulation was carried out by advertising and the drive for consumerism, they suggested that, as had happened in Germany, mass media could also be used to manipulate people into accepting particular political ideas such as capitalism. They believed that these culture industries worked against democracy and restricted people's choices and actions. (A more recent version of this argument has been put forward by Noam Chomsky; see pp. 210–11.)

This view of the media seemed to be reinforced by Orson Welles' *The War of the Worlds*, broadcast on American radio in 1938. The programme, based on the book by H.G. Wells, was broadcast as part of a regular weekly drama slot but was produced to sound like a series of news reports and newsflashes about the invasion of America by Martians. The programme appeared to include interviews with people in authority such as politicians and police officers, and contained instructions for people to evacuate their homes. Many people did in fact believe that the broadcast was a real emergency and drove out of New York State. The programme caused widespread panic and also attracted considerable criticism and complaints for being 'too realistic'. It is a good example of the power and 'authority' that the media had at the time in the minds of radio listeners. Many commentators have suggested that today we are too sophisticated to make the same mistake but a spoof broadcast of the BBC programme *Ghostwatch* on Hallowe'en in 1992 fooled many viewers into believing that they were seeing real paranormal experiences on television. The campaign to 'name and shame' paedophiles by the *News of the World* is also perhaps a reminder that we still give the media too much authority and credence.

With the introduction of commercial television and in particular advertising, the idea of 'injecting' the audience with a message seemed even more relevant. It was thought that advertisers could make people buy particular products or brands of products merely by repeating the message often and loudly – the 'hard-sell' approach. Vance Packard in *The Hidden Persuaders* [1957] (1979) identified many of the ways in which advertisers attempted to manipulate audiences. C. Wright Mills in *The Power Elite* [1956] (2000) suggested four functions that the media perform for audiences:

- to give individuals *identity*
- to give people goals, *aspirations*
- to give *instruction* on how to achieve these goals
- to give people an alternative if they failed, *escapism*.

However, studies of the various political advertising campaigns in America in the 1940s and 1950s suggested that the audience was not so passive and did not just accept what the advertisers or the programme makers said. Rather, in terms of political advertising, audiences focused on those messages that reinforced their existing beliefs and tended to dismiss those that contradicted their established ideas. This suggested that audiences in fact selected the messages that they wanted to hear and ignored others. The media's effect seemed to be one of reinforcement rather than of persuasion.

USES AND GRATIFICATIONS THEORY

Research then led to a view that audiences, rather than being simply a 'mass', comprised different social groups, with particular sets of social relations, and a variety of cultural norms and values. Several American researchers, including Paul Lazarsfeld and Elihu Katz, concentrated on providing evidence that audiences were not simply one large, gullible mass but that messages put out by the media were in fact being received by a complex mixture of different groups and that media texts were themselves mediated by these social and cultural networks. The audience was now being seen as playing an active role in the interpretation of the meaning of particular media texts.

Uses and gratifications theory was an important shift in the study of how audiences interacted with texts, and was developed by Blumer and Katz in 1975. They suggested that media audiences make active use of what the media offer and that the audience has a set of needs, which the media in one form or another meets. Through a series of interviews with viewers, they identified four broad needs that were fulfilled by watching television:

- **Diversion** A form of escape or release from everyday pressures
- **Personal relationships** Companionship through identification with television characters and sociability through discussion about television with other people
- **Personal identity** The ability to compare one's own life with the characters and situations portrayed and to explore individual problems and perspectives
- **Surveillance** Information about 'what's going on' in the world.

Uses and gratifications theory is seen to have some merit, as it supposes an 'active' audience that to some extent provides its own interpretation of the text's meaning.

However, as a means of understanding the relationship between the audience and the creation of meaning, it can appear to be rather simplistic and limited in relation to the complexity of how we the audience/reader actually works with a text. One of the main problems with uses and gratifications theory is that it assumes that the media somehow identifies these needs on behalf of the audience and then provides the material to meet or gratify them. It is difficult, for example, to imagine what the 'need' was that resulted in a television show such as *The Office* or *Heroes*. An alternative interpretation may be that we, the audience, create these needs as a response to the material provided by the media, and that in fact we could have many other needs that are not identified, or met, by existing media texts.

In fact many of our 'uses' and 'pleasures' may be seen to be 'making the best' of what is available and putting it to our (the audience's) use, which may be different from the one that the producer intended. For example, consider the unexpected popularity and fashionableness of many cheap daytime television shows, such as *Deal Or No Deal* or *Ready Steady Cook*.

It is worth thinking a little about the differences in the ways we tend to consume different media. The term 'situated culture' is used to describe how our 'situation' (daily routines and patterns, social relationships with family and peer groups) can influence our engagement with and interpretation of media texts.

If we compare our consumption of films and television, there is an obvious difference between the two in that television is generally part of what Raymond Williams [1974] (1989) described as a 'flow'. By this Williams meant that television was a constant stream available to us in the home that we can turn on or off at will, like a water tap in the bathroom or kitchen. Sometimes we have it on as background or, as it is suggested that many elderly people do, as 'company'. On other occasions we may turn the television on in order to 'share' our watching with others, particularly with sporting events or perhaps soap operas. This may be a way of sharing companionship or, like *The Royle Family*, a way of being a family.

This, Williams suggested, means that our reception of television programmes, and the media in general, is mediated through our domestic, situated culture. It means that *who* we are, our sense of our own place in the world, our views and beliefs, as well as *where* we are in terms of our social location, all influence our responses to the media.

Watching a film, in contrast to television, is generally a more carefully chosen and focused activity. A visit to the cinema requires a series of conscious decisions such as deciding to go out to the cinema, choosing who to go with, at what time, to which cinema or multiplex and which film to see. Watching a DVD or video also involves a set of deliberate choices such as deciding which DVD or video to rent, paying money, putting aside the time to watch the film, and perhaps choosing particular companions to watch it with. Even a film on television is often chosen in a much more deliberate way than the rest of the television's 'flow', which is often watched 'because it is on' rather than as the result of a series of deliberate choices.

ACTIVITY

Think about the last time you went to the cinema. List the series of decisions that you had to make. How did you make your decisions? Refer back to some of the earlier activities in this section that are about patterns of film consumption. How do you and your friends consume this medium?

Tunstall in *The Media in Britain* (1983) has suggested that the way in which we consume the media can be divided into three levels: primary, secondary and tertiary.

- *Primary media:* Where we pay close attention to the media text, for instance, in the close reading of a magazine or newspaper, or in the cinema where we concentrate on the film in front of us.
- *Secondary media:* Where the medium or text is there in the background and we are aware that it is there but are not concentrating on it. This happens most often with music-based radio but also when the television is on but we are not really watching it; perhaps we are chatting with friends, eating or

Figure 1.25 Primary media: the cinema

Figure 1.26 Secondary media: the car radio

Figure 1.27 Tertiary media: walking past advertising billboards and posters

carrying out some other activity. This could also include 'skimming' through a magazine or newspaper, waiting for something to catch our eye.

■ *Tertiary media:* Where the medium is present but we are not at all aware of it. The most obvious examples are advertising hoardings or placards that we pass but do not register.

ACTIVITY

Tunstall's ideas are based on 'traditional' media such as film, television, radio or newspapers. In what ways do you think they may also be applied to more recent digital technologies such as the web, our use of mobile phones, blogging, etc.?

Mode of address

Mode of address refers to the way in which a particular text will address or speak to its audience.

Researchers have looked at the way in which the media 'addresses' or 'positions' its audiences in relation to an event, person or idea (see section on narrative, pp. 56–71). Audiences can be positioned by the viewpoint used both verbally and visually to create a relationship between the text and its audience. Expressed verbally, this may include words like 'I' used by the narrator or broadcaster, 'you' when addressing the viewer or listener, and 'it' or 'they' when referring to an event, third person or idea. Visually this positioning can be maintained by using camera angles, where the camera follows the action in a particular way or follows a particular person. Editing the flow and sequencing of shots can also position the audience to the extent that they become observers who see more than the participants and are spectators placed outside the action. For example, this occurs in a crime drama where the audience is given 'privileged' information about who committed the crime, or in a soap opera where someone is lying or has a secret.

The modes of address used in broadcasting are often informal, conversational and open-ended because they are consumed in the private domestic world of the home. To create the necessary sense of intimacy, presenters talk to the audience as if they were individual members whom they know personally (see discussion on 'Doreen', p. 121). Although these modes of address are largely motivated by the producers' sense of their audience, they are sometimes determined by the institution's own sense of itself. For example, the BBC might consider itself to be representing the nation at a time of crisis and therefore may present its material in a particularly solemn and dignified manner.

Gendered consumption

There has been much research on how gender affects our consumption of the media. Studies such as Hobson (1982) and Gray (1992) suggest that women prefer 'open-ended' narratives such as soap operas whereas men prefer 'closed' narratives such as police dramas (see section on narrative, pp. 56–71). Soap operas are considered popular among women because they conform to what Geraghty (1991) calls "women's fiction" and have certain common conventions:

- They have strong female lead characters.
- They focus on the private, domestic sphere.
- They deal with personal relationships.
- They contain an element of fantasy and/or escapism.
  (See section on genre, pp. 44–55.)

Other research, such as Radway's (1984) study of a group of readers of romantic novels and Stacey's (1994) work with women cinema goers from the 1940s and 1950s, also explores this notion of escapism or 'utopian solutions'.

These studies suggest that female audiences welcome romantic texts as a means of reasserting positive aspects of their lives. Radway suggests that heroines in romantic novels are seen as victorious because they symbolise the value of the female world of love and human relationships as being more important than fame and material success.

"Utopian Solution" is a term taken from Dyer (1977), who suggested that entertainment genres are popular because of their fantasy element and the escapism that they provide from daily routines and problems. He suggested that particular genres such as musicals or westerns offered particular types of utopian solution.

Males are considered to prefer factual programmes such as news and current affairs, although, as Morley (1986) notes, many men may watch soap operas but are not prepared to admit it. Mulvey [1975] (2003) suggests that most Hollywood films are based on the idea of a male viewer and that the camera shots and editing are 'positioned' from a male perspective. This she calls the 'male gaze', which automatically positions women as passive and as objects.

All this research suggests the complex nature of the relationships between audience and media text. As you will have read, texts are polysemic (see p. 7) in that they have a variety of meanings, and the audience is an important component in determining those meanings.

The 'effects' debate and moral panics

There has long been concern about the supposedly bad effects that popular culture may have on 'ordinary' people. This concern has grown with the increase in 'mass media' and the availability of cheap novels, popular magazines, the cinema, popular music, television and, more recently, the internet.

In the 1950s, American comics such as *Tales from the Crypt* or *Haunt of Fear*, with their depictions of violence, were seen as dangerous, so a law was introduced called the 1955 Children and Young Persons (Harmful Publications) Act to control which comics were permitted to go on sale in this country.

In fact we can trace panics about the effects of the media back to the introduction of newspapers in the eighteenth century, when a tax or stamp duty was put on newspapers by the government to make newspapers so expensive that only rich people could afford to buy them.

The term 'moral panic' comes from *Folk Devils and Moral Panics* (2002) by Stan Cohen. Cohen looked at the media reaction to the fights between mods and rockers at various seaside resorts in Britain during the mid-1960s. His term 'moral panic' came to mean a mass response to "a group, a person or an attitude that becomes defined as a threat to society".

Once a threat has been identified, a panic is then often created through press coverage, particularly the tabloid press, and is then taken up by other newspapers and/or television programmes. Newspapers may start-up campaigns claiming 'something must be done' and then politicians may become involved, offering support to the campaigns, and legislation is often introduced as a result.

In recent years we have had panics over refugees 'flooding' into Britain from Eastern Europe seeking asylum, as well as over dangerous dogs, illegal raves and video nasties. The Columbine High School massacre in 1999 prompted a moral panic about 'goth' culture.

As a result of these 'panics', legislation has been introduced to try to control dangerous dogs, make rave parties illegal, monitor the activities of asylum seekers and the classification and distribution of certain types of video. One topical 'moral panic' was the 'naming and shaming' of paedophiles by the *News of the World*.

The moral panic over video nasties such as *Driller Killer, Zombie Flesh Eaters* and *The Texas Chainsaw Massacre* in the early 1980s led to the Video Recordings Act of 1984, which limited the kinds of videos on sale in this country (see section on Regulation of the media, pp. 248–50). Other moral panics can be more subtle; for instance, the campaigns over unmarried mothers who, it is claimed, get pregnant for the welfare benefits, or the panics about supermodels and 'heroin chic', which, it is claimed, encourage young girls to diet and can result in anorexia.

Perhaps the most well-known case is the murder of James Bulger in 1993 and its association with the film *Child's Play 3*. In this case neither the prosecution nor the police presented any evidence to support the supposition that the two boys who had killed James Bulger had actually seen (yet alone been influenced by) this film.

Figure 1.28 Scene from *Child's Play 3*

The two boys came from socially and environmentally deprived backgrounds. Jon Venables had been referred by teachers to a psychologist because while at school he banged his head against a wall to attract attention, threw objects at other children and had cut himself with scissors.

Even if it had been proved that the two boys had seen *Child's Play 3*, it is difficult to know how the court could have separated the influence of this video from all the other factors that made the two boys who they were. It was the judge in the case who, in his summing up, made the connection, which was then taken up by the tabloid press and MPs. This eventually led to the law being changed so that the British Board of Film Classification now has to take into account the influence of videos as well as their content.

There has been a large amount of research to try to identify the effects of the media on audiences, particularly in relation to violence. However, such research tends to be either inconclusive or contradictory (see e.g. Barker and Petley, 2001). Part of the problem with any attempt to prove the effects of watching violence or sex on television, video or film is trying to isolate the effect of the media from all the other factors that are involved in shaping us as individuals – family, home, education, religion, peer groups and so on. In America there were several cases of supposed 'copycat' killings following the release of the film *Natural Born Killers*. In fact many of those convicted of murder already had a history of violence before seeing the film.

Two of Britain's worst murder cases were the shootings of schoolchildren and their teacher in Dunblane by Thomas Hamilton in 1996 and the murders of elderly women carried out by the doctor Harold Shipman over a number of years. In neither case was there any suggestion or evidence that Hamilton or Shipman had ever watched any violent videos.

Much of this 'effects' debate seems to assume that somehow if we, the audience, watch a violent film, then we will carry out violent acts. This seems very simplistic in view of the complicated relationship that we, as audiences, have with the media. The most we can possibly say with certainty is that people with violent tendencies may watch violent videos, but that does not mean that everyone who watches violent videos is (or becomes) violent.

One of the moral panics today is focused around access to the internet. Over 60 per cent of adults in this country now have access to the world wide web, and it is available in schools and public libraries. There does perhaps need to be a debate about how media such as the internet is controlled and monitored, but perhaps the real difficulty lies in deciding who should be in charge of regulation. Many people are probably fully in favour of censorship – as long as they are the ones who make the decisions.

ACTIVITY

What do you understand by the term 'moral panic'? By referring to one or more specific examples, illustrate how the media may be said to be responsible for creating moral panics.

The effects of advertising

One of the most important debates surrounding the influence of the media is the effects that advertisements may have both on us, the audience, and on those who rely on advertising for their income, namely the media producers.

Since adverts are often consumed as tertiary media it is very difficult to assess the effect of advertising and the extent to which people are affected by the advertisements to which they are exposed. In the section on moral panics we discussed the difficulties in trying to isolate the effect the media may have from other influences on us – such as parents, education, peer groups or religion. This is perhaps even more difficult in the case of advertising, as we are often not consciously aware of advertisements, in that we may skim past the adverts in a magazine or newspaper or fast-forward through a DVD or film.

One of the pieces of evidence to suggest that advertising works is the fact that companies spend so much money on advertising. According to some commentators, up to one-third of the cost of a bar of soap or up to 40 per cent of the price of a tube of toothpaste may represent advertising costs. Remember that, for example, about £20 billion is spent on marketing and advertising each year.

Arguments in support of advertising

- It finances a whole range of media and provides us with a wide array of choice in terms of the media available to us.
- It may be seen as an essential part of a modern-day, consumerist society and is a very effective way of informing us about new products.
- It stimulates consumption, which benefits industry, increases employment and leads to economic growth.
- Over the years advertising has been a very effective way for government and its various agencies to provide public information about safe sex and the use of condoms, the dangers of drinking and driving or, more mundanely, changing telephone codes. The government is one of the major advertisers in this country.
- Sponsorship is an important source of funding for many sporting and artistic events.
- The advertising industry provides many people with employment.

Arguments used to criticise advertising

These are perhaps a little more subtle and complicated, as the following list suggests:

- Advertising creates false hopes and expectations.
- It works on our insecurities.
- It promotes unrealistic and dangerous role models.
- It can influence the content of media texts.
- Advertising revenue can direct programming.
- Advertising revenue is the foundation of new newspapers.

Advertising creates false hopes and expectations
Commentators such as C. Wright Mills in the 1950s and organisations such as Adbusters (http://www.adbusters.org) today are critical of the consumerist nature of our society for this reason. They suggest that advertising excludes the less wealthy and creates a 'must-have' society (advertising on children's television is often cited as one of the main examples of this). Advertising, combined with easily available credit, means that some people may buy products they cannot afford. This then may lead them into debt or criminal action to try to obtain those goods that are made desirable to us through advertising (ram-raiding is cited as an example).

Advertising works on our insecurities
The work of John Berger (1972) has been used by many people to explain the way in which advertising works upon the individual. Berger suggests that advertising works upon our insecurities and our need to feel 'esteemed' in the eyes of others by implying that we are less than perfect if we do not own a particular product or look like the models in the advertisements. The advertisement implies that if we buy that product, we will look like the models or

lead the type of life shown in the advertisements. Advertising is always working on our insecurities and making us constantly aspire to something new.

> **The purpose of publicity is to make the spectator marginally dissatisfied with his present way of life. Not with the way of society, but with his own life within it. It suggests that if he buys what it is offering, his life will become better. It offers him an improved alternative to what he is.**
>
> **All publicity works upon anxiety. The sum of everything is money, to get money is to overcome anxiety.**

(Berger, 1972)

■ Advertising promotes unrealistic and dangerous role models

There has been a considerable amount of debate in recent years over the effects of 'super-waif' and 'heroin-chic' images of models in glossy magazines. It is claimed that the constant representation of ultra-thin models in both fashion spreads and advertisements has led to an undermining of girls' self-esteem and to eating disorders.

An article published in the *British Medical Journal* in 2000 by Jones and Smith suggests that between 1 and 2 per cent of women between the ages of fifteen and thirty suffer from some kind of eating disorder and that this is directly attributable to the images that appear in fashion and 'lifestyle' magazines (see also pp. 71–82 on representation).

(We had wanted to show an illustration of an advert for Kellogg's Cornflakes that used a 'super-waif' type of model and suggested that eating Kellogg's Cornflakes was a way of staying slim but also remaining healthy. However, perhaps because of criticism that Kellogg's received as a result of this advertisement and because of the sensitivity of the whole issue, the company would not grant permission for us to use the advertisement.)

ACTIVITY

Look through back copies of newspapers and magazines and collect examples of these types of advertisements and articles about the issue of female representation. You can also access early advertisements at http://www.hatads.org.uk/.

Advertising can influence the content of media texts

Some commentators suggest that advertisers can influence the content of media texts, although there is very little direct evidence that this takes place in the British media.

One notable example is from the 1960s when *The Sunday Times* Insight Team were investigating the links between cigarettes and cancer. Tobacco companies threatened to cancel their advertising with *The Sunday Times* if the investigations were published. The then editor, Harold Evans, published the investigations and the cigarette companies did pull their advertising (a considerable amount in those days) but eventually returned to *The Sunday Times* because it was a particularly effective means of targeting their desired group.

What is perhaps of more concern is the relationship between programme content and sponsors of programmes. This is an acknowledged issue in America but has generally not been seen to be an issue in this country.

ACTIVITY

According to Williamson, "Advertisements are selling us something more than consumer goods. In providing us with a structure in which we and those goods are interchangeable, they are selling us ourselves" (Williamson, 1978).

continued

It is undeniable that advertisers do have considerable power over the media in which their advertising appears. In the 1980s the *Sport* and the *Star* ran a joint newspaper but the *Star*'s main advertisers, household names including Tesco and Sainsbury's, were unhappy at being associated with the types of stories, features and pictures that appeared in the *Sport*. They threatened to cancel their advertising if the joint venture continued. The *Star* then pulled out of the venture with the *Sport* to safeguard its advertising revenue.

Advertising revenue can direct programming

Many commentators believe that Channel 4 has become less radical and adventurous over the years and suggest that this may be the influence of advertising revenue. When Channel 4 started broadcasting it had a number of quite (for the time) radical programmes, some with fairly small audiences, and could not fill all its advertising space. Gaps would appear on the screen in the commercial breaks with a notice saying that 'Programmes will continue shortly'. Since Channel 4 has been allowed to keep all its advertising revenue instead of having to pass it on to the other commercial television companies, some commentators suggest that there has been a general shift towards more popular programmes that attract younger audiences and so raise advertising income.

Most commercial radio stations tend to offer the same mix of music and presenter 'chat' because they know that this will attract the largest number of the 15- to 25-year-olds who advertisers want to target. A commercial station that initially attempts to offer something different, as did London's X-FM, Jazz FM or Kiss, often quickly changes its format to reach a more popular market.

ACTIVITY

Look at the schedules for Channel 4. Can you identify the way in which different audience 'segments' are packaged together? To what extent do you think that the current Channel 4 schedules offer something that is 'innovative'?

Or:

■ **Advertising revenue is the foundation of new newspapers**

Figure 1.29 The logo for *Today* newspaper, which folded in the 1990s

Newspapers such as *Today*, the *Post* and the *Sunday Correspondent* all started up in the 1980s but folded in the 1990s because they could not attract sufficient income from advertising. This may have been as a result of fierce competition in the newspaper market or because the products were not good enough to attract high circulation figures, but in the case of the *Sunday Correspondent*, a left-wing newspaper founded in 1989 and lasting for less than a year, it is possible to argue that there was a conspiracy behind its demise, which occurred after advertisers withdrew their support. Other radical magazines such as *Red Pepper* or the *Big Issue* struggle to survive owing to the lack of advertisers willing to invest their money in these publications.

ACTIVITY

It is worth spending some time thinking about the criteria for 'successful' advertisements. In a television poll held in 2000 of the 'greatest' television advertisements, the Guinness 'Surfing' advertisement came top. It is interesting to speculate why so many people thought that it was 'great'. It certainly caused a lot of comment, but many people seemed unable to explain fully what the advert was about. Perhaps this is the key to its success – the polysemic nature of its message (see p. 7). Second in the same poll were the Smash 'Martians' advertisements. It would be worth trying to measure the extent to which the success of either of these advertisements will have significantly increased the sales of their respective products.

Audience participation

Recently there has been a paradigm shift in the way in which members of the audience interact with media producers and their products. Until recently producers and broadcasters had created the content of television programmes, newspapers, magazines, etc. for audiences largely to passively consume. Now, due to the growth of 'user-generated-content', this is rapidly changing and 'real people' are increasingly becoming actively involved in the production and content of television programmes. At the same time readers and listeners are being encouraged to contribute to radio programmes, newspaper and magazine articles as well as online activities such as posting photographs, writing reviews or joining in votes.

Once upon a time it was only certain privileged types of people (politicians, experts, presenters) who appeared on our screens. If the public were seen, they were tightly controlled and mediated through the use of presenters (as in documentaries) or a quiz master. (Even the early quiz and entertainment shows relied upon various types of 'experts' or personalities – for instance, the BBC's *What's My Line?*, *Juke Box Jury* or *Brains Trust*.) It was largely with the introduction of more American-type quiz shows on ITV in the 1950s that 'ordinary people' started to appear in front of cameras and then usually only to answer a well-rehearsed and tightly controlled set of questions.

Today, however, the public, ordinary people like us, are increasingly the stars of the shows. A recent popular genre has been the talent show where 'ordinary people' become stars (*How Do You Solve a Problem like Maria?*, *Any Dream will Do*, *Strictly Come Dancing*, *The X Factor*). Another popular genre is the 'makeover' show, where ordinary people change their looks (*What Not to Wear*, *How to Look Good Naked*), their homes or gardens (*Home Front* or *How Clean is Your*

House?) or try to reorganise their lives and families (*Supernanny, The House of Tiny Tearaways, Help Me Help My Child*).

Television companies are increasingly looking for 'ordinary people' to participate in shows. The BBC website (http://www.bbc.co.uk/showsandtours/beonashow/) lists shows that are currently looking for participants, for example, *Sex . . . with Mum and Dad* where the BBC is looking for "young adults aged between 16–20 and their parents to discuss attitudes towards relationships". The BBC claims to "help teenagers and their parents address relationship issues and promote discussion in a positive and constructive way" and to "offer advice and support to families in order to resolve their individual concerns".

ACTIVITY

Visit http://www.bbc.co.uk/showsandtours/beonashow/shows/sex_with.shtml and think about why the BBC might be considering producing such a show; for example, will it be popular? How does it fit with the BBC's public service remit? Think also about why people may wish to participate in the programme. Is it because it offers '15 minutes of fame'? Or perhaps because the show offers professional support and advice? Think also about why the BBC may have chosen that particular title for the show and when and where you think the programme might be broadcast.

You can also visit the websites of other television production companies such as Channel 4 (http://www.channel4.com/microsites/T/takepart/index.html or http://www.livingtv.co.uk/extrememakeover/) and see which programmes are offering the opportunity for ordinary people to participate.

Increasingly television producers are putting participants in these shows under some kind of pressure to increase tension and, some commentators argue, to make the participants behave in more extreme ways and therefore to be 'more entertaining'. A recent example has been the controversy surrounding Channel 4's *Big Brother* and *Celebrity Big Brother*. When this happens there is a question over the extent to which ordinary people are being empowered or merely exploited for commercial reasons.

There are many possible reasons for the increase in ordinary people appearing on television. One explanation is that they are a lot cheaper to use than professional entertainers and presenters. They may also help the audience at home identify with the participants and the programme, and they may help to encourage audience loyalty through their familiar situations and characters.

As more viewers switch to digital television (the analogue services are to be switched off by 2012) so we can interact more with the programmes or choose from a range of different screens. According to Thinkbox,

> **Statistics from Sky show that 93% of SkyDigital households interacted with their TV between January and June 2006. Viewers of all ages . . . will now press red with confidence, in part thanks to the increasing amount of interaction offered by programme makers . . . ITV, for example, reports that three million viewers now press red on Coronation Street every month and spending up to 10 minutes within the interactive service.**

(For further information and some examples of interactive television adverts go to http://thinkbox.tv/server/show/ConCaseStudy.637.)

There has been a lot of coverage recently about Web 2.0 – the concept of using the web as a dynamic platform where users become participators, contributing and sharing with a wider community. Web 2.0 is becoming a generic term to describe this behaviour and the technologies that enable it. One of the main ways of doing this is through the use of wikis. A wiki is a collaborative website which can be directly edited by anyone with access to it, and Wikipedia, the online encyclopedia, is probably the most well known. However, this technology is increasingly being used as a way of enabling people like us to participate in the designing of media products. For example, *Where are the Joneses?* is an interactive fictional comedy made by the production company responsible for television shows like *The Mighty Boosh* (http://wherearethejoneses.com). Members of the audience are encouraged to influence the storyline either by writing scripts or by suggesting new characters. The audience can also keep up with the storyline and the characters through the video-sharing site YouTube, social network sites MySpace and Facebook, photo site Flickr and various blogs. The characters in the comedy even have their own Twitter feeds, updating fans via their mobile phones (see http://technology.guardian.co.uk/news/story/0,,212 2547,00.html).

Like other news organisations BBC News encourages members of the public to send in material from the scenes of news stories. The BBC tries to incorporate content from its viewers and listeners. On its 'Have Your Say' website the BBC says, "News can happen anywhere at any time and we want you to be our eyes. If you capture a news event on a camera or mobile phone, either as a photograph or video, then please send it to BBC News" (http://news.bbc.co.uk/1/hi/talking_point/6238360.stm).

Traditionally, newspapers and magazines have had a reader's comments section. Sometimes it is as traditional as a letters page or the *Sun*'s Dear Sun – "The Page where you tell Britain what you think". The new technologies, however, are making it much easier for us, the audience, to also become producers and to submit material for publication.

The magazine *Nuts* works hard to encourage reader participation. It asks its readers to send in letters, emails, texts or jpegs. There is a competition for the letter or spam of the week where the winner receives a year's supply of Durex. Women can also send in photographs of themselves and the (presumably) male readers can then vote by text, online or email for the one who they think should become a future bedroom babe. Readers are asked to get their 'girl' to submit raunchy confessions and each week's winners' stories are published and they get a £50 prize.

ACTIVITY

Read the section on magazines and then look through a sample, noting the ways in which the magazines try to get their readers to contribute to the articles and features. Why do you think this appeals to (a) readers and (b) the magazine editors? Think about the mode of address, the way in which readers are addressed. What assumptions do you think are being made by the magazine editors regarding their target audience? Do you think this trend improves magazines? If yes, in what ways? If no, why not?

ACTIVITY

Go to the Zuda Comics website (http://www.zudacomics.com/?action=the_deal) where they are asking people to help create a 'web comic' using JPEG technology. They are asking for examples of comic strips and claim that they may eventually be published. Why do you think they are making this offer? Surf the website and think about the mode of address used and what this suggests about the way in which Zuda Comics envisage their audience. Think about the 'Zuda community'; what does this mean? And why is the company using this term?

And finally . . .

Let us turn to *The Royle Family*, as this programme highlights many of the key themes in this section on media audiences and how audiences interact with media texts. In one episode of the situation comedy, the family members settle down after Sunday lunch to watch the BBC's *Antiques Roadshow* but instead of admiring the antiques they bet on how much they are valued at, and the family member who is nearest takes the winnings.

This episode is a good example of how the fictional family members are using a programme as a means of both entertainment and diversion from the mundane routines of daily life as well as bringing themselves together as a family and sharing in the experience of betting on the antiques in the *Antiques Roadshow*. Their particular use of the programme, to see who can best-guess the value of the antiques, is their own 'negotiated' meaning of the programme, but one that is shared by all the members of the family. Their 'situated culture', the family together, affects the meaning of the programme, and their social background affects their interpretation of what the notion of 'antiques' means – not something to own but a way of sharing pleasure, gambling and winning money.

We could also say that in fact the members of the Royle family are making quite an astute comment on the *Antiques Roadshow* itself – middle-class people bring out their antiques and pretend surprise when told how much they are worth – but actually the money 'value' of the antiques is the whole point (and attraction?) of the programme.

So really we could say that the Royle family is getting to the hub of the programme and exposing its hypocrisy.

The Royle Family is now ten years old and it is worth speculating how the family would consume television today or in the near future. For example, would four generations of one family still all sit around in one room watching one television set? Would they continue to watch a 'live' programme such as *Antiques Roadshow*? How would the newer technologies such as Freeview or a Sky box, DVDs or interactive services change the way they 'consume' television programmes?

It may be that *The Royle Family* captured a particular mode of television consumption that has already become history.

further reading

Williams, K. (2003) *Understanding Media Theory*. Arnold.

2 DEVELOPING TEXTUAL ANALYSIS

In the transition from AS to A2 media studies you need to reflect on what your course has thus far added up to, what it has equipped you to do: "What does it enable me to do that I couldn't do already?"

One answer to this question will almost certainly concern critical skills. You have, in fact, spent much of your AS year dealing with the different ways in which mass media products, from 'SUN SAYS' editorials to computer game covers, can be approached, seen and analysed. These 'readings' may be semiotic (see Introduction pp. 20–1), focus on the technical codes of a specific medium (e.g. framing or *mise-en-scène*) or concerned with genre (such as soap opera or teen drama) or issues of representation (age and gender).

What you will have developed are your skills in reading texts. You know you are a Media Studies student because you are able to respond to the text in Figure 2.1 in a particular way.

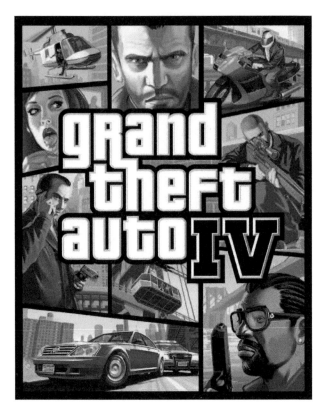

Figure 2.1 Cover of *Grand Theft Auto IV*

As an AS student you will be able to construct a detailed analysis of the cover of *Grand Theft Auto IV*.

Initial response:

■ Look at the cover as a whole – what are the most prominent features?
■ What other media forms does this layout of scenes remind you of?
■ What is the relationship between words and image?
■ Do the images appeal to you?
■ Are you familiar with the imagery – with the game itself?

Textual analysis:

1. Choose three of the scenes from the cover, and for each make notes on the following: subject matter, *mise-en-scène*, framing and angle.

Moving on from an AS approach

As an A2 student you need to develop this analysis further, taking into account a range of contexts and approaches which can add to your understanding of the text. In other words, what doesn't the detailed textual analysis of the cover of *GTA IV* tell us?

One of the most pressing contexts is that provided by the internet and new digital media, which has eclipsed our thinking about almost every aspect of media and culture. For a discipline that has sought always to address those forms where the mass audience gathers, the latest figures for computer gaming may come as an unpalatable shock. The fact that unprecedented numbers of teenagers (of all ages) (in excess of 95 per cent of 14- to 17-year-olds) are contributing to an industry worth twice as much as the music industry has led to a debate among academics and teachers about exactly what Media Studies as a subject is.

Wider contexts: production and distribution

The text that you have begun to analyse in the previous activity is the cover of a leading computer game franchise and as such is the product of a particular set of contexts. The contexts of production and distribution will be a major part of your study at A2 and cannot be understood just by analysing the front cover and these specific contexts.

PRODUCTION the production stage refers to the developers or producers of a media text (e.g. Hollywood as the producer of blockbusters, the BBC as the producer of TV news programmes).

DISTRIBUTION the distributor is an organisation which mediates between the producer and exhibitor to make the text available for consumption by an audience. For example, in film the distributor is the link between a film producer and the exhibitor (cinema, DVD, TV, etc.), who ensures that the film is seen by the widest audience possible. In media the term 'distribution' also refers to the *marketing* and *advertising* of media texts. In the contemporary media world of global conglomerates it has become more difficult to distinguish between these stages – this is clear when looking at our example of *GTA IV*.

Production and distribution of *GTA IV*

ACTIVITY

How would you research the production and distribution contexts of this computer game?

■ Which institution produced *GTA IV*? There may be more than one (clue – the company logos are usually on the cover). Can you make a distinction between the institution which produces the game and the technology it's played on?

Analysis of the production context of *GTA IV*

The *GTA* series was designed and developed by Rockstar North. This is a British company – the headquarters are in Edinburgh – which has also designed other popular games including *Manhunt* and *Lemmings*. The company is a part (a subsidiary) of a larger company, Rock Star Games. Rock Star Games is a publisher of games developed by other people rather than an originator of material. In turn Rock Star Games is owned by Take Two Interactive, an American developer, publisher and distributor of video games.

Distribution context

A study of the distribution contexts of games includes some of the key contemporary media debates:

- The competition between a few dominant conglomerates.
- The effects of new technology on revenue and profits.

The distribution context here is concerned with the future of online technology. How long will games be distributed on disc and sold in shops or online? The position of game distribution today is similar to film and music industries ten years ago.

In considering the effects of this changing distribution context you could start by asking who would benefit from the move to entirely online distribution and who would lose.

ACTIVITY

Distribution and new technology

How would new distribution techniques affect:

- Consumers?
- Manufacturers of games consoles and discs?
- Game publishers?

Some suggestions

Consumers:

- Online distribution should be cheaper than the purchase of discs (unlike films or music, games are difficult – though not impossible – to copy illegally due to the large amount of memory required for sharing and storage). There would no longer be the need to buy a console.
- Greater variety – gamers can play a range of games without having to purchase them.
- Instant access – select and play through the TV, so one no longer needs to buy a disc first.

continued

From the reference to distribution and production contexts it should be clear how at A2 textual analysis is merely the starting point for a reading of a text. The next development is in the study of the audience. Building on the work on target audience that you are used to from AS, Media Studies has developed new ways of talking about audience.

Performance context: how is a media text used?

This context represents a shift in our approach to reading a media text; rather than analysing the text from a distance (as we did with the cover of *GTA IV*) the performance context is a reflective approach, asking how people use a text and how it works. This relies much more on the idea of participation – how real people respond to media texts.

In their work on the experience of gaming, McDougall and O'Brien (2008) have devised a list of categories to suggest the different experiences participants have in playing games. Many of these refer to the way gamers use the world of the game to create and 'try on' new identities.

■ *Gaming as performance*
  Gaming is conventionally seen as a solitary occupation but the idea of 'gaming as performance' suggests that the experience is as much to do with performing skilfully and developing a particular style of gaming for the benefit of those watching. The knowledge of being watched playing *GTA IV* is likely to change the way in which the game is played.

  The performance aspect of gaming is also affected by where the game is played. The 'video' arcade, although seemingly an old-fashioned place to play games, provides some of the best opportunities to perform – and to watch. The blogger chewingpixels.com writes about the particular pleasures of the arcade:

> **A perceptive gamer can tell a great many things about the men competing at _Street Fighter_. And _Street Fighter_, like _Dance Dance Revolution_, or _Raiden 3_ or any other game that allows the performer the chance to exhibit flair, technique and character, is a game best played in public. Here the stakes are raised and the narrative becomes a communal one; the resulting stories are unforgettable.**

- _Carnivalesque_
  One of the pleasures of any kind of play is the aspect of pretending – escaping to the world of 'what if?' This form of escapism can provide a period of freedom from the rules of conventional behaviour. In this definition of experience, gamers are in an ambiguous place – neither real nor completely fantastic.
- _Frivolity – playing, picking and mixing_
  Games are often assumed to focus on darker, more violent aspects of society but participants discuss much lighter, more frivolous aspects to gaming. Examples of this may be seen in the way gamers discuss the enjoyable aspects of the games – flying, pet battles, fashionable 'vanity' clothes to wear over armour, designing tattoos, etc.
- _Morality_
  The assumption is that the world of most games is morally corrupting. In fact many gamers talk about the moral dimension of their game identities and performances – for example, see the discussion 'Should Morality be Applied to Gaming' at http://www.cheatcc.com/extra/moralityandvideogames2.html. The arguments around morality and gaming will be familiar to you from effects debates in film. It is important to consider these debates within the specific context of the game – the reward for a violent act is about power in the game – not an ethical debate.
- _Storytelling – multiple approaches_
  Despite its apparently free form, a game such as _GTA_ is to be 'completed': there are a number of consecutive missions which comprise a 'master' narrative of the game. However, this is not the end of the player's experience since there is both a broader world to explore and the set missions to 'reuse'. This comment is typical: "A linear story is easier to understand but if you have an open world, you are making the story, you feel more involved definitely because you're going to places" (Kevin).
- _The 'Baroque Showman'_
  Baroque originally referred to a style of architecture and music from the seventeenth century which had a flamboyant and highly ornamented style.

Here the term is used to describe the artificial and larger-than-life qualities of the performances of masculinity offered in and by the game. This is a kind of puppetry and, despite the graphical quality, an almost cartoonish element means that men playing these characters in the game are always aware of outing on a show. As Kendall and McDougall (2009) describe it: "A highly performed and playful 'male showing' was at work."

In your analysis of the representation of gender on the cover for *GTA IV* you probably noted the reinforcement of gender stereotypes – the rugged, macho man with big guns, the attractive female with long hair and pouting red lips. Your ideas about genre and narrative would probably also make reference to the expected roles of gangster and sex object. The idea of the 'baroque showman' suggests that there is a different way of interpreting these roles – the gender characteristics are so extreme and exaggerated in their traditional roles that they can no longer be taken seriously. This then allows gamers to try on and play with these representations – as subject (first-person position) and as object.

This research into games emphasises the way in which the players experience the world of the game, how they play it. This is clear in the following extract with a player writing 'in' rather than just 'about' *Liberty City*. He begins:

> **Starting the game from scratch isn't easy. Anyway, in between trying to sort this, this being a GTA game, I decide to take a walk down the street and fight some random passers-by. Got beaten up by a girl at one point – couldn't learn how to fight fast enough. Once I master the art of street fighting, it's back to driving the car round Liberty City. By now, about 40 minutes into playing, I'm picking up the thread a bit – I can drive, I can fight and this starts to impress the ladies.**

ACTIVITY

Participant analysis

1. Choose two games which you regularly play. The two should be contrasting in some way – the difference might be the genre, format or platform (e.g. RPG and a Strategy game, a PSP and Xbox game).

    Your aim is to produce a commentary of your experience of playing the two games. The following are some suggestions of areas that you could consider.

Figure 2.2
Playing
videogames

- When do you play the game? Is it a particular time of day? Do you choose the game depending on what kind of mood you're in?
- Where do you play? Are you usually alone or with friends?
- Which aspects of the game do you find easy? Does this make playing the game more pleasurable or boring?
- Are you aware of the games designer's plans as you play? If so, how do you respond to this?
- If it's a game which includes violent actions, how do you respond to these?
- How would you describe your relationship to the central character in the game?

Finish your commentary by writing up – or recording – your thoughts (300 words).

2. Choose a film that you're familiar with, watch the opening sequence and try the same exercise. How is the experience of watching different to playing?

Consider the following:

- What are the differences in your responses to the characters? Think about identification, sympathy. Are the characters attractive (appearance and actions)? What do you know about their personality?

continued

Suggestions for further work: reception context

A further way of developing our understanding of a media text would be to analyse its reception – how it was received by fans, critics, non-users:

■ Like films, games are extensively reviewed on release (see *Official Xbox Magazine, Game Spot*, etc.).

■ There are many online forums where gamers discuss their reactions to new games (e.g. gamerforums.proboards.com, computerandvideogames.com).

■ Games are a controversial media form in wider society and there will be press coverage of games as well as reports produced by various interested groups such as psychologists, educationalists and politicians (see e.g. *The Byron Review* into the effect of games on children at http://www.dcsf.gov.uk/byronreview and 'Video Games are Good for Children' at http://www.guardian.co.uk/technology/2009/feb/12/computer-games-eu-study).

Developing an analysis in this way demonstrates the different ways in which media texts are appropriated and used by their audiences. It helps us to understand that texts are polysemic, capable of different meanings for different audiences. It also suggests that these different interpretations are never neutral but always shaped by particular experiences and interests.

It will help your A2 study a great deal if you can begin to develop this type of exploration into wider contexts yourself. As you will have read, the ability to think for yourself and develop your own ideas and responses to media products and their contexts is a highly prized skill when it comes to taking Media Studies exams and completing your coursework. What follows is a a kind of half-way stage or, better still, a launching pad for you to start with some of your own explorations. What we have created for you is a series of questions and activities that should point you in the right direction to take your research a little further and deeper into the industry you have chosen. We start with some further ideas for discovering more about the world of computer games.

You will then find further prompts, each following a similar pattern as a way of looking at the film, TV and music industries. Don't forget that these are intended merely as a launching pad, not a final destination. You will want to add your own ideas for further exploration well beyond what we have suggested in the framework so that you move away from relying on a textbook and become confident in directing your own independent research.

COMPUTER GAMES

- *Industry*
  How do you account for the relatively low profile of the massively successful computer gaming industry?

  Part of this thriving industry is specifically 'British' but where is the British influence in specific games or game trends?

- *Audience/identity*
  Given the latest audience statistics it is impossible to see computer gamers as a niche market. They are, in fact, all of us. How and why has computer gaming become so popular?

  Which games 'define' you? Do you think these games relate specifically to your gender? What other aspects of your identity are catered for by these games?

  How attractive is the notion of 'personalisation', being able to project yourself into games?

- *Genre/form*
  Is genre in computer games more about game formats (RPG, first-person shooter, strategy) or contexts (historical period, horror, sci-fi)?

  How important is the multiplayer (online) version of computer games?

- *Narrative/representation*
  To what extent do you find representation in mainstream computer games similar to that in mainstream Hollywood films and prime-time TV?

  Despite the attempts to allow 'freestyle' play, all adventure/action games are forms of disguised linear narrative. Do you agree?

  What does it mean for a computer game to have a 'good story'?

- *Values/ideology*
  What are the different meanings of violence in computer games and computer gaming?

  What are the values exhibited by games such as *The Sims* and *SimCity*, which are concerned with creating families and communities?

■ *Issues*

What are the opportunities and dangers associated with 3D and digital technologies?

Are computer games harmlessly escapist or dangerously addictive? If neither of these, how would you describe them?

Where do you see computer games going in the immediate future?

The textual analysis and work above gives you some ideas about the games industry. Below we have added some further questions for you to use as jumping-off points for study of the film and music industries.

FILM

■ *Industry*

What is the future for the British film industry? What kind of films should we be making?

What are the connotations of the tags 'British' and 'Independent' when applied to films? Find examples of both and then reconsider your answers.

Choose three films which you think epitomise Hollywood film at the moment.

■ *Audience/identity*

Ricky Gervais recently said in an interview on Radio 1 that it was important primarily to make stuff for yourself rather than second-guessing what audiences want. He was suggesting that the alternative never brought long-term success. Is it useful (or even possible) to discriminate between those films that see us as a mass audience and those that 'speak for themselves' and hope we will want to listen?

Which films 'define' you? Do you think these films relate specifically to your gender? What other aspects of your identity are catered for by these films?

What impact do film 'fans' have over which films are made?

■ *Genre/form*

Genre study came out of film studies, yet does it have anything very much to tell us about contemporary films?

Paul Watson talks of a post-generic cinema with a different set of prompts: "The blockbuster, special effects movie, event cinema, spectacle cinema, summer movie, even action cinema." Are these more appropriate names for the cinema of the twenty-first century?

Is *Avatar* best described as (1) a sci-fi film, (2) a film about conservation/ecological issues, or (3) a special effects movie? What difference does it make?

Avatar has been criticised for being too long. In what ways might the length of a film matter? (Remember: film is not just an art form but also a social/cultural practice in which people participate.)

■ *Narrative/representation*

Stephen Poliakov has argued that "People like to be told stories" whereas 'technology' seems to be offering a greater involvement/immersion: who do you think is right? Which films would you offer as evidence?

One of the issues that *Looking for Eric* emphasises is how little concerned mainstream film is to represent 'ordinary people' (preferring a world of the significantly attractive/funny/charismatic). Is this inevitable?

What does it mean for a film to have a 'good story'?

■ *Values/ideology*

It is assumed that, as a committed socialist filmmaker, Ken Loach makes films with political messages/meanings. How useful is this information to you as a Media Studies student?

What are the values exhibited by a film like *Twilight: New Moon* and how appropriate are they for its young audience?

Ideology is usefully described as a system of representation, a code through which specific meanings are privileged/delivered. What is the ideological 'delivery' of a Hollywood blockbuster like *Avatar*?

■ *Issues*

What are the opportunities and dangers associated with 3D and digital technologies?

It has been suggested that film was the dominant art form of the twentieth century. Where do you think it stands one decade into the twenty-first century?

Films are now available to us in more formats than ever. In which contexts do you watch films (cinema, TV, computer, phone)?

MUSIC

■ *Industry*

The 'music business' has been changed significantly by downloading. In what specific ways have things changed for (1) producers (music companies), (2) artists, (3) audiences?

To what extent is the age of the music video over?

■ *Audience/identity*

What does your i-pod (including its contents) say about you?

How important is live music to the contemporary pop scene?

■ *Genre/form*

With tribute bands and reality TV sing-offs there are fewer places at every level for up-and-coming artists to perform. Does this matter?

Music is perhaps the one area of the mass media where genre remains a potent force in the ways people define themselves. How are musical genres different to those in other media?

■ *Narrative/representation*
How are the girl-made stories in songs different to the boy-made stories?

Popular music in the modern sense is more than 50 years old and is continually making reference to its past by way of its retro-tendencies. Is this history, in your opinion, well known and respected or merely exploited and plundered?

■ *Values/ideology*
Despite unparalleled success in the British charts female artistes still find themselves judged as much by image as by music. Why is progress so slow in this respect?

■ *Issues*
Rage Against the Machine got to number one at Christmas in 2009 by way of a protest against Simon Cowell. Not one physical copy was bought and the song had never even been released. What does this tell you about the contemporary music scene?

3 THEORETICAL PERSPECTIVES

Media Studies is a discipline full of theories. On one level this is great news because it allows you lots of opportunities for looking at theoretical perspectives. Any text you look at is likely to lend itself to a whole lot of different tools with which to prise it open. Marxist, feminist or postmodernist theories are all likely to be applicable to the texts that you want to explore.

However, slavish adherence to what these theories propose or tell you is not always the best way to use them. The hallmark of a really good 'active' Media Studies student at A2 is a willingness to question what has gone before. This does not mean that you have a licence to go around rubbishing every theory you have encountered. There will be theoretical issues that you will feel will remain useful and have an important application today. Equally you must realise that it is not an act of heresy to call into question some of the received wisdom that underpins Media Studies. You need to adopt a healthy scepticism about the ideas that you come across. Better still, be prepared to test them out against your own experience of texts and contexts.

Your study of the media should have made you aware of the vast extent to which it is used socially. Media output is a common talking point whenever people meet and exchange ideas, be it physically or in cyberspace. Just about everyone has something to say about the media, especially contemporary topics such as the latest reality TV show or a controversial new film showing at the cinema. On this basis, the majority of the population could wander into a Media Studies exam and have a go at many of the questions on an A2 paper. Some of the better informed might even scrape a pass. The reason the majority would probably fail, however, is that their knowledge and understanding of the media would lack the important theoretical framework that is crucial to an academic study of the media. It is your ability to show that you have grasped at least some of this theoretical base that is such an important ingredient of your success at A2.

Of course, there is an argument which suggests that theories exist for no other purpose than to be shot down. Well, perhaps you are not quite at the stage of your academic career when you feel equipped to challenge the major theorists. What you are in a position to do, however, is to question and test out the validity of the theories you come across. More simply, you are in a position to question whether they are theories that are true on the basis of the products and issues you have studied.

Don't forget that you are studying Media Studies at a time when the discipline is in a state of flux. A lot of the theories and ideas that have been taken for granted for many years are being questioned, not least because they have become out-dated in the face of the vast technological changes that have taken place in the way in which media texts are both produced and consumed.

Of course at this point you are hoping for a list of key theories that you can learn and show off in the exam. You have probably guessed, however, that being Media Studies it is not quite that simple. You will be glad to hear that there is an expla-nation of some of the more important theoretical perspectives coming up but it is not the sort of thing that you can just learn and trot out in the exam.

Most theories or perspectives by their nature are designed to explore texts and issues from a specific point of view. Far from being an objective take, they seek to put forward and support a particular perspective from which to consider media output. One thing you may note is that different perspectives often invite you to look at an issue in terms of how power is distributed within society. In other words, how media output may be seen to serve or not to serve the interests of different groups within our society.

A good example of this would be feminist theory which, as you will read, sees media output from the perspective of women. Clearly this is a complex issue, but at a simple level many media texts can be interpreted through their ideological function of supporting, reinforcing and preserving the patriarchal social order in which power is vested in men. Media output may be seen as a mechanism for diverting and controlling women in order to ensure they remain in a position in society which is subordinate to men. A survey of advertising, for example, by a feminist would point to the representation of women in advertisements in ways that are very different compared to those represented by men. The conclusion might be that the media does this in order to gain our acceptance that this way of representing women is natural or inevitable and therefore in some way acceptable or 'right'.

So where does that leave you as a Media Studies student in relation to theory or critical perspectives, as they are often called? The simple answer is that if you know and have a basic understanding of a perspective, it is a good idea to apply it. However, you should only do this if you are convinced it is appropriate. Nothing looks worse in an exam or coursework essay than a half-understood theory contrived to fit a particular situation in a vain and simplistic attempt to show off some nodding acquaintance with said theory. It is probably better to use no theory at all than to use it inappropriately or merely for the sake of trying to show off.

You may like to think about what is implied by the term 'perspective'. It is a term often used in painting which describes the way in which a two-dimensional painting is created to give the illusion of three-dimensionality. This is not to suggest of course that perspective is merely a shallow trick. What a perspective does is offer a vantage point which invites the spectator to see the universe as complex and multi-dimensional rather than merely as a flat surface. So perspectives, or theories, offer to you the student vantage points from which to identify the complexities of the media and its output. It is for this reason that they are important. What they allow you to do is to move from the individual or particular to the general. So in Media Studies that can empower you to move from close study of one particular product to feeling confident about making broader statements about the cultural, social and ideological functions of the media more widely.

For example, look at Figure 3.1 and make a list of some of the issues it raises for you beyond the image itself and into broader cultural and social issues.

Figure 3.1 Advert for Tom Ford for Men

What do we learn about the values of our society from looking at what is in the advertisement or perhaps what isn't in it? Or does that depend on what we want to learn about the values of our society? Do you think different social groups within our culture would see different values according to the perspective which forms their point of view? Where are you standing in relation to the advertisement?

Much of the theory you need you already know from your AS study. One of the chief perspectives that informs any study of the media is that of structuralism. Structuralism suggests that there are certain structures that underpin much of human activity including the production of media output. Look back at the Introduction and you will see that at AS you learned about genre, narrative and semiotics. All are examples of structuralism, a perspective that allows us the vantage point of seeing common and often universal strands in the construction of media products. There is a refresher of these in the Introduction. If you need more detail you could refer to *AS Media Studies: The Essential Introduction for WJEC* (2011).

We have tried to identify and highlight for you some of the key critical perspectives that we feel you will need to enhance your A2 study. This is not an exhaustive list – you can find something akin to that in the WJEC specification (http://www.wjec. co.uk/index.php?subject=22&level=21) at least for the purposes of your A2 course. What it does offer is a series of accessible ways of applying theoretical perspectives to your study by offering some basic guidance on key perspectives.

For the moment, perhaps a short quotation taken from an earlier edition of this book might persuade you that exploring critical perspectives a little more deeply is worth the effort:

> **Rather annoyingly, theories often suggest that something which had always seemed perfectly simple and straightforward is actually complex. As we shall argue later, the mass media have a particular knack of making things seem so obvious and so natural that it would be just plain daft to criticise or ask for explanations. In those areas, especially, it is important to have theories which never take anything for granted, theories which ask *how* and *why* we see things as obvious or natural.**

(Bennett *et al.*, 2005)

What follows is a brief introduction to some of the key theories that should inform your study of the media. They come in no particular order; none should be considered more important than any other. This introduction should be seen as a starting point to your study of theory, especially if you are intending to pursue media or an allied discipline to another level when you have completed A2.

Marxist perspective

Marxism! Something we have all probably heard of, but what exactly is it and what is its importance to the study of media?

wake up to the smell of class struggle

Marxism Coffee Mix

Figure 3.2 Marxism, what is it?

Social and political ideas which are products of the Marxist tradition have affected the lives of millions of people, not simply because they are influential in themselves, but because they formed the core of the communist ideology which was central to the Soviet Union until its collapse and which remains part of the social fabric of China and North Korea today.

The writings of Marx gained more widespread acceptance after his death in 1883 than they did during his lifetime and this influence appears to have continued beyond; but in reality, Marxism as a theoretical perspective has evolved and developed over time and it now incorporates many different perspectives. The body of Marxist thought is much more than the writings of Marx alone; rather, it is a body of work with many contributors among which there is by no means complete agreement or harmony.

Any detailed examination of the topic of Marxism is a huge undertaking since the perspective has something to say about almost all facets of human existence and societies in the world. However, a basic knowledge of the main principles of the topic will help in gaining a deeper understanding of media theory, not least because the mass media is one of those facets of human existence about which Marxism is concerned.

At its heart, Marxists believe that all societies have an economic 'base', a system through which production occurs or services are offered. From this economic base, people get paid for their work and those who own the means of production take home the profit. Emanating out from this economic base is the 'superstructure', which consists of the social and cultural institutions such as the family, the education system, the judiciary or legal system, and of course the media. Marxists argue that the superstructure is shaped and determined by the economic base, so in modern Britain the economic base is founded upon capitalist and consumerist ideas, and the superstructure reflects this. However, in pure Marxist ideology, the superstructure is not only a reflection of the ideology at the heart of the base but also acts to protect and legitimise the economic base, and it is in this area that Marxism offers most to the study of media.

Marxists believe that in capitalist societies such as ours, there exists a state of conflict between those who own and control the economic base, the 'haves', and those who work for them, the (at least relative to the haves) 'have-nots'. In Marxist terminology, those who own or exert control are called the bourgeoisie while the workers are called the proletariat. For the proletariat there is relative poverty, a feeling of being exploited, inequality and a distinct lack of power or a sense of control over their own lives, whereas for the bourgeoisie there exists a healthy sense of well-being and satisfaction at becoming wealthier and more powerful thanks to the hard work of the workers who are rewarded with low pay and minimal prestige.

If the picture painted by the Marxist perspective concerning the relations between those who own and control the means of production and those who work is true, then it is hardly a happy picture. Yet, despite outnumbering the bourgeoisie hugely, despite the sense of angst that Marxists believe the proletariat have a right to feel and despite the certain and inevitable collapse of the social system if the workers downed tools and protested, the status quo is largely maintained and the workers tend to continue to work, the odd strike or two excepted, while the owners, chief executives and directors continue to grow richer. This inactivity on behalf of the proletariat is, in no small part, due to the workings of the super-structure which protects and legitimises the base and, through a process whereby the proletariat seem to succumb to their position which Marx called 'false con-sciousness', the inequitable and exploitative relationship between the ruling class and the working class is maintained.

ACTIVITY

To what extent do you feel the Marxist perspective on society is reflected in television's soap opera and drama? For a more widespread and thorough investigation, you should look at British soap and compare it to American and Australian TV.

The Slovenian philosopher Slavoj Žižek offers an interesting viewpoint on the Marxist ideas in his work on the evolution and development of an ideology. It is useful to consider the development of an ideology rather like a narrative unfolding over the course of a film or a book. Each ideology begins as a 'doctrine' by which it is formed following a set of ideas or beliefs. It is here that the ideology is in its purest state. The next stage is 'belief' whereby the key points of the ideology become apparent in wider society before the ideology finally moves to the 'ritual' point whereby individuals in a society regard themselves as examples or the embodiment of the ideology.

In the evolution of Marxism, which itself began as an ideology based upon the beliefs of Marx, it became accepted as an established ideology and is reflected in the workings of the superstructure, especially in certain communist societies, before finally leading to a feeling of exploitation and powerlessness by the working classes.

The relevance of Marxist theory may now quite feasibly be called into question. Writing over 150 years ago and referring to a period of time when industrialisation was in its infancy, Marx saw squalor, poverty, a lack of esteem and low wages among the working classes which were far more a feature of Victorian England than of today's society. The companies and businesses of Marx's time were much more likely to be owned by an individual person or by a small partnership of two or three people. Today's companies are likely to be owned by shareholders who

INFORMATION BOX i

Figure 3.3 shows how the social and cultural structures within a society stem from the economic base at that society's heart. This is the basic premise of Marxist theory. The media is one of the many elements which make up the superstructure.

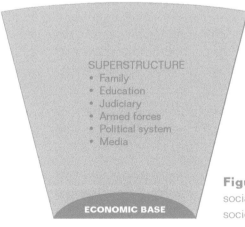

SUPERSTRUCTURE
• Family
• Education
• Judiciary
• Armed forces
• Political system
• Media

ECONOMIC BASE

Figure 3.3 Diagram showing how the social and cultural structures within a society stem from the economic base

are drawn from a variety of backgrounds. Privatisation and flotation on the stock market of large companies and organisations means that companies can be owned by several million shareholders, many of whom will be the very workers who Marx regarded as exploited. Later Marxist thought is much more concerned with a 'ruling elite' rather than with the factory and business owners of Marx's day. Members of this ruling elite at the heart of the economic base may not own the means of production or services, but they control it and, through the workings of the super-structure, they ensure their survival as the most powerful and influential group in contemporary society.

Marxists also believe that the objective of survival as the most powerful group can lead to members of the ruling elite acting in their own self-interest rather than in the interests of the wider society. A good example of how the role of those who hold positions of power and influence in media can be affected by their position to the detriment of their society is offered by Edward Herman and Noam Chomsky in their book *Manufacturing Consent* (1988) in which they argue that the decisions which are made by the American news media in setting an agenda: (literally deciding the content and the discourse for news coverage in American news) is determined by the need for the news institutions to remain profitable. In the newspaper industry, for example, the main source of income comes from adver-tising; in some instances this can account for up to 80 per cent of all revenue. The newspapers are less likely to cover items which cause offence to or upset the advertisers if they feel that by covering these items of news they could jeopardise their relationship with advertisers and thus threaten their own profitability.

BASE in Marxist terminology, the base refers to the economic core upon which a society is organised. It is the central means by which wealth is created and distributed among the people within that society.

SUPERSTRUCTURE this is the name Marxists give to the institutions that exist in a society other than those associated with the economy, and which would be part of the base. These institutions include religions, the law, education, the political system and the media. Marxists believe not only that these institutions are shaped by the economic base but also that the superstructure helps to legitimise the base and ensure its future as the economic system of that society.

PROLETARIAT the name Marx gave to those who work the means of production and provide the services offered in a society – the working classes.

BOURGEOISIE the Marxist name for those who own or control the means of production or services – the middle classes.

FALSE CONSCIOUSNESS a term which suggests that the working classes are not fully aware of the exploitation they endure at the hands of the ruling class. It is regarded as a reason why those who are exploited do not rise up and rebel against the ruling elite.

CAPITALISM the economic system in which a society is focused upon the pursuit of capital (wealth). In Britain and other Western countries, capitalism may be said to be at the heart of the economic base. The main criticism is that it does not seek to create wealth for all people. For there to be wealthy people, others have to remain poor. Therefore critics of capitalism argue that while it is good at creating wealth, the unavoidable consequence of capitalism is inequality: the rich get richer and the poor get poorer. As capitalism has spread across the world, this inequality is no longer confined to within a country but is seen on a global scale.

Figure 3.4 The haves and the have-nots: the inevitable consequence of global capitalism

The media plays a pivotal role in the function of maintaining the power and influence held by the ruling elite, according to Marxist theory. Just as is the case with institutions in other sectors of British society, the media institutions, organisations and businesses are themselves controlled by members of this group of the ruling elite, and those who work in the media industries are themselves exploited by their managers just as they are in other industries. In addition, the media is used to indoctrinate and influence people into accepting their role and so the Marxist perspective of the media is not only to make money for those who own or control the media institutions but also to preserve the interests of the ruling elite and to keep the workers in their place and accepting of capitalism as the natural and best way for the economic base to be structured.

ACTIVITY

Despite the glitz and glamour often associated with media industries, not everyone who works in the sector benefits from high-profile, glamorous and well-paid jobs. Conduct some research into the experiences of people who work in a variety of media jobs which lack the glitz and the glamour frequently associated with the media sector; for example:

- Production runner
- Hospital radio DJ
- Freelance photographer
- Fanzine editor
- Local news reporter
- Session musician.

Examples of the Marxist perspective in media

Let us begin to apply this Marxist perspective in a simple way, by looking at the media platform of film. Marx himself claimed, though obviously not by means of a direct reference to cinema, that there is often a disconnection between the maker and what is made. This is perhaps nowhere better illustrated than in the world of cinema. Take a look at the film poster for the 2008 film *Body Of Lies* (Figure 3.5).

On this poster, as is the case with most film posters, there is a hierarchical approach to the personnel involved in its production not unlike the hierarchy Marxists believe exists in wider society. At the top of the poster we see the surnames of the two lead actors. Leonardo DiCaprio, by virtue of having his name to the left, is given billing precedence over Russell Crowe. The importance of the two actors to the film may be seen not only in the prominent position of their names

Figure 3.5 Poster for *Body of Lies*

but also in the fact that theirs are the only faces we see on the poster's image. Again, in this respect it is DiCaprio who enjoys the more prominent representation; despite Russell Crowe's Oscar success in *Gladiator* it is clear that the producers feel DiCaprio is their most prized asset for marketing the film. The next piece of written information is the film's tagline followed by the details of the director. A kind of ownership is ascribed to him by the term "A Ridley Scott Film". Although, in the film industry, Scott is a very influential and successful director with numerous credits to his name, he is less likely to be as instantly familiar to as many people as either DiCaprio or Crowe, and so the audience is reminded of some of his earlier work. Finally, the fourth item of written text from the top is the film's title. Last, we see a billing block with certain key members of the cast and crew, including DiCaprio, Crowe and Scott once again to finally confirm their place among the ruling elite, but if you have ever stayed until the end of a film in the cinema, you will know that several hundred names have been omitted from the poster's billing block but who were involved in the film's production.

This is a crude and rather simplistic application of Marxist theory and of course the reasons for the layout and design of the poster are fairly obvious. The film was made to make money for those who produced and made it, which in itself can be justified by the capitalist context in which Western media operates. Under these circumstances, it makes sense to emphasise the selling points of the film; hence the mention of a director's previous successful work such as *American Gangster* and *Black Hawk Down*. However, if it is the case that referring to previous work can help to sell a film, then why just the director? Why does it not make reference to the electrician's previous work or the lighting rigger? Surely the make-up artist, the set designer or the solo violinist for the musical score have a body of work worthy of inclusion for advertising the film. The reason for their omission is simple: they do not form part of the ruling elite of the world of cinema. That accolade is the honour of directors, actors and writers, and herein lies the key point in the Marxist perspective. For a ruling elite to remain as a ruling elite, it must remain a small and exclusive club. If entry into this elite club was open and membership widened, it would by definition cease to be a small and exclusive club.

INFORMATION BOX *i*

Take a look at the homepage for the BBC Radio 2 website, an example of which is shown below. There is a clear emphasis on the presenters of the shows but many of them in this example, such as Claudia Winkelman, Paul O'Grady and Alan Titchmarsh, are arguably at least as well known for their work in other areas, especially TV, and yet they are represented here as the main force behind the show. Most of the staff who work behind the scenes as editors, sound engineers and technicians will have dedicated a large part of their careers to radio work and they will remain largely uncredited for their work. This is perhaps understandable, as listeners will be attracted to the show by the presenter rather than by those who work behind the scenes, but as you will see if you visit the websites for any radio station or listen to a show, those who present the shows enjoy a high level of coverage while the station's other staff remain unknown. The hierarchy of power and influence as proposed by the Marxist perspective may be seen in this example just as in a film poster.

Figure 3.6 Website for BBC Radio 2

A further area of media where the Marxist perspective is particularly relevant is in news. Watching a news bulletin on the TV or reading a newspaper, it becomes clear just how much coverage is given to the main areas of politics, business and commerce, which all help to define the kind of society which Marxists believe the UK to be – consumerist, capitalist and 'Western'. The theory of news values which ascribes newsworthiness to events suggests that if an event is deemed to be important, then it will be covered more widely. Put simply, the dominance of politicians, business leaders and other key members of the ruling elite in news coverage serves to remind audiences just how important they are and to reaffirm their status as that ruling elite.

ACTIVITY

- Watch news bulletins on TV over the course of a few days. How much of the content involves one or more of the three areas of business or commerce or politics?
- Now repeat the same activity but this time for a newspaper over the course of a couple of days. Again, coverage of news (as opposed to sport or reviews) should be studied to get a picture of the content.
- To what extent do you feel that the coverage of the 'ruling elite' from the worlds of business, politics and culture serves to reinforce and legitimise their positions as the ruling elite?

The Marxist concept of hegemony, coined by Antonio Gramsci, refers to the power and influence held by an influential and powerful though usually smaller group over a weaker, larger group. This domination can be on a local scale, such as power held by politicians over the rest of a society, or on a much larger scale, such as in the case of the domination of the USA on the world stage relative to the rest of the world. In the case of news, Anthony Giddens writes, "Control of the world's news by the major western agencies . . . means the predominance of a 'First World outlook' " (Giddens, 1993, p. 559). There is also evidence which suggests that this domination, especially by America, takes place on a cultural level too. Consider the huge influx of American culture in British society with American film, music and television. This serves to reinforce America's position as the dominant global force for cultural exports. The media in these examples is being used as a means of ensuring that members of the ruling elite, both nationally, and internationally, can maintain their hold on power and protect their position as the ruling elite.

- Conduct some research into the TV shows currently showing on British television. Do not limit your research to any one genre; make sure you include comedy, drama, children's shows, documentary and so on. How much of the TV we receive in the UK is American? How well represented are other countries on British TV?
- Now do some further research into radio schedules on BBC and commercial radio stations. Which cultures are the most represented on mainstream radio shows?

There are, as is the case with every theory, criticisms of the Marxist perspective. It is rather a simplistic theory, a factor which may make it attractive as a concept to students compared to some of the more complex viewpoints. This simplicity may be regarded as a strength but it could equally be regarded as a weakness. What Marxism assumes is that the proletariat are too poorly educated to know that they are being exploited. The belief that the media serves to reinforce the position of the ruling elite to a passive and inactive audience which does not realise it is being duped is rather outdated and has been discredited by a wealth of media theorists. Marxist theory has also suffered somewhat from the seismic changes in British society today compared to when Marx was writing. Social mobility has increased, people born into a working-class family are not as entrenched in this existence as they once were and, for those who hold traditional working-class occupations, there exists an improvement in pay and conditions and a level of contentment and affluence which did not exist in Marx's day.

Summary of Marxism

- Marxism is a theory which regards the relations between those who rule and those who are ruled as one of conflict.
- Marxists see the media as one of the means by which the inequality which exists in a society is legitimised and propagated and by which members of the ruling elite remain in their position of privilege.
- The media industries themselves offer a working model of Marxism as they are generally hierarchical with a ruling elite (overpaid?) and a working class (underpaid?).
- Marxism's pessimistic view of society and its relevance in the modern world has been called into question as social mobility, higher standards of living and the blurring of the distinction between the middle and working class have become more of a feature in modern Western societies.

Useful website: http://www.lacan.com/zizekchro1.htm.

Feminist perspective

Feminism is the belief that women should have equal rights to men. In consequence, the feminist movement fights for equal rights and opportunities for women.

There are many different kinds of feminism, and feminists themselves tend to disagree about the ways in which women are disadvantaged and what exactly should be done to get equal rights. For example, 'socialist feminists' believe that women are exploited by the capitalist system both at work and in the home.

However, it may be argued that there have been some real improvements in the way that women are now represented in the media, possibly owing to the increase in women working in the media, sometimes in positions of power. However, many would argue that women are still represented in a negative and stereotypical manner and are still a long way from enjoying equal power in media institutions. Feminists would argue that this reflects and reinforces the unequal social, economic and political position of women.

A brief history

The history of feminism can be divided up into three main movements or waves.

- *The first wave* in the nineteenth and early twentieth century in the UK and US. It won improved rights for women in marriage and property. Its biggest achievement was winning some political power. In the UK the *Suffragettes* and *Suffragists* campaigned for the women's vote, and in 1918 women over age 30 who owned property won the vote and in 1928 it was extended to all women over 21.
- *The second wave* – 1960s and 1970s. It extended the fight beyond political rights to education, work and the home. In *The Feminine Mystique* (1963), Betty Freidan argues that women were unhappy because of the feminine mystique. She said this was a damaging ideal of femininity which she called "the Happy Housewife" and it restricted women to the role of housewife and mother, giving up on work and education. This may be seen in the US drama series *Mad Men* in the character of Betty, and similar themes are explored in *Desperate Housewives*. Both of them show women trapped in the stifling role of homemaker and the damage this does to women, men and society. The book was seen as one of the main forces of the second wave of feminism. Freidan also co-founded the National Organization for Women which concentrated on winning equal legal rights for women, such as the Equal Pay Act and legalising abortion.
- Another important second-wave feminist book was *The Female Eunuch* by Germaine Greer (1970). She argued that women are 'castrated', the eunuch of the title, by society. In particular she attacked the nuclear family, romantic love and the limits on women's sexuality. She argued that gender roles were not natural but learned. They conditioned girls to conform to a very restrictive

femininity. The book has been criticised for not offering any realistic solutions to women's oppression, because it proposed action by individual women rather than organised political action.

▪ *The third wave* – 1990s to the present – widened the feminist movement and its ideas beyond middle-class white women, addressing the different disadvantages women experience owing to, for example, their race, ethnicity and class.

Seeing the history of feminism in these three waves can ignore the fight for equal rights and the end to discrimination by women outside the large feminist movements in the UK and US, including working-class women and black and ethnic minority women.

▪ *Post-feminism* – 1980s to present – includes a wide range of reactions to the feminist movement and is often critical of feminist ideas. The word 'post' suggests that feminism is something that has already happened. Some post-feminists argue that feminism isn't relevant any more because women have won equal rights. Other post-feminists argue that younger women don't see feminism as relevant to them now. They may still believe in equal rights for women, but either see themselves as individuals, not part of a feminist movement, or don't want to use the word feminist. This has been criticised by feminists as a way of 'manufacturing consent' for the fact that women are still unequal, by getting women to accept their unequal position in society.

ACTIVITY

Some post-feminists would argue that the sexually explicit images of female pop stars are empowering to women because they show them as sexually confident and active, using their sexuality on their terms. Analyse the images of a number of female pop stars online and list arguments against this view.

Recent developments in feminist ideas

ANGELA MCROBBIE

McRobbie has written several books, especially about young women and the media. She argues that many feminist ideas from the past aren't seen as relevant by young women now. Her first famous study was on the teenage girls' magazine *Jackie*. Then, in *Feminism and Youth Culture: From Jackie to Just 17* (1991), she came to more positive conclusions about media representations of young women.

Figure 3.7 *Cosmopolitan* Magazine cover, March 2010: www.natmags.co.uk

She argued that there were some positive aspects to, for instance, women's magazines, with ideas that could empower their young female audience, for example, how to enjoy sex or learning about their bodies. In *The Aftermath of Feminism* (2008), she explored how the media encourages women to consent to and play a part in negative media representations, for example, lads' mags competitions to appear on front covers or makeover programmes that ask the female audience to be critical of other women's bodies.

ACTIVITY

Analyse the front cover of a women's lifestyle magazine. List the positive and negative representations of women.

Do you agree or disagree with McRobbie's ideas?

THE BEAUTY MYTH (NAOMI WOLF 1991)

Wolf argues that women are oppressed by the pressure to fit into a myth or false ideal of beauty. Feminism may have won women new rights, but they are still held back by an obsession with physical appearance and a very narrow definition of beauty, for example, to be white, thin and made up. This beauty myth is socially constructed and helps to maintain patriarchy, where men still have power in society. Women buy into this myth, helping to create hegemony, where the values are accepted even by those that are harmed by them. Wolf attacked the *fashion and beauty* industries, and the advertising and media industries that support them, for exploiting women. Women's magazines make their profits from advertising that depends upon women feeling inadequate and being critical of themselves.

Women can never achieve the ideal of beauty because it is an unrealistic, air-brushed construction. There have been many recent examples of images of women in the media that have been manipulated to conform to this unrealistic ideal. For example, in 2003 Kate Winslet complained that her legs had been made thinner and longer when she posed for the front cover of *GQ* magazine. Keira Knightley was given larger breasts in the marketing posters for the film *King Arthur* and in her Chanel campaign.

Figure 3.8
Keira Knightley on the UK and US film posters for *King Arthur*

In an article in the *Guardian* in 2009, Emine Saner discussed the controversy over *Glamour* magazine in the US publishing a photo of a model that hadn't been touched up. The model Liz Miller said, "People don't ever see images like this in *magazines*. It shows how hungry the world is to see all different body types." At the other extreme gossip magazines and websites are very critical of celebrities' bodies; for example, www.perezhilton.com calls his website "Hollywood's Most-Hated Web Site!" and scrawls comments all over photos of celebrities, while *Heat* magazine has its famous Circle of Shame. Mark Frith, the former editor of *Heat*, said he believed the reality pictures actually made his readers feel better about themselves.

This unrealistic body ideal has been accused of contributing to women's negative body image and leading to physical and psychological problems, such as eating

Figure 3.9 Model Liz Miller's picture was published in the US edition of *Glamour* Magazine without airbrushing: www.guardian.co.uk

disorders. It has been argued that young women in particular use the media to construct their identity and are especially vulnerable. It is very difficult to prove a direct causal link between the media and audience behaviour, and many active audience theories argue against it.

ACTIVITY

What do you think?

On your own consider the following questions. Alternatively, split into groups, each group discussing one of the following questions and reporting back to the class the arguments for and against and their own views.

1. Does the representation of women in the media lead to women having a negative body image?

continued

RAUNCH CULTURE (ANDREA LEVY 2005)

In her book *Female Chauvinist Pigs: Women and the Rise of Raunch Culture*, Levy attacks the increasingly sexualised culture that objectifies women. She argues that women are encouraged to see themselves as objects and to see sex as their only source of power. This can be seen in lads' magazines like *Nuts* and music videos of female artists like Shakira.

Figure 3.10 Homepage of Katie Price's website: www.katieprice.co.uk

ACTIVITY

1. Is Katie Price a good role model for young women? Is she a successful and wealthy business woman who uses her body on her terms? Or does she show that society only values women who see and sell themselves as sex objects?

Zoe Williams in the *Guardian* in November 2009 argues, "She colludes with – no, encourages – the commodification of her body, values it out by the pound to whoever pays the most in whatsoever state of undress, and this makes her a very neat icon of raunch culture."

In *Media, Gender and Identity* (2002), David Gauntlett argues that audiences are active, and role models "should not be taken to mean someone that a person wants to copy. Instead, role models serve as navigation points as individuals steer their own personal routes through life."

2. List five people who you like or admire in the media; try to include a range of different people. Then swap your list in pairs. What does the list suggest about the other person and the values they have?
3. Then divide your class into young men and women. Are there any names that were repeated? What does your list suggest about the values that the media communicates about gender? What exceptions were there?

Feminists argue that sexualised images of girls and young women now saturate the media and are widely available in mainstream media, such as advertising, magazines and television. This damages women's self-image and it also distorts men's views of women. The internet has led to increased and easier access to pornography, whose message is that women are sexually available and their bodies are for sale.

GENDER AND IDENTITY (JUDITH BUTLER 1990)

Butler argued that feminism has contributed to a binary view of gender, where men and women are divided into opposing groups, with fixed ideas about what it is to be masculine and feminine. This has narrowed down the choices people could have about their own identity and excluded people who wanted to be different. She emphasised that because gender is socially constructed, rather than something that men or women are born with, it should be flexible, able to change at different times and in different circumstances. She argued that gender is only a performance; it's how we learn to behave and our society rewards us for behaving in what are seen as gender-appropriate ways. She argued that gender identities should be challenged by subversive action or what she called gender trouble, where people create or perform their own new identity, so that there are lots of different identities, not a narrow and restricting one. This is seen in queer theory, which challenges what is considered 'normal' ideas about gender or sexuality. You can read more about queer theory on page 198. The media can be one of the main places where new ideas about gender and sexual identity may be explored.

ACTIVITY

The games industry is dominated by male characters with dominant representations of men as competitive, violent or heroic. In *Gender Inclusive Game Design: Expanding The Market* (2003), Sheri Graner-Ray questions why the game industry is still producing computer games that primarily target males aged 13–25. She argues that game developers must start looking at expanding their market, which means designing titles that are accessible to a female audience.

There are some alternative representations of women in gaming. Collect a range of images from game covers, game websites and shots of game play from games that you think are challenging gender roles.

How are they creating gender trouble, challenging 'normal' gender roles and behaviour?

The game blog www.vgfreedom.blogspot.com lists their *Top 5 Coolest Women in Video Games* as:

5. Nariko from the *Heavenly Sword* Series
4. Princess Zelda in *The Legend of Zelda*
3. Joanna Dark in *Perfect Dark*
2. Lara Croft from *Tomb Raider*
1. Samus Aran from Metroid

Figure 3.11 The coolest women in videogames. Left to right: Joanna Dark, Lara Croft and Samus Aran

Self-representation

Developments in new and digital media have led to an increase in the number of representations of women, some alternative, and an increase in self-representation.

There are now lots of feminist webzines that are critical of existing representations of women in mainstream media and which offer alternative representations.

ACTIVITY

Compare the representation of women in the homepage of a feminist website with the homepage of a mainstream women's lifestyle magazine online; for example, www.mookychick.co.uk or www.fbomb.org, with www.glamourmagazine.co.uk or www.graziadaily.co.uk.

1. How do the two websites represent women? What are the main differences? Are there any similarities?
2. What values do they communicate about femininity and how society constructs what it is to be a woman? How is mookychick a feminist product?
3. What effect could this have on their audiences? However, because alternative representations are often only seen by a small audience does this mean they don't have the power or influence of mainstream dominant representations?
4. Is it possible for women to get a negotiated reading from either of the websites?
5. Who is producing the two products and why are they producing them? How does this influence the representations?

Figure 3.12 Homepage of feminist website www.mookychick.co.uk

Figure 3.13 Homepage of *Glamour* Magazine website

Postmodern perspective

One of the great attractions of postmodernism is that it roundly dismisses almost all the other theories on the grounds of irrelevance. According to postmodernists, any theory which makes claims about universal or underlying truths is just missing the point. Those 'big stories', like Marxism or Christianity, are no longer convincing in a world that is ever more confused and fragmented. Jean-François Lyotard called these discredited 'big stories' metanarratives in his 1979 book *The Postmodern Condition* and stressed the breakdown of values that this entailed.

Postmodernists also reject the idea of cultural value: the notion that some cultural practices and products are simply and intrinsically *better* than others. "We live," said Lyotard, "in a cultural Disneyland where everything is parody and nothing is better or worse." Here the old distinctions between high and popular culture have broken down and the construction of cultural identities is an active process of *bricolage*, of tinkering with the debris. We have, according to John Storey, "an audience of *knowing bricoleurs* who take pleasure from this and other forms of bricolage". This is a 'do-it-yourself' world of meanings where popular culture is no longer seen as the poor relation but simply as another means of expression. It is a world where William Shakespeare's *Romeo and Juliet* is a gangster movie and *Jerry Springer: The Opera*.

We can see evidence of this kind of *bricolage* and recycling everywhere: pop songs which sample riffs and licks from the 'classics' of popular or serious music, the 'instant nostalgia' of television programmes such as *Mad Men* or even *Life on Mars*, advertising's appropriation of the icons of visual arts such as the 'Mona Lisa'. Of course, the meanings originally attached to these 'borrowings' from the past can be accepted, rejected or manipulated, often in the name of 'postmodern irony'. Lads' magazines, stand-up comedians, schlock films and homophobic rap artists have all dismissed the criticism that they are being offensive and tasteless on the grounds that they are expressing a form of 'postmodern chic'.

ACTIVITY

Mix and mashup

Bricolage is no more or less than what in contemporary terms would be dubbed a 'mashup', something (song, video, file) created by recombining existing material. YouTube, for example, is a treasure house of these things. Think of your favourite mashups and then consider what is being said about:

- the identity of the creators
- who owns the material
- ideas about originality
- the nature of the audience.

ACTIVITY

Cultural implosion?

Jean Baudrillard argues for "the implosion of meaning in the media", suggesting that the old structures of 'high' and 'low' have been replaced with something of a 'bombsite'. What examples can you find where high art and popular culture (or 'old' and 'new' culture) are confused or combined (think TV and pop music and film and computer games).

Despite the energy and excitement sparked by this active approach to meaning, both Lyotard and Baudrillard are fundamentally pessimistic, worrying where this succession of breakdowns will lead. Recycling old meanings in new combinations is all very well but it may have implications for our understanding of what is real and particular for our sense of the past. This is Lyotard's point about us inhabiting "a cultural Disneyland", an idea developed in Baudrillard's work on hyperreality and the simulations which create it.

For Baudrillard, we live in an era of media saturation in which we are bombarded with information and signs. So much of our experience is in the form of media texts rather than first-hand, direct experience that the signs become 'more real than real'. This is *simulation*: the part of our lives that is dominated by television, computer games, DVD, internet chatrooms, magazines and all the other image suppliers. This is a very big part of many people's lives, perhaps even the biggest and most important part. Consequently, Baudrillard argues, the distinction between reality and simulation breaks down altogether: we make no distinction between real experience and simulated experience. Hyperreality refers to the condition where the distinction between them has not only blurred, but the 'image' part has also started to gain the upper hand.

HYPERREALITY

Here is an example which may help to explain the rather baffling concept of hyperreality. Let us imagine that I have never visited Paris. In spite of this I have a huge fund of impressions based on the simulations of Paris that I have seen in films and on television, usually to the accompaniment of accordion music. I have looked at magazines, travel brochures and my friends' holiday snaps. I have read about the entertainment, the food and the nightlife. The simulated Paris I know so well is a vibrant, exciting

Figure 3.14 A trip to Paris: reality or hyperreality?

and stimulating city. One day I decide to visit Paris for the first time. It is drizzling, my hotel room is cramped and dirty, nobody is particularly friendly and I get ripped off in a restaurant. Now I have a fund of rather negative 'real' experiences to add to my very positive simulated experiences. Which of these will win out to form my overall impression of Paris? If Baudrillard is right, they will all merge into one undifferentiated set of experiences, but the image-based simulations will be just that little bit more powerful than my direct experience. My Paris is hyperreal.

Baudrillard's argument is that in a media-saturated world, representation has been replaced as the dominant mode by its opposite, simulation. John Storey summed it up well when he wrote, "In the realm of the postmodern, the distinction between simulation and the 'real' continually implodes; the real and the imaginary continually collapse into each other. The result is hyperrealism: the real and the simulated are experienced as without difference' (Storey, 1998, p. 347). If hyperrealism reflects a hyperreality, reality itself is forever lost to us.

ACTIVITY

Standards of realism

The idea of hyperreality does not presuppose that we have lost our capacity to discriminate between the real and the simulated, but rather that we are implicitly not encouraged to do so. Media standards have

continued

become the norm: we talk of video-quality computer graphics and of the height of the realistic being 'photo-realistic'. Both 'video' and 'photo' are, lest we forget, one step removed.

Computer games make an interesting case study, as part of their essence is to strive for greater 'realism'. Select *three* games which depict an observable reality and describe:

- the ways in which they are 'realistic'
- the models on which this 'realism' is based
- the differences between your experience of these 'worlds' and your own.

Baudrillard revives the biblical term 'simulacrum', which refers to an identical copy without an original. He proposes that we are surrounded by representations which have no real reference to reality; they are images of images. Baudrillard considered representation the opposite of simulation, which is interesting to us as Media Studies students. Representation, he argued, works on the principle that "the sign and the real are equivalent" whereas simulation divorces the sign from its original subject. This process through which images are degraded works in four phases:

This would be the successive phases of the image:

- it is a reflection of basic reality;
- it masks and perverts a basic reality;
- it masks the *absence* of a basic reality;
- it bears no relation to any reality whatever: it is its own pure simulacrum.

(Baudrillard, 1998, pp. 353–4)

This is the cut-and-paste world of parody and pastiche which is the modern mass media experience. It is a world in which 'comic book films' have become a viable (and lucrative) film genre: the reflection of a reflection of a reflection. It is a world in which image and images have lives of their own; unanchored to any 'basic reality', they constitute their own. This is not just about virtual realities and other computer-generated environments but about the worlds represented by film, advertising and television. Think of the Manchester presented by *Coronation Street* since 1960 or the East End offered up by *EastEnders* since 1984. They have become significantly more and less than realistic realisations of reality. Like pubs in living museums or theme parks, the Rovers Return and Queen Vic, for example, are simulations, part of a hyperreality.

In the same way depictions of female characters in blockbuster Hollywood action films can hardly be seen as representational. In the codes of these films there is a paradigm of female types, which as they are progressively used progressively undermine the motivation of the images.

Figure 3.15 Film poster for *Indiana Jones: Kingdom of the Crystal Skull*

Figure 3.16 DVD cover for *Pulp Fiction*

ACTIVITY

Look at the three women depicted in the posters above and decide, irrespective of your knowledge of the films themselves, what you can confidently predict about their character and function. What else do you notice about them?

The representation of women in these texts, Baudrillard would argue, has been superseded by a process whereby mythic features have taken over from the desire to be realistic. Thus what might have started out as a realistic portrayal is soon conventionalised away from its reality and into the service of the hyperreal. Take either of the stock representations of 'evil' women/bad girls above (Cate Blanchett's 'manly' bitch or Uma Thurman's *femme fatale*). Both may have been coined as representations of a perceived aspect of 'womanliness' or of individual women but as they are continually reproduced across media platforms and genre (they will feature just as readily in news as in drama) their link to these realities is eroded. And the precession begins:

- It is a reflection of basic reality.
- It masks and perverts a basic reality; the original image is adapted and developed in a way that moves it further from its basic reality.
- It masks the *absence* of a basic reality; ultimately it comes to be understood as marking the absence of any real 'evidence' of meaning making.
- It bears no relation to any reality whatever: it is its own pure simulacrum. It is now merely a counter in a world of claim and counter-claim.

One thing that is masked in this process is any sense of where these simulations have emerged from, any historical context. *Bricolage* may be about plundering the canon of 'great works' and recycling the past but this accumulation happens on the surface and in the present: it has no depth or past. Postmodernism concerns itself primarily with surfaces. As you will be aware, the media consists largely of 'shiny surfaces' that give the illusion of depth, like a film set. The form of a film or an 'alternative' CD may give us the impression that it is weighty and meaningful, but this impression may very well be limited to the form rather than to the content; the text *looks* very significant, but that is as far as it goes. A postmodernist take on this would be to say 'So what? What you see is what you get.' In other words, we shouldn't even expect depth or meaningfulness. Just as there are no 'deep structures' there are no 'underlying meanings'; the signifier has detached itself from the signified. The cultural form which exemplifies this approach perfectly is the pop video. A dense array of suggestive signifiers may be compiled, drawing on all sorts of cultural reference points. But what does it all mean? If you are asking the question, you have already missed the point!

Now this is a very positive take. Most postmodernist theorists are more concerned with the impact that the unreliability of reality as a concept might have. Freed from history, the modern audience seek further simulations and these are primarily fuelled by nostalgia.

> **When the real is no longer what it used to be, nostalgia assumes its full meaning. There is a proliferation of myths of origin and signs of reality: of second hand truth, objectivity and authenticity. There is an escalation of the true, of the lived experience.**

(Baudrillard, 1998, p. 354)

Prophetically this is a manifesto for reality TV, that "escalation of the true, of lived experience". In reality a show like *Big Brother* (now axed) has itself gone through a period of 'degradation' as its initial purpose, to teach us something about social interaction, gives way to something far more expedient. Here postmodern play-fulness only serves to expose a further masking of reality.

Postcolonialism as a perspective

"Rule Britannia! Britannia rules the waves.
Britons never, never, never shall be slaves."
(Adapted from the poem 'Rule
Britannia' by James Thompson, 1740)

History books tell us that the British used to have an empire which at one time spanned half the globe. Among the parts of the world which Britain colonised were the USA, Canada, Australia, South Africa, Jamaica and the areas which now form the countries of India and Pakistan. Patriotic songs like 'Rule Britannia' are replete with references to our domination of the seas and many nations of the world. The building of an empire with such a global reach was made possible by the military might of Britain in the eighteenth, nineteenth and early twentieth centuries. Less developed countries would be entered, a new system of governance established and the resources and labour exploited by the colonising power. Over time, colonial territories declared their independence, often after war or revolution, and the empire declined. While it is true to say that relative to the position it once held, British influence on the world stage and that of other colonising countries such as Spain and France have declined significantly, there exists a belief that in the aftermath of the empire, the effects of colonisation have by no means vanished completely. This standpoint forms the basis for the theoretical perspective of postcolonialism.

Among the areas where these effects may be seen most obviously are in language, sport and culture. English is widely spoken across all the countries which were once imperial territories just as Spanish is across most of South America following the colonisation of that continent by Spain. Australia, India, New Zealand, the

West Indies, Pakistan and South Africa all excel at either cricket or rugby or, in some cases, both. These sports were exported by the British to these countries during the times when they were colonies. Although Britain and other Western countries no longer have an empire where through military might they enter and take control of a country in the way they once did, the postcolonial theoretical perspective is concerned with the view that in terms of media and culture there is still a sense of Western domination, or as Marxists would term it, 'cultural imperialism', and that this echoes the empire building of old. While the tool of empire building was once a sword or a gun, today it is far more likely to be culture, consumer products and media production.

INFORMATION BOX

Figure 3.17 Even in the furthest reaches of Africa, the influence of the American global giant Coca-Cola can be felt, as these images show

Arguably the most evident sign of cultural imperialism in the contemporary world is the area of cinema, a media platform which is dominated by the USA. Even a cursory glance at the film schedule of your local multiplex at any time will reveal a preponderance of American film showing on the screens. Even countries like France with a well-established national cinema has expressed concern at the effect the influx of American imports might have upon its own film industry and it has taken steps to address this by limiting the number of non-French films shown in cinemas across France. The influence of US media and culture can be evidenced in a wide range of other media platforms such as music or television and also in the organisations which produce the media. However, the US influence is just part of what might more broadly be regarded as Western influence which, in addition to the media output of the USA also includes European and Australian media. Through recognising the East/West divide in media, postcolonial theory involves looking at how Eastern and Oriental culture is viewed through the eyes of the dominant Western media. Edward Said in his highly influential book *Orientalism* (1978) argues that Eastern culture is habitually seen as inferior to Western, a phenomenon he calls Orientalism. The West, he argues, terms Eastern cultures as the 'other' and contests that this perception can be traced back to the work of, among others, Shakespeare, Byron and Chaucer. At best, argues Said, when represented by Western culture, Orientalism is seen as exotic which is relatively harmless, but of more concern is the manner of this representation – a deliberate and aggressive exploitation by Western culture which perceives itself as stronger and perpetuates a doctrine that has legitimised this imbalance of power and the relative weakness of the East. Elizabeth Poole supports the main points of Said's study in her research into representations of British Muslims in the media. Political Islam, she argues, emerged as a consequence of the oppression of the colonisation of Islamic countries and has "allowed the West to construct Islam as the new enemy" following the collapse of communism in the late 1980s. Within the Marxist perspective, the media is seen to act as a tool of hegemony, a means by which the interests of a powerful group – the West – are both legitimised and enforced over the weaker group, in this case Muslims. Similarly Poole suggests that the media is instrumental in demonising Islam and both reproducing and sustaining the ideology which subjugates Islam and those who follow the faith (Poole, 2002).

This is perhaps nowhere more evident than in the representations of Islam in Western media. The film *Executive Decision* (1997) portrays a radical Islamic group who hijack a plane with a view to crashing it into an American city, thus releasing nerve gas which will kill millions of people and, having pitted his wits against aliens, communists, machines and private armies, Arnold Schwarzenegger took on a radical group of Muslim extremists in *True Lies* (1994). Recently, the hit TV show *24* which has been praised by many critics as an innovative and original concept whereby the action takes place in real time has also attracted its critics for its representations of Muslims. During the fourth series of the show, the Council on American–Islamic Relations complained to the show's producers, Fox TV, about the negative portrayal of Muslims in the show. This complaint led the show's star, Kiefer Sutherland, to announce at the start of one of the episodes that "the American Muslim community stands firmly beside their fellow Americans in denouncing and resisting all forms of terrorism. So in watching *24*, please bear that in mind." Nevertheless, the criticism continued when Muslims were again portrayed as terrorists in the sixth series. The eighth series which first aired early in 2010 once again saw radical Muslim characters involved in terrorist plots with dissident Russian characters.

These characters, from top left Tarin Faroush, Farhad Hassan, Habib Marwan, Ahmed Amar and Abu Fayed, have all attempted to bring terror upon the USA in the name of an Islamic cause in the TV show *24*. This has led to criticisms of the show for the negative and stereotypical manner it portrays Islam but do characters like these on TV demonise Muslims and help spread a sense of Islamaphobia?

Figure 3.18 Muslim characters in TV series *24*

Research conducted by the Islamic Human Rights Commission (http://www.ihrc. org.uk/show.php?id=2493) counters further that the demonisation of Islam is not limited to fictional media but may be found in the way Muslims are represented in TV news, current affairs and more broadly in literature. Coverage of Muslims in TV news seems to be dominated by issues of terrorism, radicalisation, illegal immigration and a general representation, as Said argues of Muslims as the "other". In his book *Hegemony or Survival: America's Quest For Global Dominance* (2004), Noam Chomsky explains how America sought to portray Saddam Hussein as an imminent threat to the USA and as responsible for the terrorist attacks in New York on 11 September 2001, accusations which with the benefit of hindsight appear to have been inaccurate at best, if not completely false. This was part of the USA's strategy through which it reserved the right to resort to force to protect its global hegemony. Chomsky concludes that this campaign was highly successful in America in shifting attitudes and that the media was partly responsible for this. However, it could be argued by taking an institutional viewpoint that the purpose of all media, including that concerned with news and current affairs, is to make money, and so it is simply reporting the events which are deemed newsworthy, a process which is based upon the application of a set of news values to an event. This was a concern of Noam Chomsky in his earlier book *Manufacturing Consent* (1988) where he argues that American news media in its drive to make money reports those events which will attract the largest audiences and so attract the greatest number of advertisers upon whom they rely for revenue. Clearly the feeling with this perspective is that the demonisation of Muslims in news media helps to sell news media.

What Elizabeth Poole, critics of shows like *24* (e.g. the Council on American–Islamic Relations and the Islamic Human Rights Commission) are referring to here is perhaps better known today as Islamaphobia or a fear of Muslims borne out of the actions of a few radicals who have perpetrated a number of atrocities including the 9/11 terror attacks and those in London in July 2005, and which has intensified to a fear of the entire faith of Islam. It is argued that the media plays a key role in influencing opinion on this issue; certainly it has been quite widely reported in the press and a wealth of negative coverage has led to the belief among some that Islam is dangerous. Yet the figures do not support this fear. The overwhelming majority of Muslims across the world do not engage in any terrorist activity, nor do they actively seek to be in a state of conflict with the West as has been reported in the media.

Can negative newspaper coverage of Muslims also contribute to the Islamaphobia many now feel has taken hold in Western societies?

Figure 3.19 Negative coverage in the *Daily Express* and the *Sun*

This takes us back almost full circle to the Marxist consideration of media as part of the mechanism by which the ruling elite legitimises and maintains its control and power over the rest of society. The postcolonial perspective fits neatly as a parallel to this since it seeks to explain how the West, which regards itself as the ruling elite, legitimises and maintains its power over the East and exerts its cultural influence around the world. This cultural imperialism is further strengthened when the West is willing to invade countries and to impose Western democratic political ideology upon the population, as is the case in Afghanistan and Iraq. Portraying Muslims in the media as terrorists, a threat to Western values and principles and as the 'other' to be feared and mistrusted, becomes an important way in which consent for the dominant ideology and the wider military objectives can be won.

Summary of postcolonialism

- Postcolonialism offers a useful viewpoint on the modern world in which the developed countries of the West exert huge influence over the developing countries.
- Postcolonialism shares with Marxism an interest in the exploitation of a weaker group by a more powerful and influential group.
- The postcolonial perspective of media criticises the reference to non-Western culture as the 'other' and the inherent superiority which Western culture demonstrates over Eastern culture.
- Some theorists, Said, Poole and Chomsky among them, argue that these media representations of the 'other' help to win consent for the wider military, economic or political ambitions Western countries have over those in the developing parts of the world.

Queer theory and queerness

Queer is an academic theory of popular culture (originally about film); it is the name given to a small range of media texts (queerness) and a radical activist movement which includes groups such as ACTUP and Outrage.

Queer theory and queerness in popular culture is difficult to reduce to one definition. This is partly because one of the arguments of queer theory is that as an audience it is possible to take up queer and straight positions at different times, that media texts can be straight and queer, films with gay characters can be straight (in the context of queerness) while a film about straight characters can be queer. This rather confusing outline does reinforce the fact that queer is not a synonym for gay but rather a position which rejects conventional or mainstream expressions of all types of behaviour – including sexual identity. A characteristic of queer theory has been a debate about what a queer text is and what it should look like. This argument has often been structured around the differences between mainstream and alternative institutional contexts of popular culture – asking whether there can ever be a queer mainstream text.

Queer theory has a close relationship to feminist theory and gender studies. In some ways queer theory continues the approaches of those areas but it also rejects some of the assumptions underpinning these more traditional perspectives. Like feminist theory and gender studies, queer theory is interested in studying non-normative expressions of gender and sexuality. In opposition to these approaches queer theory rejects the essentialist nature of theories of identity which are expressed through binary oppositions – male/female, gay/straight, etc. Queer theory argues that people do not simply categorise themselves in this way; representations don't conform to either side of these divides – instead, there is another space outside of these oppositions and it is this space which is 'queer'.

Queer positions: androgyny, cross-dressing and reception

This concept of a queer space may be applied to the example of androgyny and cross-dressing. A film which has been discussed a lot in queer theory is *Sylvia Scarlet* (Cukor, US, 1935). In this film, Katherine Hepburn, an actress whose star persona emphasised her unconventional gender characteristics (trousers, suit jackets, athleticism, strong features) plays a young woman who dresses as a man (Sylvester) in order to avoid arrest. Straight male audience members who gain

Figure 3.20 Katherine Hepburn in *Sylvia Scarlet* and Hilary Swank in *Boys Don't Cry*

sexual pleasure from looking at Katherine Hepburn in male dress are having a queer moment – something which cannot be simply categorised as gay or straight (Doty 1995).

This analysis could be tested with reference to a more recent film, *Boys Don't Cry* (Kimberley Pierce, US, 1994). The central character – Brandon – is a female who identifies as and performs the role of a heterosexual male. Brandon's girlfriend identifies as a heterosexual female rather than a lesbian, even when she knows that Brandon is biologically female. *Boys Don't Cry* isn't necessarily queer though; Brandon's attempt to 'pass' in society as a heterosexual male could be read as a reinforcement of conventional definitions of gender and sexuality and therefore not queer.

What is a queer text?

Queer texts are defined in two ways:

- Those which deal with explicitly queer themes and characters.
- Those which are read as queer; the accumulation of queer readings 'queers the text' whether it is explicitly queer or not.

The definition of a queer text – or persona – as one which 'has accumulated queer readings' (Doty 1998) means that texts portraying gay characters may not be queer but gay, while texts without gay characters may be queer.

There is of course a great deal of disagreement about what constitutes a queer text, but an independent film movement in the US in the early 1990s which was named 'new queer cinema' by critics is generally agreed to be queer. These films had in common a central character that was on the margins of society – an outsider – usually due to their sexuality but issues such as race, gender, class and physical disability were also referred to. While there had been films which featured gay characters and storylines before, new queer cinema was different in that it rejected the idea of positive representations which would be acceptable to the heterosexual, mainstream audience and instead deliberately attempted to shock and anger that audience. In a similar approach, the term queer which had previously been used as a form of abuse was appropriated by some organisations and individuals and used as a positive form of identification.

Poison (Todd Haynes, 1991); *My Own Private Idaho* (Gus Van Sant, 1991); *Swoon* (Tom Kalin, 1992); *Go Fish* (Rose Troche, 1994); *The Living End* (Gregg Araki, 1993); *Savage Grace* (Tom Kalin, 2007).

Figure 3.21 Film posters for *Go Fish* and *Swoon*

Queerness and the mainstream

The debates around definitions of queerness in mainstream texts can be illustrated by the career of Gus Van Sant. Gus Van Sant was a leading figure of new queer cinema, an out gay director of independent, experimental films as well as star-driven Oscar winners (*Good Will Hunting*, 1997). *Milk* (2008), which is a bio-pic of Harvey Milk, the first openly gay elected politician in the US, has been defined as a gay rather than a queer film. This is partly due to its mainstream institutional context, star performance (Sean Penn won an Oscar for the title role) but particularly because it focuses on themes of equality and acceptance, the idea that everyone is the same and can be assimilated into mainstream society. Queer is instead a celebration of difference and is unapologetic in foregrounding that difference – whether it is uncomfortable for the audience or not. Gus Van Sant's films which deal less explicitly or not at all with gay themes are, conversely, queer in their representation of outsiders, drifters, criminals and addicts (see *Drugstore Cowboys* (1989), *Last Days* (2005), *Paranoid Park* (2007)).

This approach to queerness means that films such as *Rebel Without a Cause* (Nicholas Ray, 1955), *Edward Scissorhands* (Tim Burton, 1990) and *Donnie Darko* (Richard Kelly, 2001) are queer due to their focus on and sympathy for characters who do not conform to the conventional expectations of their society.

Queer genres

A diverse range of style and content may be characterised as queer but many queer texts do share a particular characteristic – the subversion of traditional genre rules. This form mirrors the other unconventional representations in the films. *Brokeback Mountain* (Ang Lee, US, 2006), a film which caused controversy for a variety of reasons, has been the focus of a gay vs. queer debate among critics and academics.

BROKEBACK MOUNTAIN AS QUEER TEXT

- The use of melodrama, which is traditionally structured around heterosexual relationships to tell the love story of Jack and Ennis (the central characters in the film), places the audience in a queer position, identifying with characters who are queer rather than gay (they don't self-identify as gay – the concept hardly exists in the world of the film).
- The melodrama – also known as the woman's film or weepie – is intercut with the western. This placement of the two genres together reveals meanings which had always existed in the western but which had not been acknowledged. *Brokeback Mountain* takes the homoerotic aspect of the western and puts it centre stage. This queering of the western is not the uncovering of a subtext but acknowledges a meaning which had always existed alongside dominant, straight readings. (The truth of this analysis is perhaps evident in the delight a variety of audiences and media got from describing the film as the 'gay cowboys movie'.)
- The concept of 'queer space' which is neither gay nor straight is symbolised in the geographical space of Brokeback Mountain.

BROKEBACK MOUNTAIN ISN'T QUEER

- The concept of queer positioning carries with it the idea of pleasure for the audience. As a melodrama the audience is positioned to suffer with the characters.
- Gay relationships are represented as a source of suffering; the best you can hope for is a few weeks of happiness. The silent endurance of Ennis is completely at odds with queerness which refuses to be quiet.
- The audience empathises with Alma, Ennis's wife, and the misery caused to her by Ennis and Jack's relationship.

Figure 3.22 Ennis Del Mar (Heath Ledger) in *Brokeback Mountain*: Queer?

IT'S NOT GAY, IT'S QUEER: *I LOVE YOU PHILLIP MORRIS*

There has clearly been an identifiable shift in the representation of gay characters in mainstream texts in the past 20 years. Stereotypes have been challenged and gay characters (although with the exception of *The L Word* it does tend to be gay male characters who appear) are more common and are no longer defined simply by their sexuality. Popular TV series *(Brothers and Sisters* (ABC, 2006–present), *Glee* (Fox, 2009–present), *Nurse Jackie* (Showtime, 2009–present)) feature central and supporting gay characters. Queer theory questions the meaning of these representations however, arguing that too often they are based on assimilation and the need for acceptance by straight society. The recent Hollywood, star-driven film *I Love You Phillip Morris* (Glen Ficarra and John Requa, US, 2009) seems to represent something different; a mainstream film about gay men which is actually queer. The film is based on the true story (as the tagline puts it 'no, really, it is') of Steven (Jim Carrey), a con man who, after a happy marriage and family life, comes out as gay and embarks on a career as a conman. In prison he falls in love with Phillip Morris (Ewan McGregor), and the rest of the film is about their relationship in the context of Steven's outlaw lifestyle. Despite its mainstream context, *I Love You Phillip Morris* may be read as queer in a number of respects:

Figure 3.23 Film poster for *I Love You Phillip Morris*

Figure 3.24 Scenes from *I Love You Phillip Morris*

- The outsider theme of queer is clearly evident in the poster and plotline; the heroes are convicts who continue a life of crime on release.
- There is no moral judgement made about their lifestyle (as criminals or gay men) leading to the film being described as 'morally reprehensible'.
- This disregard for the conventions and morality of mainstream society is typical of queer.
- Sexual desire and the physical pleasures of gay sex are dealt with in a cheerfully frank, explicit way. Gay sex is represented as different to straight – gay films usually try to minimise the sense of difference.
- The difference between gay and straight lifestyles is celebrated throughout. As an out gay man Steven lives a totally different life to his straight, suburban existence (he's 'living high on the gay hog'). When he prepares to play golf with his boss in order to get on in the corporation, Phillip cries out in horror: *"But you're a homosexual!"*
- A characteristic of queerness is the subversion of genre conventions. *ILYPM* is a hybrid of romantic comedy, crime film (there are similarities with *Catch Me if You Can* (Steven Spielberg, 2002)) and the prison film. As with *Brokeback Mountain* the mix of traditionally male and female genres queers the text. The romcom narrative structure means we root for the happy couple, and the references to the prison film acknowledge the homoeroticism of that form.
- The use of the comedy genre – rather than the drama or melodrama – constructs an audience response of happiness and celebration. Steve and Phillip's

relationship is romantic, joyful and public – in direct contrast to the tortured 'gay cowboys'.

Summary of queer theory

- Queer is used as an overarching term to describe the way in which a range of identities (sexuality, race, gender, disability etc.) intersect; it is not synonymous with gay.
- Queer theory shares with feminism and gender studies an interest in unconventional gender characteristics.
- Queer theory rejects the concept of essentialism and binary oppositions in defining identity.
- Queer texts can be defined through content and the accumulation of queer readings.

Conclusion

ACTIVITY

Based on your understanding of theoretical perspectives in this chapter, how useful do you find them:

1. Collectively?
2. Individually?

Do you think these perspectives have enriched your study of the media in any way? If so, how?

Look back at the Tom Ford advertisement on page 165. Consider how each of the theoretical perspectives about which you have read might further develop your understanding of it. Where do you stand now?

part 2

PREPARING FOR THE WJEC UNITS

1 PASSING MS4: TEXT, INDUSTRY, AUDIENCE

2 PASSING MS3: MEDIA INVESTIGATION AND PRODUCTION

·

4 PASSING MS4: TEXT, INDUSTRY, AUDIENCE

In this chapter we consider the following industries in preparation for MS4:

- News
- Film
- Computer games
- Television

On the companion website you will find work on the music and radio industries which should also be useful for this unit.

MS4: the components

This unit is assessed by an exam which is structured in two sections:

- **Section A: Text**
- **Section B: Industry and audience**

You will answer three essay questions – one (from a choice of two) from Section A and two (from a choice of four) from Section B – and you must write about a different industry in each answer.

Rationale: what are the aims of this unit?

One way of understanding the aims of this unit is to look at the assessment objectives (what the unit is 'testing'):

AO1 Demonstrate knowledge and understanding of media concepts, contexts and critical debates.

AO2 Apply knowledge and understanding when analysing media products and processes, to show how meanings and responses are created.

This unit forms part of the synoptic assessment which is central to A2 study. It is designed to develop your understanding of the connections between media texts, their audiences and the industries which produce and distribute them.

Progression from AS is demonstrated through the emphasis on this interconnection and the debates surrounding the nature of that relationship. Your understanding of the media should also be more informed by appropriate theoretical perspectives.

The 'mind map' in Figure 4.1 demonstrates the approach to texts at MS4.

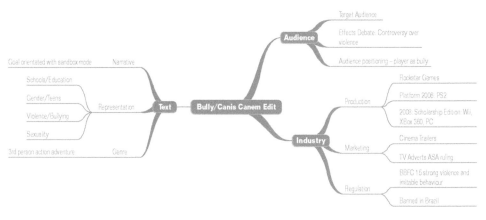

Figure 4.1 A 'mind map' demonstrates the approach to texts at MS4

If one of your three industries was computer games, then you would also need to study two other games in as much comprehensive detail.

Due to the nature of the exam – questions which can be answered across texts, industries, audiences, etc. – there can't be a definitive list or plan of how you should prepare. The exam board expects you to be a much more developed and free-thinking student than at any other time in the past. In some ways, this examination represents the culmination of everything you have studied in this subject so far and doubtless you will be using information which you first encountered even as far back as your GCSE.

Synoptic assessment

MS4 is a synoptic unit – it draws on all the knowledge and skills you have developed at AS and A2 including the key theoretical concepts, research skills, technical and creative ability.

What does it mean to be synoptic?

The first step in developing a synoptic approach is providing a synopsis of your subject, drawing together everything that you have covered so far on the course. The next stage is to use that synopsis to develop your knowledge and understanding further.

A synoptic approach should:

- Be based on knowledge, understanding and skills specified in the MS4 unit but also draw on those in previously studied units. Part of the skill of a synoptic approach is to select relevant areas from previous study – not just to mention everything!
- Demonstrate the ability to construct, evaluate and support an argument. It isn't enough to have the subject knowledge; you must also demonstrate the skills of critical thinking and apply these to the industries studied in response to a specific exam question.
- Engage with ideas, issues and debates which go beyond the limits of the knowledge, skills and understanding studied on the course.

The following areas to consider on the TV industry illustrate the wide-ranging textual and theoretical approaches you need to consider to be able to demonstrate your in-depth knowledge of a particular industry.

GENRE

What are the dominant TV genres today? Do these genres have anything in common?

Formats are more important than genre in contemporary television. How far do you agree?

NARRATIVE

TV has been described as a narrative medium. What is meant by this?

How have traditional TV narratives been affected by digital technologies?

INDUSTRY

To what extent are the BBC and ITV still the dominant companies in British television?

The movement to television programmes endorsed by advertisers was a response to changing viewing patterns. What potential problems might it hold for makers of TV programmes?

Has television been marginalised or consolidated by convergence culture?

AUDIENCE

Is not having a TV unthinkable?

Where do you watch television and with whom?

VALUES/IDEOLOGY

Fiske and Hartley, writing in the 1970s (when Britain boasted only three TV channels), suggested that television was a vital source of cultural information. To what extent do we still get a significant slice of our cultural information from television? Where else do we get it?

ACTIVITY

Draw up a similar range of questions/issues for debate for one of the other industries you are studying.

Preparing for the examination

MS4 provides a great opportunity for you to demonstrate your skills of critical thinking and autonomy. This is due to the large amount of choice in this unit which places the emphasis on your own selection of texts, industry, approaches, etc. For example, you need to sit down at your table in the examination room with detailed knowledge of three different media industries, say, film, radio and newspapers, and have three example texts from each of these industries of which you also have detailed knowledge, so that's nine texts in total. You will then be asked to answer three questions, one each from a choice on the topics of text, industry and audience.

In addition to your knowledge of your three media types from the viewpoint of text, industry and audience, one further element which the board is keen to test is this flexibility, literally being able to answer any of the three types of question (text, industry and audience) for any of your three industries. While it is true to say that many candidates may have a broad idea of the approach they intend to take in the exam beforehand, the final decision should be delayed until you see the questions. Consider the student who enters the exam having prepared to use film for the text question, radio for industry and newspaper for audience, only to find that the set questions do not facilitate the answers the student had prepared. Those students who are able to look at the questions and then decide which areas of media they have studied best lend themselves to the questions asked will be in a far stronger position than those who are not able to do this.

There are a number of approaches to preparing for this exam given this requirement for flexibility, and it will very much depend upon the approach taken by your teacher. It is most likely that your preparation for the exam will be primarily through taught texts which have been studied by the entire class and will examine the key issues of text, industry and audience, thus allowing you the flexibility of using all of the three studied texts for each area in any of the three questions you ultimately answer. However, in order to allow for some flexibility, you may, in consultation with your teacher, be encouraged to pick some of the texts yourself, say, one for each of the three areas covered, so that you have some input into the texts you refer to in your exam and can explore those you would choose alongside those chosen for you. It is also possible that you have total freedom of choice over more of the texts, and in extreme cases you might be choosing them all.

Either way, which ever approach your class is taking, there are certain limitations and areas of advice which you must be aware of.

- For each industry, you must study three main texts in detail.
- You should aim to choose contrasting texts.
- No individual texts which formed part of your MS3 research can be used here, although the same industry may be studied.
- At least two texts for each industry must be contemporary (this means no more than five years old).
- At least one text must be British (this can be a grey area in the case of film so, if in doubt, it is worth checking with your teacher or directly with WJEC).
- Finally, you should be aware of time allocation for the examination. A 15-minute reading and planning period should be observed at the start of the examination. It is important to spend this time in any context but especially in this exam, since you have crucial decisions about which media you are going to use for which questions and you cannot realistically make these decisions until you have read all the questions. This will then leave you with approximately 45 minutes on each of your three answers.

The texts selected for the following case studies are arranged in groups according to the media industries that produced them. Each set of three is prefixed by a mini-essay which leaps into what might be considered interesting and perhaps significant themes and trends:

Industry: Film: text, genre and gender
Industry: News: industry and audience
Industry: Computer games: text, narrative and audience
Industry: TV: text, industry and audience

These examples provide a foundation for A2 study but must be supplemented by examples of your own.

Case study 4.1

FILM: GENDER AND HORROR: EVERYTHING BUT THE GHOUL!

Figure 4.2 The horror genre. Left to right: *Bram Stoker's Dracula*, *The Descent* and *The Dark Knight*

Media industry:	Film	Context
Focus	Genre (horror), gender	
Texts	*Bram Stoker's Dracula* (1992)	Hollywood, historical context
	The Descent (2005)	British contemporary
	The Dark Knight (2008)	Hollywood contemporary

This case study demonstrates one approach to the MS4 examination, but remember: you don't have to use the films in this example; neither the genre of horror nor gender representations have to form the basis of study and film doesn't have to be the chosen industry.

Genre: is it a horror film?

As a concept, genre is a useful analytical tool and especially so in Unit 4. It has an obvious application as a textual device through which students can analyse a range of texts and identify those with common generic features or signifiers. This is a convenient method of categorising media texts and allows trends over time to be observed; for example, the rise in popularity and then decline of the body of work known as punk music in the 1970s or of the western genre of film in the 1950s to 1960s. As a textual device, genre also allows common features to be identified cross-generically when features usually found in one genre are observed in other genres. This idea is developed later in this section. However, using genre in this way is not without its limitations or pitfalls; for example, not all texts fall neatly into a generic category, and even among those that do seem to belong to a genre, there may be huge differences between texts, as is the case in the gritty 'realism' of British soap opera such as *Coronation Street* compared to the wealth and glamour of American soaps such as *Dallas* or the focus on youth and affluent setting of many Australian soaps such as *Home and Away*, yet each could conceivably be identified as soap operas. However, when the idea of subgenre is introduced, these TV shows perhaps sit more comfortably in the category of soap opera; it's just that they stem from different areas of the genre.

In addition to the textual uses, genre also presents excellent opportunities to analyse texts from the industry and audience perspective. Our knowledge of genre allows us to make decisions about what we like to consume as

continued

audiences. No doubt many of us would define ourselves by our generic preferences, for example, a rock fan or sci-fi enthusiast. In addition, the media industry is run, by and large, along the same lines as any business in which products are made and sold to consumers, and the prime concern is the creation of income. As a concept therefore, genre offers media producers what Branston and Stafford call a chance to "minimise risk and predict expenditure" in a commercial setting which they describe as particularly "costly and volatile" (2010, p. 106).

The table below looks at some of the main areas in which genre may be applied to industry and audiences.

The usefulness of the concept of genre	
To audiences	To industry (producers)
■ Genre allows decisions to be made about consumption. Literally we know what we like and so we consume the films, TV, music, magazines, etc. which fall into the categories which appeal to us. ■ Our knowledge of genre and the genre conventions presents us with a sense of satisfaction when they are fulfilled. The repetition of generic elements is what keeps audiences flocking to see James Bond films or the latest entry into the *Saw* franchise because audiences know what to expect and they have these expectations satisfied. Yet despite this desire for repetition in media products, audiences also demand a certain amount of difference. The extent to which this balance between repetition and difference is successfully achieved can only really be seen thanks to knowledge of the genre of the texts in question. ■ Genre also gives audiences the chance to do what you as a media student are doing in this unit: to analyse media texts, to pass	■ Media is, as Branston and Stafford suggest above, volatile and unpredictable. Take film, for example. The entire product must be completed with all of the costs associated, salaries for the cast and crew (several millions of dollars in most cases), expensive post-production such as special effects and musical scores added and then a costly marketing campaign which includes posters and trailers for both TV and cinema. Companies cannot make the first ten minutes of a film as a sample and, if the audience like it, make the rest of the film. The entire product must be completed and distributed, and all this happens before a single ticket has been sold and there is no guarantee that the film will break even let alone show a profit. With this backdrop, companies are keen to make those products with the highest chance of being successful. This, probably more than any other reason, accounts for the popularity of fantasy and romantic comedy and the scarcity

judgement on the content and to make sense of the wealth of output that is available for consumption. The modern audience member often approaches their media consumption in a sophisticated way and has knowledge of such concepts of highbrow and lowbrow culture, all of which is fuelled by their generic knowledge and expectations.

of westerns in your local cinema. Westerns simply do not sell tickets.

■ Genres provide a blueprint which can be followed by producers. If a producer is going to make a horror film, they have a wealth of examples which can be drawn upon to create the repetition which audiences crave.

■ Genre also assists producers with marketing their products. With a genre comes a target audience and once a producer has identified a target audience they can aim their marketing strategy more directly and with greater accuracy. Have you noticed that when you open a new magazine, a wad of paper usually falls out? This is frequently advertising a range of products, including new media products, which are specifically aimed at the target audience of the magazine you are reading.

■ From a wider industry point of view, genre can be expanded into a debate about those genres, especially horror, gangster, pornography or action which are frequently at odds with the codes of practice of regulatory bodies.

In looking at genre from the audience and industry point of view, it may be worth considering to which of these two is genre the more useful as a concept. Clearly it has uses to both, and whether it is more useful to one or the other is a topic capable of debate and development for this unit, but in this particular case study, which it is worth reiterating once again offers just one possible approach to the unit, the focus for genre will be as a textual device.

Many people reading this may well be thinking that *The Dark Knight*, the sequel to *Batman Begins*, is not a horror film and this is indeed a valid point of view. This illustrates one of the problems with adopting such a definitive

continued

approach to textual analysis. *The Dark Knight* might conceivably be labelled as a super-hero or comic book film and placed alongside other entries into this 'genre' such as the Superman, X-Men and Spiderman franchises, but to simply label *The Dark Knight* as such would be to miss an opportunity for wider comparative analysis. Indeed, this is an example of an interesting feature found increasingly in contemporary film, namely the tendency for film texts to include features from a range of genres. A horror film, it may be argued, is a text which uses elements from a set of features defined as signifiers from the horror genre, chief among them knives, dark corners, blood, masked killers and so on but it is an equally valid point of view to argue that horror may be defined by the effect it has on an audience. If we consider Stanley Kubrick's *The Shining* (1980), this film had very few of the ingredients normally associated with horror. It was bright and open through-out most of the film, we see only one bloody death, that of the chef who is killed by an axe blow, although we hear of more, the psychopathic killer appears not to be out of control and randomly killing as happens in many slasher-type movies and there are very few sudden appearances of char-acters accompanied by a burst of music designed to frighten the audience. Nevertheless, *The Shining* stands out as an excellent example of a horror film and frequently finds itself towards the top of polls designed to establish the greatest horror film ever, precisely because of its effect on the audience. Thus categorising *The Shining* as a horror film is not necessarily a guarantee that you will see all the elements you might expect to see in such a film and, likewise, not being categorised as a horror film does not necessarily guarantee an absence of those elements. As we will see when we delve more deeply into *The Dark Knight*, there are elements from within that film which are straight out of the repertoire of generic elements of the horror genre. The table below looks at what these features might be identified as.

The most common generic features of horror

- Death, usually in a gruesome or particularly unpleasant manner, and, in most subgenres such as slasher, in fairly large amounts.
- Settings designed to unnerve, often dark, small or conversely very large, haunted or gothic settings are those common in the genre.
- Knives, axes and other sharp instruments which are designed to be used by invading the victim's personal space and to result in copious amounts of blood (victims do not tend to be shot or killed by bombs in horror films – it's just not unnerving enough!).
- A recognisable musical style which features disjointed and screeching sounds with loud and sudden interjections (which are designed to make you jump).
- Teenage victims.

- Masked or at least mysterious psychopathic killers who derive enjoyment from the murderous activities.
- Ineffective authority figures.
- Scenes or set pieces designed to frighten the audience.
- The theme of good vs. evil.
- Supernatural elements (in some subgenres) which may in the case of *The Exorcist* or *The Omen* have a foundation in religious belief or, as in *The Blair Witch Project* or *The Sixth Sense*, folklore, superstition and mythology.
- Crazed scientists whose pursuit of a dream has disastrous consequences.
- In terms of the narrative, an open ending or even the triumph of evil over good is quite normal to allow for the sequels for which the horror genre is notorious.

Approaches to 'text'

Let us begin this case study by looking at the three films chosen from the point of view of Section A in the WJEC MS4 examination, that of text. Naturally, there is a need for students to have a thorough and detailed knowledge of the films which are going to be used to answer the questions and there is really no substitute for acquiring this detailed knowledge than watching the films several times and making detailed notes about the generic features, the narrative structures, the characters and the filmmaking techniques such as cinematography, editing, the use of sound and the *mise-en-scène*. In each case it is worth considering not simply how these elements are presented in the films, but also asking whether the way they are presented challenges the conventional norms found in films in general and more specifically in the horror genre. An example of this is found in the film *28 Weeks Later* where the film's hero, Don, played by arguably the film's biggest star, Robert Carlyle, is infected with the deadly Rage virus about half-way into the narrative and is killed shortly afterwards.

GENRE the French word which simply means 'type', used to categorise media texts such as films into recognisable groups.

REPERTOIRE OF GENERIC ELEMENTS/GENERIC FEATURES the features we normally associate with media texts that belong to a certain genre which a text *can* demonstrate but which in some cases may not. For example, space is a feature of some science

continued

fiction films but there are many sci-fi texts which do not have space as a feature. However, some generic features are more prescriptive; for example, it is hard to envisage a western film which does not feature cowboys and which is not set in the western and southern states of the USA in the 1870s or 1880s.

CAMERA WORK the use of the camera in filmmaking. This includes the shots used and the camera movements.

EDITING for some people, editing simply refers to removing sections which are not needed but in truth there is much more of a contribution to the overall feel of the film from editing. It refers to placing the shots in a sequence which is understandable to the audience and also the length of the shots. As a result, the job of the editor is to ensure the correct pacing for a sequence (e.g. fast and with quick cuts for a chase sequence or slower and with fades for a dream sequence).

FILM SOUND often overlooked compared to the more visual elements but crucial to creating the atmosphere for a film. Generally, sound may be divided into two sections. Diegetic sound refers to that sound which both the audience and the characters in the film can hear, and includes dialogue and sounds made by objects in the scene such as a gunshot, a car engine or a character striking a match, whereas non-diegetic sound refers to that which just the audience can hear, and includes narration or voice-over and incidental music.

MISE-EN-SCÈNE another French term which, translated, means 'put in the scene'. It refers to the control the director and the set decorators have over the visual elements of the film. In films set in the contemporary world, this is much more of a straightforward task than setting a film in Roman Britain when costume, transport and the general everyday objects must all reflect the era in which the film is set. Lighting can also play an integral part in the *mise-en-scène* as mood and atmosphere are created by the use of appropriate lighting which, together with the camera work, forms the area of filmmaking expertise known as cinematography.

Some theoretical knowledge will always be of help when looking at film study as it provides a framework from which to approach your analysis of the texts. However, overreliance upon theory at the expense of original and independent thinking should be avoided. You should aim to use theory as a starting point for a discussion or a debate or to back up a more general point. What MS4 is most definitely not is an exam which asks you to apply theory after theory to a set of texts looking for similarities or differences in the use of genre, narrative or language. Among those general film theories which are relevant to the study of narrative you might consider using in Section A example are:

- Tvetzan Todorov's Narrative theory
- Robert McKee's Classic Five-part Narrative theory
- Roland Barthes' Narrative codes
- Claude Lévi-Strauss' Binary Oppositions theory

INFORMATION BOX *i*

The theories of Todorov and McKee refer to the common narrative structures found in film. Each is laid out in detail in the Introduction to this book on page 10.

Binary oppositions occur when there is a presence in a media text of opposing qualities or forces. Through these, the audience is able to attach a greater sense of meaning to what they see; for example, the role of a hero is much more clearly defined and recognisable when set against the presence of a villain and a scene of horror in a film has a heightened effect on the audience if it is placed next to a scene of innocence and peace in the editing process.

Codes help us again with building up our understanding of a media text and attaching meaning to what we see. Barthes offers five codes which are of interest to us here:

- *Action codes* How our understanding is created by the action which takes place in a text (e.g. smiling, winking or punching) and are all actions that the audience understands as meaning something.

continued

- *Semic codes* How our understanding is shaped by our knowledge of the semiotic devices we see in a text. Among them are the use of colour, intertexuality, verbal and non-verbal communication; in fact most of what you did during your preparation for the unseen media text task for WJEC AS Level MS1.
- *Symbolic codes* How our understanding of a text comes from recognising metaphorical and allegorical references such as in the case of George Orwell's *Animal Farm* which is a metaphorical representation of the events of the Russian Revolution.
- *Cultural codes* How our understanding of a text comes from our understanding of the cultural context of that text; for example, we in Britain derive more understanding from an American text since we share many cultural similarities than we would of, say, a Middle Eastern text, the context of which would be more culturally different.
- *Enigma codes* These are perhaps the most intriguing from a film point of view. At several places in the telling of a narrative the audience will encounter many unanswered questions, riddles and mysteries, called enigmas, which are strategically placed by the director to achieve two goals. First, to add an extra level of interest to the text which will keep the audience interested; and second, to reveal in an indirect way information which we may need later on to allow all the pieces to drop into place. These enigma codes are frequently used in thriller and horror media texts.

These theories will form a solid starting point from which to approach the text section when using narrative and will help to demonstrate that there are often several different theories, some of which are quite different to each other, which may be applied to the same text and offer different perspectives. Attaining the right balance, however, between your own original writing and using theories such as these poses something of a dilemma, and you may be wondering why you need to refer to theories such as these at all. However, consider when consuming a film or a TV text how much meaning comes from the narrative. A basic approach of beginning, middle and end can help us to understand how the plot unfolds and, when looking at a text in which the plot unfolds non-chronologically, a plot which you could argue challenges the conventional manner in which stories usually unfold, a more complex map of the narrative may be called for. It is through narrative that audiences are exposed to the notion of cause and effect, the idea that an action in a media text has a reaction or a consequence. This is fairly evident in fictional media where, for example, in a soap opera a character divorces her husband (action) and the husband sinks into a depression (consequence or reaction) but it is also used in factual media, such as in the case of news items in which the known facts are presented (e.g. an earthquake wreaking havoc on a city (the action) followed by the impact this has on the people who live in that city (the consequence)). However, as is the case with all theory, they should be used sparingly to provide a starting point from which to develop and explore your own autonomous responses to texts or to back up the points you have made.

However, the real success of your answer will come from your critical autonomy, your own reading and exploration of the texts and your use of theory simply as a means of substantiating your points rather than as forming the main part of your answer. In order to see how we might do this, we perhaps need to look at some specimen questions for Section A.

Specimen questions provided by WJEC for Section A (text)

1. Explore the ways in which your chosen texts reinforce or challenge typical representations of gender. [30]

Or:

2. How do your chosen texts use genre conventions? [30]

(*source*: http://www.wjec.co.uk/uploads/publications/6052.pdf)

These questions are clearly focused upon the need to concentrate on either gender representations in the first case or genre in the second. The decision about which question to answer will most likely depend upon the three texts you plan to write about in your response. In this example, the focus is the horror film genre which, at face value, may lead you towards the second question, and this would certainly make sense. However, it is also the case that among film genres, the representations of gender in horror are certainly noteworthy, and students who have sufficient knowledge of both how males and females have been represented in horror and how many of the stereotypes have been challenged may well be tempted to venture down the path

continued

of the first question, not least because this is perhaps the less obvious path to take.

Categorising horror as a genre

Any effort to relay the history of the genre of horror in this book cannot possibly do justice to the topic. Suffice it to say that stories which scare people pre-date cinema by several hundred years and, since the earliest years of cinema, horror has been one of the most enduring, alluring and controversial types of film, and yet to define a horror film remains a difficult task. Some people regard a horror film as one with lots of deaths in it, but if this were enough to consign a film to the genre of horror, most of Arnold Schwarzenegger's action film output would be included, and yet it is not. Another measure may come from the presence of a masked killer who victimises innocent teenagers on a bloody and violent rampage, and yet many horror classics such as *Frankenstein*, *The Wolf Man* and more modern offerings such as *The Omen*, *Misery* and the previously mentioned *The Shining* feature no such character. The truth is that there is no single homogeneous genre; certainly there are some features as identified earlier in the table on page 218 which many horror films tend to have (e.g. certain dark settings, a predilection for stabbing weapons, a certain music or musical style) but, rather like many genres, horror consists of several subgenres: slasher, vampire, ghost, alien, etc. In an interesting study, Charles Derry (1977) counters that there are three types of horror. He terms these the horror of personality, the horror of the demonic and the horror of Armageddon.

In the horror of personality, the source of the horror (or to put it more simply, the 'bad stuff') originates from within humanity itself. It is quite simply the evil that people can do; it is internalised within the human and not, as Derry himself argues, "'externalised' through the presence of a monster or a demon". In *The Dark Knight*, a film which revolves around the age-old battle between the forces of good and evil as embodied by the heroic and gallant Batman (Christian Bale) and his nemesis, the sinister and malevolent Joker (Heath Ledger), much of The Joker's character can be traced straight back to the repertoire of horror. He is masked (both in terms of his garish face paint and by his disfigured mouth) and very enigmatic, as are many film psychopaths such as Michael Myers, Jason Vorhees and Freddy Kruger. He has a fondness for knives and sharp instruments which facilitate a more invasive and slow death and, in common with many murderers found in horror, takes a sense of pride and enjoyment in his work. The source of the horror in *The Dark Knight* has entirely human origins, just as it does in other films such as *Hallowe'en*, *The Silence of the Lambs*, *Psycho* and *Saw* which are perhaps more instantly recognisable as horror films.

Figure 4.3 The Joker – a typical horror villain

In the horror of the demonic, Derry argues that the source of the horror is a higher evil force; it literally emanates from a supernatural force of malevolence akin to the Devil. Stories of the struggle between God and the Devil with humanity caught in the middle are among the oldest on the planet and are found in many horror film classics, among them *The Omen*, *Rosemary's Baby* and *The Exorcist*. The story of Dracula which was remade in 1992 by Francis Ford Coppola tells of a Transylvanian Count, Dracula, who was tricked by his enemy into believing that his wife committed suicide while he was fighting to defend the Church. In anger at this betrayal, he turned his back on God and sold his soul to the Devil. His penalty was that he should live eternally in the shadows and was made to survive entirely by drinking human blood in the tradition of the mythology we know as the vampire. Several hundred years later, Dracula believes that his dead wife is reincarnated and he sets out to find her. Dracula's powers include the ability to become invisible, to change his shape and appearance and to control the minds of animals, all of which are as a result of the relationship he has with this supernatural force of evil.

Derry's final classification, the horror of Armageddon, requires a little more explanation. The term 'Armageddon' is usually associated with the end of the world, but for Derry, the horror of Armageddon is found in any film where normality turns abnormal and the world we think we know is replaced by a more unknown, enigmatic and darker reality. Derry argues that such films act as a metaphor for the potential destruction made possible by nuclear proliferation (the Armageddon link) whereby all we knew and took for

continued

granted would be wiped away and replaced by uncertainty and bleakness. Some obvious examples of this might be *Outbreak*, the *Terminator* franchise or even *Jaws* (despite their reputation, great white sharks are not quite the voracious predators they are made out to be in the film and the events of Spielberg's masterpiece are very much abnormal). In *The Descent*, a group of female pot-holers lose their way in a series of underground caves. When some are injured, paranoia and fear take hold of the group and when it seems that their plight cannot get any worse, they are attacked by a race of subterranean humanoid creatures called crawlers who need their blood to survive. These events clearly represent a sense of Armageddon from the characters' points of view if, as Derry suggests, Armageddon represents the end of any concept of normality.

The most conventional way to approach the study of a genre could be through the presence of certain visual signifiers. These may be called icons or common features and this is something which could quite easily be done for the horror genre with its preponderance of castles, dark rooms, stabbing instruments, masked killers and gruesome death although, as we have seen in Derry's work, we may need to go further into subgenres to gain an understanding of the genre more fully at this level.

One very interesting alternative approach is taken by Thomas Schatz (1981) who approaches genre from a point of view which does not begin with the visual icons but rather from the other features found within the film's text. This approach has the added benefit of being able to identify generic similarities from among films which visually, in terms of their icons, have little or nothing in common. Schatz identifies two categories which he terms "Genres of Order" and "Genres of Integration". The table below outlines the main features of these genres.

	Genres of Order	Genres of Integration
Space/ environment	Contested	Civilised
Resolution	Conflict and violence	Consensus and emotion
Characters	Male-dominated	Maternal
Society	Individualistic	Familial
Examples	western, gangster, horror	musicals, melodrama, comedy

It is perhaps this theory, together with many of The Joker's horrific acts, that allows us to argue for the similarity between *The Dark Knight* and other films which are seen to belong to the horror genre. That is not to say that *The Dark Knight* is the same as a horror film, it is just that it is one of the many genres of which it demonstrates features. This is becoming more common in films as they seek to create a new angle from which to tell their stories and to maximise their audiences by offering something of more than one genre in a film release.

GENDER IN HORROR FILM

Among film genres, horror has been the centre of much attention and research in terms of the way gender is represented. Women in horror have arguably been represented in ways which both challenge and reinforce many of the existing gender stereotypes to a greater extent than in any other genre. When you consider victims in horror, you invariably think of a female, whether it is a teenage girl in a slasher movie or a virginal, prim gentle-woman, the victim of choice of the illustrious Count Dracula. Nevertheless, it was a film with horror elements that first introduced the idea of a female action hero. The character of Ripley in the *Alien* franchise helped revolu-tionise the way women were represented in film and laid the foundation for future female action heroes such as Lara Croft. Stereotypical represen-tations of women were again challenged in horror films such as *Misery* (1990) and *Single White Female* (1992) where women assumed the role of the psychopathic killer, and in the former case, the role of the victim also challenged the stereotype as it was a male.

In *Bram Stoker's Dracula*, a film which may conceivably be seen as a hybrid between gothic horror on the one hand and a love story on the other, gender plays a very important part. While the motivation for horror in many nar-ratives can be traced back to evil or malevolence, the overwhelming motivation for Dracula, played by Gary Oldman, is his love, and it is this which leads to the consequences of horror. Dracula is represented at various times in the film as passionate and charming, and in his polite wooing of Mina (Winona Ryder) and his more animalistic wooing of Lucy (Sadie Frost) he proves to be quite irresistible. Herein lies a criticism of the female characters within the film. Jonathan Lake Crane argues that the female characters in vampire films in general are seduced a little too willingly. *Bram Stoker's Dracula* is, he argues, a film "where women are dying to sleep with a monster . . . whenever women think about Dracula, they seem compelled to don décolletage and writhe against any available male should the Count be otherwise detained. No film is more obvious in demonstrating

continued

the vampire's appeal to the fairer sex" (Lake Crane, 1994, p. 70). This representation may in some ways be accounted for when contextualising the story. *Dracula* was a Victorian gothic horror classic and, in seeking to remain faithful to the source, Coppola could be accused of reinforcing a somewhat outdated stereotype of women both as easy prey for the charming male and, since both of the two principal female characters are kept women yearning longingly for marriage, as the stereotypical wealthy female lacking ambition or career aspirations. The sexualisation of women is heightened even further by the presence of Dracula's three sensual and voracious brides to whom the previously faithful and honourable Jonathan Harker (Keanu Reeves) succumbs while captive in Dracula's castle.

The male characters, on the other hand, engage in more masculine endeavours. Their occupations are science, the military, medicine and business. Never slow to engage in a fight, the male characters again represent the stereotypes one would expect from a story written in Victorian times. Nevertheless, their efforts to defeat the Count by their conventional methods generally fail as his powers prove too much for them and it is only after the intervention of Mina that Dracula finally allows himself to be defeated so that he may die and be reunited with the soul of his wife.

In a sense, then, it could be argued that in *Dracula*, the end to the horror is brought about by a female character after the male characters have failed to bring about his demise. In a highly influential study, Carol Clover argued that in slasher movies there is a key character, called the Final Girl. While maintaining many of the features associated stereotypically with femininity in certain parts of the horror narrative (for example, she is fairly weak and naive, and spends a lot of time screaming), the Final Girl pulls through in the end. In fact, in films such as *Hallowe'en*, *Scream* and *Friday the 13th*, the Final Girl does so much more. She manages to unmask the killer, she injures him, protects others, and succeeds where other male characters fail. Although she may not kill the villain (after all, he is needed for the sequel), she does gain a victory within that narrative context and crucially she survives. Parallels may thus be drawn between this character from the modern slasher film and the character of Mina in *Bram Stoker's Dracula*.

Unfortunately from the point of view of this example, *The Dark Knight* would appear to offer less to our investigation of gender. The film is overwhelmingly male-dominated with the only significant female character, Rachel, played by Maggie Gyllenhaal, adopting a fairly conventional role as the protagonist's girlfriend which, in a super-hero action movie will invariably bring her into the line of fire of the villain, as indeed it does. However, the film offers much in the study of masculinity. The character of Batman has in the recent film offerings had to be completely repackaged following the camp and rather ineffective portrayal of the character in the 1960s TV series.

Figure 4.4 Repackaging Batman, from 'Camp Crusader' to fearsome and menacing Caped Crusader

The modern Batman as played by Christian Bale speaks only when required and then in a gruff and forceful manner quite in contrast to the Batman of the TV show and to his own alter-ego Bruce Wayne, who represents a decadence far removed from the warrior-like approach of Batman. In *The Dark Knight*, Batman inflicts pain on others, and in his scene with The Joker in the police interview room this borders upon torture. In every way, Batman is the masculine hero, and this juxtaposes well with the stunning Oscar-winning portrayal of The Joker by Heath Ledger.

The Joker, whose persona is based loosely on a clown, is brought to a different level in *The Dark Knight*. Ledger injects a kind of femininity, or at least a lack of masculinity which serves to make The Joker much more terrifying. Whereas Batman's violence is externalised and brutal, The Joker's is subtle and at times even humorous, a criticism which led some to question the granting of the film its 12A certification in the UK. Batman is masculine and strong and, as Bruce Wayne, he is impeccably smart in the James Bond mould and possesses the same charm, wit and sophistication, whereas The Joker is unkempt, wears mismatching colours, smears poorly applied make-up on to his face (the wearing of make-up is not an exclusively feminine trait in the modern world but one which is still often associated by some with those in touch with their feminine side!) and, when needing to assume a disguise to gain access into the hospital, he poses not as a male doctor, orderly or office worker, all of which would be unremarkable in a hospital, but rather as a stereotypical nurse complete with short white skirt and stockings. In many ways The Joker may be argued as having something in common with the modern metrosexual male. He is single (presumably), has high disposable income, not necessarily legally acquired however, he has his clothes tailor made – the absence of a label in his clothing is remarked upon as adding to his anonymity – and he is concerned with his

continued

appearance: although it is untidy and unkempt, it is deliberately so. He is also concerned to maintain his reputation. Not only is The Joker Batman's nemesis, but he is also his polar opposite in terms of the way masculinity is portrayed in the film.

The final film in this example, *The Descent*, is rare among horror films; in fact it is rare in film texts in general, in that it features an almost entirely female cast. This in itself is remarkable since, although women have long featured in horror, it is usually as a victim. To have an entire female cast means that the typical roles of horror characters, victim and hero, must necessarily be female characters. What *The Descent* offers is an interesting look at how a group of friends find themselves in a truly awful situation, the setting for many people's ultimate nightmare, being trapped underground and lost in a series of caves. Matters are made worse when people start to get injured and then finally they are attacked by the crawlers, cave-dwelling creatures which presumably have evolved in parallel with humans in their enclosed setting. As a British horror film, *The Descent* may be counted among other classics such as *The Wicker Man* and *28 Days Later* but there are influences of the American 'schlock' horror franchises of *The Texas Chainsaw Massacre, Hostel* and *Saw* with very graphic and horrific scenes of death. Where *The Descent* is useful for this example is in how the female protagonists are extreme sports enthusiasts which may be regarded as a departure from the stereotypical representations in film and how their friendship is represented in the film. Throughout most of their traumatic experience the characters stick very closely together, forming a kind of 'sisterhood' and a bond which helps them survive the fact that they are lost and the injuries some of them sustain. At this point they even begin to see the funny side of their predicament. The characters show, however, that they are in possession of the decidedly masculine traits of strength, resilience and ruthlessness when the crawlers attack them. Sarah, played by Shauna Macdonald, could again be argued to assume the Final Girl character as she survives, a little ambiguously perhaps, and manages to defeat many of the crawlers, the source of the horror, in the process. Liza Lazard (2009) criticises the film's portrayal of feminine friendship as being heterosexualised and counters that the film offers little by way of challenging the heterosexist view of femininity; in other words, the friendship is very conformist to the dominant heterosexual ideology of British society.

Many of the stereotypes one might expect from a group of women are refreshingly absent in *The Descent*. Cattiness and bitchiness and the usual findings from research into women in horror, such as naivety, mental instability and as purely victims, give way to practical and clear-sighted thinking, strength and fortitude. In many ways, the characters may be seen as British extensions of Ripley from the *Alien* films or as Thelma and Louise in Ridley

Scott's film of the same name. We could conceivably be seeing the dawn of a new era of strong women in horror as female characters who challenge some of the existing stereotypes have been seen recently in the psychopathic character of Amanda in the *Saw* films. *Hostel II* (2007) features a character called Beth who is lined up to be a victim in the film but in a bizarre twist turns perpetrator, and 2009 saw the sequel to *The Descent* in which Sarah once again faces the feral and gruesome crawlers.

To conclude, this section has looked in detail at some of the main arguments which might be made in the context of generic features and gender representations of three films for the WJEC Section A: Text question. It acts as a guide to some of the issues and debates which might be included. Naturally your answer will depend upon the texts; they may not even be films which you are using to answer Section A. However, from this section you should have acquired an understanding of how to be critically autonomous, use theory and other people's ideas to help back up or form your answer without relying upon it and to make sure that you comment on each of your texts, at least one of which must be British and at least two contemporary; that is, no older than five years from the date you sit your exam.

References

Branston, G. and Stafford, R. (2010) *The Media Students' Book* (5th edn). Routledge.

Clover, C. (1992) *Men, Women and Chainsaws: Gender in the Modern Horror Film*. Princeton University Press.

Derry, C. (1977) *Dark Dreams: A Psychological History of the Modern Horror Film*. A. S. Barnes & Co.

Lake Crane, J. (1994) *Terror in Everyday Life: Singular Moments in the History of the Horror Film*. Sage.

Lazard, L. (2009) ' "You'll like this – it's feminist!" Representations of strong women in horror fiction'. *Feminism and Psychology*, 19 (1): 132–6. Sage.

Schatz, T. (1981) *Hollywood Genres; Formulas, Film Making and The Studio System*. McGraw-Hill.

Case study 4.2

Figure 4.5 Newspapers

Media industry:	Newspapers	Context
Texts	*Daily Mirror*	Tabloid, Labour-supporting, owned by Trinity Mirror
	The Times	Broadsheet, conservative, owned by News Corporation
	Metro	Free paper, mid-market tabloid

The focus for Section B of MS4 is the concepts of industry and audience. (Remember: Section A looks at the style and content of the texts themselves, applying the concepts of language and representations.) Although news, and newspapers in particular, is an area of Media Studies which tends to inspire less enthusiasm from students than other, more entertaining media (e.g. computer games, film and music), it is a very good media industry from which to approach Section B. This is due to the following:

- The almost unique way in which newspapers are regulated.
- The challenges of declining readerships.
- The adoption of digital and interactive media, such as online versions of their products.

News remains a very important part of our lives. News programmes occupy prime TV and radio slots, millions of copies of newspapers are bought and read in the UK every day, 24-hour television news is now part of the packages which come as standard on Freeview and subscription satellite and cable TV packages, and one of the first things people do when they go online is check to see what's happening in the world on one of the many internet sites dedicated to news.

Audience focus

DAILY MIRROR, THE TIMES AND METRO AND THEIR AUDIENCES

You are no doubt familiar with the idea that media products have target audiences, a group of people from within a much larger potential audience which the producers of media texts have in mind when they plan and produce a media text. Having a target audience for a text makes the job of deciding the content and the style easier, especially if those responsible for audience research have accomplished their job well and have managed to build up a clear impression of the interests and preferences of the audience as well as their habits and personal lifestyle choices. This enables producers to make sure that the content of the text they are making appeals to the target audience as much as possible.

Due to the competitive nature of newspapers, they are niche market products. That is to say that generally speaking a newspaper cannot hope to be all things to all readers, and so each identifies an audience and aims its content at that audience. In the case of national newspapers, this target audience is defined largely by such factors as occupational type (manual, professional), social class, political persuasion (both ideological and in terms of party politics), and age and gender. The table overleaf details the target audience profile for the two national newspapers being used in this case study.

continued

The target audience profile for the *Daily Mirror* and *The Times*

	Daily Mirror	The Times
Gender	Male	Male
Age	18–25	40–50
Social class	Working class	Middle class
Typical occupation	Skilled and unskilled manual	Professional, management
Political persuasion	Left-wing leaning, Labour	Right-wing leaning, Conservative*

The Times, as a product of the News Corporation media conglomerate together with the *Sun*, publicly switched its allegiance from Labour to the Conservatives in 2009. This could be due to the possibilities either that *The Times* moved ideologically further to the Right and away from the ideological standing of the Labour Party or that Labour under Gordon Brown moved to the Left away from the ideological standing of *The Times*. Either or even perhaps both of these theories are possible, or maybe it was simply that News Corporation, sensing how unpopular Labour were in late 2009, decided to switch allegiance in the hope of attracting the wider audience of Conservative supporters which opinion polls seemed to suggest existed in this time period and into the election of May 2010.

Readership and competition

Despite having such clearly defined target readerships, national newspapers do have broader appeal. It would be wrong to suggest that those targeted are the only ones who actually read the newspaper. Each one will have much more variety in terms of the actual audience, and likewise, all 18 to 25-year-old working-class males who support Labour do not always buy or read the *Mirror* exclusively.

Since they are so politically biased in their content and these two newspapers target such vastly different audiences, it would be almost impossible to imagine either of them trying to steal each other's readers by adjusting their content to cater to the other's audience. This, with a red-top popular newspaper and a quality title, is an extreme example, but how about two more similar newspapers such as *The Times* and the *Daily Telegraph*? These two newspapers do seek to attract audiences that are more similar and mobility between the readers of these newspapers is much more likely, but both newspapers are old and recognised titles and have established loyal readerships that become the focus for the content, the niche; therefore, in addition to age, gender becomes defined partly as readers of *The Times* or the *Daily Telegraph*.

In the case of local newspapers, they tend not to demonstrate the same partisan approach to politics as do their national counterparts and, since the demographic they target is more a matter of geographical location than any other factor, the niche they target is a local community or the population of the town or city they serve. They adopt a more matter-of-fact approach in the way they present their content compared to the heavily biased and, in the case of the red-top newspapers, sensationalist approach of the national titles.

Metro, as a free newspaper, is perhaps less concerned with the idea of selling but it still has to maintain its circulation so that the companies and organisations which buy advertising space in its pages and who provide the main source of revenue continue to do so. In terms of audience, *Metro* adopts the same less partisan and less opinionated approach as local newspapers.

News values and newsworthiness

One of the main debates which surrounds newspapers and certainly one which students should be aware of when analysing any news media is that of newsworthiness. This becomes clearly important here since the question on newsworthiness is very much focused upon what the audience will regard as newsworthy. There are literally millions of events which occur in the world every single day. These events themselves are not actually news unless they are reported as such. Clearly then a decision has to be made about which events will become news and which will be ignored, or to put it another way, which events are newsworthy and which are not.

It is perhaps understandable that you might think that an event is news-worthy if it is important or if it is a major event. However, this is only partly satisfactory as an answer because it doesn't account for the fact that events which may seem very important to some people are actually not very important to others. When, for example, the football team you support is relegated, people who do not follow the sport of football, much less your own team, are likely to disagree with your assessment of how important that particular event is. Even large events which affect a lot of people, such as a rise in unemployment in China, may not be deemed sufficiently impor-tant to feature prominently in a newspaper in the UK, especially if a different event which does affect the UK to a greater extent has also occurred, although, in practice, both the football and the unemployment stories would probably feature in the newspaper somewhere.

continued

The news media is not one homogeneous mass; rather, it is a body of different outlets related by their pursuit of news stories but in many ways quite different. There are many significant differences among newspapers themselves and among newspapers and other sources of news in the media such as internet news and broadcast news in terms of the content, style and delivery designed to appeal to a target audience. It is important to recognise therefore that not all events which could form part of the news content have the same appeal to all target audiences.

Figure 4.6 The *Daily Star* and the *Guardian* cover the same news story in different ways

Audiences are an essential part of the communication process but the relationship between media producers and audiences may hardly be said to be an equal one. Generally speaking, the communication is largely one-way, although many more opportunities for interaction from audience to producers now exist through the 'red button' and through innovative websites such as YouTube or Twitter, and the distinction between producer and audience has become a little less distinct. However, with newspapers, the communication process is overwhelmingly one-way.

Agenda-setting: the passive audience?

The Marxist point of view as espoused by theorists such as Louis Althusser is that the media, along with other institutions such as the government, the judiciary and business, operates as an apparatus for the power elite, members of whom own and control the media to legitimise and maintain their power over the rest of society. It is perhaps more the remit of the social sciences to evaluate that particular perspective but the effect of the communication process on the audience is certainly something with which media students should be concerned.

One particularly relevant area for the study of news is the issue of agenda-setting, the idea that the media, in this case the news media, not only tells us the message but in the fact that it is telling us that very message, as opposed to any of the other messages that may have been recounted to us in the news, we are also being told that the message is important. This is most obviously demonstrated in a newspaper by the lead story on the front page. Figure 4.7, which is based upon work in the area of agenda-setting by McCombs and Shaw (1972), shows how the public's perception of reality is shaped by both reality itself and the 'reality' as portrayed by the media.

Recent examples of how the public's perception of reality may have been shaped by the media include the increased threat both in our country and abroad from terrorism, the numbers of migrant workers and illegal immigrants coming to Britain, threats to our safety from knife crime and

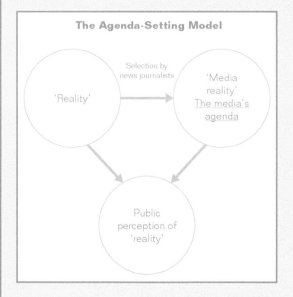

Figure 4.7 The Agenda-Setting model

continued

antisocial behaviour especially from 'feral' gangs in 'hoodies', and the dangers of binge drinking. These are all very real issues and the newspapers are right to report on them; however, it has been argued that the serious nature of some of these issues has been exaggerated, which has led to a blurring of the extent to which they really are the issues they are made out to be. The newspapers have been criticised for their coverage of these issues and this point of view is further strengthened when the content of investigative documentary programmes such as *Panorama* or *Tonight* which increase the coverage the issues receive are considered along with the news coverage. Stan Cohen in his work *Folk Devils and Moral Panics* (2002) argues that when the values which a society cherishes are threatened by "a group, a person or an attitude", then the result is a moral panic. In his documentary *Bowling for Columbine*, Michael Moore investigates the belief that the purchase of guns in America is due to a moral panic over security and immigration, and that the Columbine High School shootings of 1999 were linked to a moral panic over 'goth' culture, violent films, video games and rock music.

INFORMATION BOX *i*

The agenda-setting model suggests that we are told what is important by the fact that it is in the newspaper, and that the amount of coverage given to an event or an issue has an impact upon our perception of the item or issue's importance. In this example, the news is presented in such a way that readers are being subtly told how they should feel about the news items, in both cases a sense of disgust and revulsion.

Figure 4.8 The front cover of *The Times* presents news in such a way as to subtly tell the reader how to feel about the story

If moral panics exist as described above, a reason for this is the influence the media has on its audiences. If we look at a number of hypothetical events or issues such as those which could occur on any given day, each one labelled X1, X2, X3, etc. (see Figure 4.9), then the coverage given to each in the media may help us to decide how important each event is. The perception of importance of each event or issue as shown in the final column is to scale. Clearly, because of its coverage, X2 is the item which would be seen by the audience as the most important, whereas X4 (which is given far less coverage) is seen by the audience as having less importance. This model not only works for news in general, taking all news media into consideration collectively, but can also be useful when analysing the content of one newspaper compared to the content of another. What one newspaper sees as important a different newspaper may not.

INFORMATION BOX

In agenda-setting, the amount of coverage given to each item of news can influence us in attaching importance to events. If something attracts extensive coverage, the model suggests that it must be important and relevant.

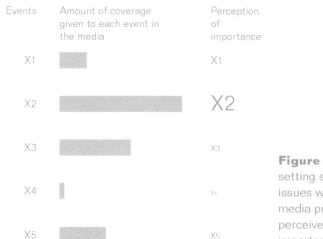

Figure 4.9 Agenda-setting suggests that issues which are given media prominence are perceived as more important

Source: adapted from Nicholas and Price (1998), p. 66.

MS4: TEXT, INDUSTRY, AUDIENCE

X2 might be a story connected to immigration or the rise of Islamic Fundamentalism, issues which currently receive extensive coverage. X3 could be a fairly important story such as the resignation of a football manager or a company announcing record profits. In contrast, X4 is a story which receives minimal coverage and so is perceived by the audience as having far less importance.

ACTIVITY

Conduct some research into the content of three newspapers. Consider how they address their audience and use news articles within as evidence. You should consider the following points:

- The audience the content is aimed at (political ideology, gender, age, etc.).
- How the content or style of the articles is helping to form opinions about the items and not simply informing the audience about what happened.

What are newspapers for?

As a method for communicating items of news, it is hard to imagine a less efficient way than newspapers. When you read a national daily newspaper, you are in fact reading about events which happened the day before and the content cannot be updated once it has been printed. The audience in the modern digital world have demonstrated a desire for more immediate and up-to-date news reporting. So bad are newspapers at achieving this that the owners, eager to remain a player in the huge news media market, all operate online versions of their products which, unlike their printed cousins, can be updated frequently. (Online versions of newspapers will be examined in more detail later in this chapter.) News may be sent via text message to a mobile phone which incidentally is likely to have access to the internet where online news sites are readily available from news broadcasters such as SKY, CNN or the BBC, and from newspaper producers. TV news is broadcast 24 hours a day on channels such as BBC News 24 or SKY News, and radio news is usually broadcast at least once every hour. In both instances of broadcast news, any breaking events can be incorporated at any time should they be deemed to have enough news value.

For a list of the online versions of English-language national and local newspapers in the UK and in the rest of the world, visit http://www.thebigproject.co.uk/news. The site provides links to each newspaper's homepage.

So where does this leave newspapers which, apart from the addition of photography and colour, have remained almost unchanged since they first appeared in the seventeenth century? Well, a useful staring point is to analyse the word 'newspaper'. If we assume that news is generally taken to mean new information, then newspapers are generally misnamed. Well over half the content even of the most information-packed newspapers consist of advertising and non-news items such as interviews, obituaries, entertainment and so on. In a content analysis conducted for her book *The Language of Newspapers*, Danutah Reah found that in their editions of Thursday, 6 September 2001 the *Guardian* had a news content of 41 per cent while for the *Sun* the figure was only 28 per cent (Reah, 2002, p. 3). Notwithstanding the ephemeral nature of newspapers, the content is, if these figures are found across the full range of British titles, mostly not actually news.

Newspapers then should perhaps be more accurately called 'journals'; that is, a record of the day they are printed, or more accurately the events of and the issues which existed on the day before they were printed. Newspapers are, according to Danutah Reah, artefacts of the commercial and political world, and, it may be argued, the ideological and cultural world too; that is to say, they are a physical record or a journal which reflects the time in which they are printed and not a serious competitor for the kind of interactive, dynamic and up-to-the-minute news found elsewhere.

Nevertheless, newspapers are still sold in the UK in their millions every day. There is still quite an appeal to sitting down with a favourite drink and biscuit to read the paper. Thousands of people enjoy them on coffee breaks at work and for many, Sunday afternoons just wouldn't be the same without the crossword or the previous day's sports results. In these respects, news-papers quite undeniably have the edge over TV or internet news. Circulation figures are measured by the Audit Bureau of Circulation (ABC) and are published in a variety of places. Perhaps the most accessible source for the

continued

data is the *Guardian* newspaper, which publishes the figures for each month's sales in its media supplement. The table below shows the figures taken from the *Guardian* for August 2009 with an analysis of the circulation compared to the same month from 2008.

Newspaper	August 2009	August 2008	Percentage change
Sun	3,128,501	3,148,792	−0.64
Daily Mirror	1,324,883	1,455,270	−8.96
Daily Star	886,814	751,494	18.01
Daily Record	347,302	390,197	−10.99
Daily Mail	2,171,686	2,258,843	−3.86
Daily Express	730,234	748,664	−2.46
Daily Telegraph	814,087	860,298	−5.37
The Times	576,185	612,779	−5.97
The Financial Times	395,845	417,570	−5.2
Guardian	311,387	332,587	−6.37
Independent	187,837	230,033	−18.34

These figures make for interesting reading. The only national daily newspaper not to suffer a fall in sales over the 12 months to August 2009 was the *Daily Star*. The general trend for sales of national daily newspapers in Britain is according to these figures one of decline. It would be too simplistic to say that the decline was due entirely to the fact that news is more readily available elsewhere since, as we have seen above, newspapers have not really been at the forefront of news dispensation for some time. There are other reasons which may account for this decline. It is possible that during the economic downturn and recession which affected most of the world throughout 2009, people decided that little luxuries such as a daily newspaper were dispensable as they sought to cut down on expenditure, or perhaps it was due to the closure of small newspaper shops which have for years provided delivery services and which, unlike supermarkets, tended to be located in heavily populated areas within walking distance of most of the residents. However, the current dominant position of the supermarkets, which are argued by many to have adopted aggressive competitive practices, has also jeopardised the future of local newspaper shops. On the other hand, the fast-paced modern world does not, for many, allow for quite so many coffee breaks and quiet moments in which a crossword or anagram puzzle is attempted. Perhaps it is a combination of all these factors but, whatever the reasons, an industry cannot afford to sustain such losses over a long period of time; indeed, the most pessimistic commentators estimate that the next five to ten years will effectively see the extinction of the traditional daily newspaper.

Free papers: *Metro*

Against this rather gloomy backdrop of decline and a shift towards inter-active news services is *Metro*, which literally millions of people take (and sometimes read) while travelling on the public transport network. Having hit the seats of London transport in March 1999 as a free colour newspaper, *Metro* is now available in 16 of Britain's biggest cities. Drawing on an idea from Sweden (where the franchise was Metro International), this product from the Associated Newspapers stable (which also produces the *Daily Mail*) actually outsold the newspaper which inspired it, which became a rival in late 1999 in Newcastle. It has also triumphed over a couple of significant rivals in London during the past decade: both Associated's *London Lite* and Murdoch's *thelondonpaper* closed within weeks of each other in 2009. *Metro* currently rates as the largest free newspaper in the world and with a daily distribution of 1.3 million copies is the fourth largest newspaper in Britain (with the *Daily Mirror* in its sights). This is made more remarkable when you think it is only distributed in urban areas.

Although the *Sun* still has the larger circulation, it almost seems only a matter of time before *Metro* exerts its influence further. This is partly because 'exerting its influence further' here only means giving away more copies, a solution which is at present not available to those newspapers that are paid for. While the national bought newspapers are all fairly loyal to a political party, notwithstanding the *Sun*'s dalliance with both main parties over the past 20 years and the *Guardian*'s rather unexpected support of the Liberal Democrats in the 2010 election, and with tight and clearly defined ideal types of reader which act as a constraint in terms of content and style, *Metro* could not be more different, as its own press release points out:

 Metro's news stories are tightly written, so that the reader can take in all the key facts quickly. And *Metro* has no political axe to grind.

continued

This is not the only way in which *Metro* differs from other newspapers. Few people choose to take it home; instead, it is designed to be read almost as a relay whereby people read it on their daily commute and leave it on the seat for the next occupant to pick up. Short on detail and bereft of opinion, *Metro* offers general items of news simply presented with a healthy dose of travel, health and internet issues and, of course, plenty of advertising.

ACTIVITY

What might the advantages be of a newspaper that, put simply, doesn't take much reading? Think of how newspapers are principally funded.

This significant change in models of usage and readership, on top of the dynamic created by giving the newspaper away, has produced excellent results economically. The audience statistics suggest significant penetration into 'hard-to-get' groups such as the young as well as sound returns among working people (who are largely the ones using the transport network). This resulted in very sound advertising receipts and *Metro* adding, unwittingly, to the pressure on London rival and Associated Newspapers stable mate, the *London Evening Standard*. The *Standard* had been published as a paid circulation since 1827 but in selling their majority shareholding to the paper in January 2009 Associated Newspapers were paving the way for an unprecedented transformation. In October 2009 the *London Evening Standard* became a free newspaper and immediately doubled its circulation.

The future of the industry: declining sales and new technology

It is not inconceivable that national newspapers, many of which have already lowered their cover prices, may also follow suit and enter into the realms of giving their printed product away free. This may not seem to make sound business sense; indeed, giving away your main product for a business could be regarded as economic suicide. Coca-Cola would not remain the company it is if it were to offer free cans of its products every day, but Coca-Cola does not obtain around 70 per cent of its revenue from advertising, whereas newspapers do. Therefore, the main concern is to attract advertisers who pay for space in the newspaper and the only way it can do this is to keep the circulation figures high. In adopting the free approach, newspapers would only be mirroring the model similar to that of commercial radio stations whose product is in essence free to consume (provided you have access to a radio or the internet) and which relies almost entirely on advertising revenue.

ONLINE NEWSPAPERS: THE GLIMMER OF HOPE

Nevertheless, drastic as this approach may be, it may still not be enough to save the newspapers from the decline and extinction towards which many feel they are heading. One glimmer of hope is offered by online news which is a market that newspaper producers are looking to exploit. Currently, online versions of all Britain's national newspapers are available, and these, unlike their printed counterparts, offer news which can be updated as events occur. However, there are major issues for the owners of the newspaper in terms of switching their content to an online version. Primarily, although advertising space is available, the websites are in essence free to access for the consumer. Although the costs of printing and distribution are no longer applicable, the actual cost of gathering the news and presenting it online such as paying journalists and photographers, buying news items from agencies such as Reuters or photographs from photo journalists and the cost of maintaining a website all have to be met.

One solution to this issue which has already been adopted by some American newspaper sites is for the consumer to pay a subscription for accessing the news through a newspaper's website. In an article in the *Guardian* newspaper on 6 August 2009, Rupert Murdoch, CEO of News Corporation, the organisation behind the *Sun*, *News of the World*, *The Times* and *The Sunday Times* and one of the foremost media conglomerates in the world, made it clear that it is his intention to charge a subscription for online newspaper content.

Rupert Murdoch plans charge for all news websites by next summer

The billionaire media mogul *Rupert Murdoch* suffered the indignity of seeing his global empire make a huge financial loss yesterday and promptly pledged to shake up the newspaper industry by introducing charges for access to all his news websites, including

continued

This is a brave move by News Corporation. To charge for something which had previously been available for free is risky. Media industries are not generally known for being forgiving when costly errors are made, and so it demonstrates how perilous the production of newspapers is in the UK for such a step to be taken. The risk is further heightened by the fact that other newspapers are not currently planning to introduce subscription charges for their online versions and by the fact that news is available from other online sources. In the case of the BBC, the website is part of the package together with BBC TV and radio which we already pay for through the licence fee, and so too the individual browsing the internet in search of news; there are other options besides having to pay a fee for news content.

However, what this argument does not take into consideration is the loyalty that many readers feel towards their newspapers. Newspapers are not just vehicles for news; indeed, the points made earlier in this section argue that they do not do this particularly well, but with their political and ideological bias (which is not acceptable in TV news as it must remain neutral), cultural and entertainment content and the mode of address designed to appeal directly to their idealised type of reader, for many, reading a newspaper is not just about reading *any* newspaper, but reading *their* newspaper, the one which speaks to them and their interests and views directly. Organisations such as News Corporation are banking on this loyalty and reader identity with newspaper titles continuing into their online news ventures. The BBC, as a Public Service Broadcaster, and other TV-based news sites such as those provided by SKY and ITN offer news websites which, like their broadcasts, are bound to be impartial and politically unbiased, and if the history of newspapers in the UK tells us anything at all, it is that this is not necessarily how the audience want their news presented to them.

Of course, even if there is an explosion in the online newspaper market and charging proves to be successful, this may not solve the problems facing the print versions, and the shift to online versions of newspapers may serve to preserve the organisations which produce newspapers without saving the actual print versions themselves if they fail to offer attractive opportunities to those who pay for advertising space.

MODE OF ADDRESS the language and style in which a media product is presented so that it appeals directly to its intended audience. For example, red-top popular newspapers adopt a chatty and informal mode of address to appeal to their readers.

IDEAL TYPE OF READER an absolutely typical and average member of the target audience. Newspapers tend to present their content aimed at this idealised person and so all the articles, despite being produced by a number of different contributors and on a variety of topics, has the same mode of address and reflects the ideology, interests and perspectives as the ideal type of reader.

PUBLIC SERVICE BROADCASTER a media organisation which is funded directly by the public and which has a duty to provide a service. All sections of the public both majority and minority audiences must be addressed and the organisation is non-profit in its nature. The BBC, funded by the public through the licence fee, is such an organisation. The lack of advertisements on the BBC is a direct result of its non-profit creed.

ACTIVITY

- Examine the ways in which newspapers differ from other news media. What constraints exist for newspapers which online, TV or radio news are free from?
- What is your assessment of the online news revolution? Do you regard it as a glimmer of hope for newspapers or a further nail in the coffin of the printed versions?

continued

Regulation

Like all media, newspapers are regulated and controlled by a regulatory body, in this case the Press Complaints Commission (PCC). The PCC was set up in 1991 and consists of 17 members, most of whom have no connection with the newspaper industry, which ensures that the PCC is independent of the newspaper industry. However, some of its members are connected to the industry so, at the same time, the PCC allows newspapers to have an element of self-regulation which helps to ensure the freedom of the press and enhance the role of the press within a democratic society. This makes newspapers unique among media types in that its regulatory body is made up partly of people involved in the industry. Governmental interference in the press is not only a threat to democracy but could also be an inhibiting factor in allowing journalists to call to account those in positions of power and authority.

The main functions of the PCC are twofold. First, it has a Code of Practice which acts as a kind of guide for editors and reporters to follow (in theory at least). If a newspaper flouts the Code of Practice, the PCC will then fulfil its second function and adjudicate on a complaint which can be made by a member of the public or a person about whom an article is printed, and it may ask the newspaper to print its adjudication and to publish an apology. The full details of the PCC's code of practice, its members and current cases may be found on its website (www.pcc.org.uk).

Specimen questions provided by WJEC for Section B (Industry and Audience)

The following are typical of the types of questions you can expect to get in your exam (you have to answer two in Section B from a choice of four). It is clear that with newspapers as a case study you would be able to address any of the following questions:

1. Briefly outline the ways in which your selected industry is regulated. What impact has regulation had on your chosen texts? [30]
2. Explore the impact of digital technologies on your selected industry. [30]
3. How do your chosen texts attract their audiences? [30]
4. Explore the marketing strategies used by your selected industry. Use the examples you have studied to illustrate your answer. [30]

(source: http://www.wjec.co.uk/uploads/publications/6052.pdf)

For each question list three or four points you think would be central for a successful answer. For example, for Question 1 you might include:

- PCC: regulation and self-regulation – definitions, debates around the different types of regulation.
- Code of Practice: guidelines for content and journalistic practice – effect on types of stories covered.
- Regulation and new technologies – discuss the role of regulation in the context of online editions.

These are just a few of the many issues and debates that are related to newspaper audiences and industries media but it is important to look at them as examples. Students preparing to use newspapers for MS4 will need to be familiar with three newspaper titles and have a general appreciation of what those newspapers represent, their readerships and their place within the newspaper industry, and copies of each should be examined for more details and examples of current stories. These should allow the student to look at audience- and industry-based issues (if newspapers is one of the media chosen for Section B; any student choosing newspapers for Section A will need to be much more focused upon the text itself, the use of language, employment of news values and generic considerations).

Newspapers constitute an area of the media which has an uncertain and unpredictable future. What is certain, however, is that people's desire to know what is happening in their world and to know it quickly remains undiminished. It is the responsibility of those people involved in telling us what we want to know to find ever more efficient and reliable means to satisfy this desire while remaining viable and ensuring their own survival in the process.

References

Cohen, S. (2002) *Folk Devils and Moral Panics* (3rd ed). Routledge.
McCombs, M. and Shaw, D. (1972) 'The Agenda-setting Function of Mass Media', *Public Opinion Quarterly*, 36 (summer), 176–87.

continued

Nicholas, J. and Price, J. (1998) *Advanced Studies in Media*. Nelson.
Reah, D. (2002) *The Language of Newspapers* (2nd edn). Routledge.
The Guardian online. www.guardian.co.uk. 6 August 2009.

Useful websites

http://www.pressgazette.co.uk/section.asp?navcode=161
http://www.abc.org.uk/
http://www.newspapersoc.org.uk/
www.pcc.org.uk

Typing the name of a newspaper into a search engine will lead to its online version.

Case study 4.3

COMPUTER GAMES: KILLING YOURSELF TO LIVE

Figure 4.10 Computer games. Left to right: *Call of Duty 4: Modern Warfare, Just Dance* and *Football Manager 2010*

Media industry:	Computer games	Context
Texts	*Call of Duty 4: Modern Warfare*: first person shooter	Infinity Ward (US) Xbox, PS3, Wii
	Football Manager 2010: third person/manager mode	Electronic Arts (UK) Xbox, PS3, Wii, Windows
	Just Dance: music video game	Ubisoft (Fr) Wii

Audience: theory and practice

The statistic that more than 97 per cent of teenagers, boys and girls alike, regularly play computer games is a wake-up call to older parents and Media Studies students. Here is an experience as universal as prime-time TV once was. Even for the current generation of parents of teenagers, Sonic and Mario are as familiar as '*Corrie*' and *EastEnders*.

ACTIVITY

What were your first experiences of playing computer, console or video games? What games, what systems? Did you visit game arcades?

How have games changed since? What do you miss about the old days?

Philip Auslander writes about the mediatisation of modern life, the degree to which we see and talk about our lives in the same ways we talk about those lives created on TV or film. This suggests that our ideas of the real and the imaginary, even of fact and fiction, are breaking down or at least becoming blurred. Computer games are always looking to give us a more vivid and encompassing experience, and with video-quality graphics and surround sound it becomes more and more like you are there. To those outside of this experience the 'places' that we visit in computer games may therefore seem especially disturbing since they are often violent and urban.

continued

This leads to a 'job-lot' of panicked responses to content, as ultraviolent or problematically sexist and an almost total neglect of the ways in which these activities might be perfectly comprehensible and negotiable to those who play them. We visit dark and violent places in books but attention is not drawn to this by flashing lights and Dolby sound. Equally the zombie-like state of the avid reader is seen as 'absorption' in a valued activity. Part of the value here is attributed to the idea that when reading we are actively engaged, whereas the equivalent hour in front of your television, for example, merely makes you a 'spectator' and implicitly less active (or even passive!). Computer gaming seems, interestingly, to sit somewhere between the two since it involves both watching and doing.

ACTIVITY

What do computer games give you which is more than 'watching'? You may like to consider the difference between watching the cut scenes of a game and playing it.

Compare playing a game to watching a film and reading a book.

Which is most/least likely to be done with others?

Which is the most demanding and which the most relaxing?

Is reading a book justifiably the activity that is considered most valuable by other people/society in general?

While it may be fatuous to talk about the development of hand–eye communication as a rationale for hundreds of hours of Pro-Evo, it is vital that we address the essence of this 'consuming passion'. This will mean addressing those who do it a lot rather than those who do it a little or not at all.

ACTIVITY

Why do people play computer games?

Consider this as a research question. What other questions do you need to ask to get usable answers to this enquiry into the functions of gaming for computer gamers?

One thing which surveys of gaming tell us is the significant amount of time expended on these activities. This means that so-called 'digital space' has become very much a place where we are socialised, "where users learn about how to become consumers and how to become boys and girls . . . lessons about skills and values, and broad socio-cultural and political lessons about gender and social power" (Luke, 1996). The media has long been thought to be an important site of socialisation. Hartley and Fiske wrote in the 1970s about the 'bardic function' of television, for example, the special role that TV had for our 'tribe' in delivering cultural information. What is new is the horror that this cultural 'teaching' might occur through 'fighting the Vietkong', 'skippering Chelsea to the Konami cup' or entering the bizarre world of Second Life. It's as if all of our anxieties about an ever-changing world are met in the 'horrors' of digital culture.

ACTIVITY

'About gender and social power'

Think about your three favourite computer games and what they might be able to tell you about:

- Potential differences between the genders (in terms of status, attitude, character or role).
- Who more generally is important and/or has power in society.
- What should be valued and/or what 'works' or gets you reward.

Like any collection of games or pastimes, computer games potentially take us from childhood to adulthood, though perhaps with a greater edge since, despite age-limited certificates, the lines are blurred. It has meant that computer gaming has featured heavily in debates about what Sefton-Green (1998) describes as "concerns about the changing nature of childhood – or indeed about its apparent 'disappearance' ". The worry is that children are becoming less active, less outdoor oriented and more isolated (i.e. less social), and computer games can be blamed for all of these. Moreover, these negative implications come with an undesirable content into the bargain: a diet of sex, sleaze and violence to a hard rock beat. At the same time 'the media' is blamed for a broader sexualisation and commodification of

continued

childhood, when it should perhaps principally be charged with treating young people as a homogeneous group and thereby stirring up moral panic.

ACTIVITY

Narcotysing dysfunction?

One aspect of critical theory's attacks on the culture industry was to suggest that mass culture was a harmful drug that kept people helplessly addicted. Some have applied this argument especially to the popularity of computer games among young people.

Do you consider computer gaming a harmful activity (to your intelligence/mental health/social standing)?

In fact there are many more interesting things to explore and discover in the visceral video-quality graphical world of the computer gamer. These developments call into question our working definitions of concepts such as 'narrative' or even 'reading'. Yet the first thing to say is that much is unchanged. Games work within highly diverse but specific generic conventions, drawing on literary, filmic and other references across a range of cultures, utilising familiar structures of variation and repetition. Maligned, as all technologies seem to be, by critics as enemies of literate culture and reading in particular, it is interesting to first consider gaming as an active process of meaning making. Beavis (1998) puts it this way:

> The text literally only comes into existence when engaged by the reader/player. The reader is an active participant in the joint construction of meaning, with the meaning, or at least the action, created only through the player's physical participation. While each level has a prespecified configuration, and the traps, fights and puzzles are written into the program, it is also true that one never plays quite the same game each time, one never reads the same text twice.

One narrative aspect familiar to all gamers is point of view (here 'voice' becomes 'view') with the conventions of first and third person central to many games. The FIFA football franchise, for example, as well as offering numerous takes (literally camera angles) on the third-person experience, offers the 'Be a Pro' feature which puts you at the heart of the action in a developing career narrative. And during 'Be a Pro' gameplay you can switch between 'player' and 'ball' options to represent the experience of being at the centre of the action. Buttons also allow limited dialogue with team mates though the main language, as ever, is action.

The idea of immersion within this point of view is also true of the Football Manager series which attempts to create an accurate portrayal of professional football management giving you 'the greatest job on earth'. The game offers an overview of the action, presenting players with data and statistics about the success or failure of their team on the pitch. Thus the players' decisions have direct consequences upon the action they are witnessing, giving them a uniquely interactive experience. Equally the success of the franchise is based on the player's ability to feel the genuine tension and stress of management ("the most immersive pitch-side experience ever"), which is created through the painstaking building of teams and the perfection of tactics.

Figure 4.11 *Football Manager 2010*: the greatest job on earth?

continued

Modern Warfare 2, which offers a relentlessly first-person view, also offers masses of onscreen information, which needs to be effectively processed for optimum game performance. These include positions of destinations and enemies, health checks and inventories of equipment and ammunition. It's a screen reminiscent of the Terminator view in the film franchise and increasingly the offer to DVD viewers of advanced systems like Blu-ray. Here is a different kind of reading, which rather than promoting inactivity in fact promotes a differently active engagement. Perhaps this 'new' reading is closer to that which Barthes proposed was our relationship with the constructed environment when he wrote: "The city is a writing and he who moves through it is a kind of reader." So it is with these 'constructed environments' that gamers enter, visit, remake and transform.

ACTIVITY

Landscapes of the mind

Many computer games involve us in 'visits' to magnificently detailed locations in pasts, presents and futures, both real and imagined. What is this 'visiting' like? (How would you describe it?) What might we learn from these 'visits'? How do these visits compare with visits you make to real places?

Computer games are sometimes described as archetypal postmodern texts, since they offer explicit hyperreality worlds created out of simulacra, substance-less images. Some would argue that the changed consciousness that results from this is as significant as the change caused by the invention of printing in the mid-fifteenth century. For some, therefore, computer games are an essential part of a contemporary education since in playing computer games young people learn to deal with the media-saturated and digitally mastered reality they inhabit: a world of possibility, multiplicity and uncertainty.

It is argued that successful game playing requires a postmodernist sensibility, whereby players "are capable of working such chaotic environments from within, moment by moment". This is a considerable shift of perspective: "their domain is space rather than time. They exist within time, dancing across it, rather than being subordinated to it" (J. Johnson-Eilola, 1997, pp. 195–6). This last point may explain in a small way the degree to which real time is abandoned to game time: a common experience for young people and their parents. A game like *Call of Duty 4: Modern Warfare* will offer an immersing experience which even in its first phase as a structured set of single player campaigns will last for many hours. And this of course is nowhere near the end of it. Not only are there the almost endless possibilities of multiplayer online (and the potential of many more game scenarios) but once 'finished', the game is also open to the potential to be creatively replayed. This player of *Grand Theft Auto* (*GTA*) is typical:

> **Having completed the game the other day, I decided there wasn't much else to do, but to start the entire thing again. I completed the first few missions with no problem whatsoever, but then, probably out of impatience I started messing the missions up by just generally messing about on them, including punching the women in the face in 'first date'.**

(Dean)

continued

This response also opens up the thorny issue of in-game violence, a discussion that is familar to Media Studies students as the Effects Debate. Given that no research has established unequivocably the causal links between images and effects, we seem forever to be moving between a moral panic and a casual disregard. Most would agree that discussing in-game violence with the perpetrators makes good sense as does understanding that these are still texts to be read. It also seems likely that this will be best achieved if the whole gaming experience is better incorporated into what we deem valuable (and therefore 'valued') activity.

Specimen questions provided by WJEC for Section B (Audience and Industry)

Briefly outline the ways in which your selected industry is regulated. What impact has regulation had on your chosen texts? [30]

(source: http://www.wjec.co.uk/uploads/publications/6052.pdf)

To respond to this question consider the link between concerns over violence in games and the response by regulatory bodies. Has the form of regulation affected the content and types of games produced? Which audience is regulation concerned with – how does this link to audience theories?

ACTIVITY

Digital slapstick

Most of us who play computer games play games in which violence is a means to an end: a way of winning. What for you is the character and function of violence in computer games? (What is it like and what does it do?)

As the answer, of course, is 'it depends', consider the question for different games.

Is violence a necessary part of the games you buy and play?

Gee has argued that the relative freedom and plurality/multiplicity (openness) of games such as *Modern Warfare* and *GTA* (and even more online) offer the conditions crucial for active learning to take place:

- First, we "learn to experience (see, feel and operate on) the world in new ways";
- Second, "since domains are usually shared by groups of people who carry them on as distinctive social practices, we gain the potential to join this group, to become affiliated with such kinds of people (even though we may never see all of them, or any of them face to face)";
- Third, "we gain resources that prepare us for future learning and problem solving in the domain and, perhaps, more important, in related domains" (Gee, 2003, p. 23).

This is the basis on which Kendall and McDougall offer their studies of the ways *GTA* is 'used': it's about listening to the views of those who actively 'read' games because "as players of games they felt licensed to be creative and innovative". Like Dean earlier, Kevin is innovating:

> **A linear story is easier to understand but if you have an open world, you are making the story, you feel more involved definitely because you're going to places, you're having to literally get out and travel to see those places so you're getting to learn the area.**
>
> (Kevin)

With this clearly established critical perspective (this is not the voice of a mindless addict) we can better appreciate these professional academic responses:

> **Videogames offer narratives that are formative in terms of individual and social understandings of race, youth and citizenship in the modern, neoliberal, globalized world. They allow players to step into a new identity and to 'perform' the world from the perspective of an 'other', so the way in which that world, as well as that 'other' is constructed, is extremely important.**
>
> (Barrett, 2006, p. 96)

continued

What Kendall and McDougall call "this playing at the 'other' within the 'unreal' " is very much a theme in all of the responses of gamers:

> **What appeals to me about it? I think it's just real light-hearted fun and you can get a good laugh out of it even though it's crime and it's probably not morally correct, you know there's not really that much of a consequence you know? You just get to have a little bit of fun and have a little joke with your mates when you're playing it.**

(Dean)

This element is also that which makes the experience social since these 'performances' are the staple of the numerous blogs devoted to all these games. This notion of being centre stage is another indicator of the sophisticated way readers of all social classes 'get' the game (and through it other rule-governed activities in everyday life). There is also a playfulness here which contradicts the stereotype of the narcotised addict with the hyper-realism adding as much to the 'show'/spectacle as the isolation.

Figure 4.13 *Just Dance:* old-fashioned games

This is what allows us to explain why the other major innovation of the moment (alongside ever more convincing game graphics) is the modest and old-fashioned Nintendo Wii. Here again the attraction needs identifying. How in a world of high-resolution graphics and surround sound can we be transfixed by clunky cartoon characters playing ping-pong? In *Let's Dance* we are invited to disco along with a series of brightly coloured guys and chicks who take us through routines which are part gym workout and partly reminscent of your grandad dancing at your sister's wedding. Yet we keep coming back for more since we are actively reminding ourselves what family and friends are for. Just as *The X Factor* scores because it's something parents want to watch with their children, so *Let's Dance* offers kids something to do with their parents. It also further contradicts associations of computer games with inactivity.

References

Auslander, P. (1999) *Liveness: Performance in a Mediatized Culture.* Routledge.

Barrett, P. (2006) 'White Thumbs, Black Bodies: Race, violence and neoliberal fantasies in Grand Theft Auto: San Andreas', *The Review of Education, Pedagogy and Cultural Studies*, 28: 95–119.

Barthes, R. (1997) 'Semiology and the Urban' in N. Leach (ed.) *Rethinking Architecture*. Routledge.

Beavis, C. (1998) Computer Games: Youth culture, resistant readers and consuming passions. Accessed at http://www.aare.edu.au/98pap/bea98139.htm.

Gee, J. (2003) *What Video Games Have to Teach Us About Learning and Literacy*. Palgrave Macmillan.

Johnson-Eilola, J. (1997) 'Living on the Surface: Learning in the age of global communication networks', in I. Snyder (ed.), *Page to Screen: Taking Literacy into the Electronic Era*. Allen & Unwin.

Kendall, A. and McDougall, J. (2009) ' "Just Gaming": On being differently literate', *Eludamos. Journal for Computer Game Culture*, 3 (2): 245–60.

Luke, C. (ed.) (1996) *Feminisms and Pedagogies of Everyday Life*. State University of New York Press.

Sefton-Green, J. (1998) 'Introduction: Being Young in the Digital Age', in J. Sefton-Green (ed.), *Digital Diversions: Youth Culture in the Age of Multimedia*. UCL Press.

TV: the art of reinvention

Media industry:	TV	Context
Texts	*X Factor* (ITV)/*The Apprentice* (BBC)	Reality TV, convergence
	Torchwood: Children of Earth (BBC)	Scheduling
	Peep Show (C4)	Narrative and storytelling

The reasons that television survives as a mass cultural experience are many and complex but one stands out. It is the fact that television occupies a specific – one might say special – position within our culture; no social history of the twentieth century could ignore the impact of TV. Whether you visit a living museum of the twentieth century or your local IKEA, our 'living' spaces are orientated around the 'gogglebox/all-seeing eye/etc.'. No other medium has so many different names, which suggests it's something with which we have an uncomfortable even perhaps a love–hate relationship. When we speak of television therefore we are addressing very much an extended signifier which operates semiotically something like this.

Television:

- **Denotes**: the technical equipment, all of its output, a mass medium.
- **Connotes**: something oppositional – a source of information and entertainment, an asset and a danger, a social activity.
- **Myth**: much of the above has become enshrined in our culture – particularly the dichotomy of 'help' and 'harm'. It has been argued that television presents "social values as if they were social reality". This reduces the discussion of TV to its content and makes all of its issues those of representation.

Marshall McLuhan was particularly interested in the ways in which communication technologies developed in relation to one another and in relation to our needs and intentions. He theorised these relationships in a model he dubbed 'the tetrad' (because it has four parts). Actually they are four questions to ask of any communication technological innovation:

- What will it enhance?
- What will it impair?
- What will it recover/rejuvenate?
- What will it make obsolete?

Technological innovation led to predictions that television as we had known it was likely to find itself in slot 4's obsolescence. These innovations included ever more affordable and powerful home computers and ultimately laptops, films and now even TV programmes on demand, ever more powerful games machines, mobile phones and internet access, personalised video recorders (e.g. Sky+) and on top of all this the internet itself as a visual archive. All these innovations might have contributed to a slow but terminal decline in the importance of television. In fact there is a counter-argument which suggests that television is in a particularly healthy state and that its apparent competitors have paradoxically become its most significant benefactors. To understand why this set of events produced this rather unexpected set of results, we need to first remind ourselves of some key audience theories. We might summarise these as being of three types:

- text-based (effects) theories
- use and gratifications theories
- context-centred theories.

In the contemporary media context of developments in new technology which affect how we watch and use TV, the third set of theories is the most useful. For example, it reminds us that what we watch on television is often not television and that paradoxically, the use of PVRs (e.g. Sky+) actually increased the amount of television watched. Similarly, the massive popularity of games machines that need screens (and the bigger the better) has returned TVs to use.

> **CONVERGENCE** an attempt by industries to maximise profit by making a range of media companies work together, i.e. digital and satellite television and film channels, DVD, mobile phones, internet and broadband, personal computers.
>
> The ultimate ideal would be for the consumer (audience member) to be able to use one piece of technology (e.g. a PC, a mobile phone) for all their media needs (watching television, internet surfing, listening to radio programmes, downloading music and films, making telephone calls, taking photos, etc.).

However, there is also something more significant going on that is clear from the work of context-centred theorists such as Morley and Lush. Fiske summed up this approach very clearly when he wrote: "The important thing is rather than trying to understand what the text is, is trying to understand how people use it." Lull and his team of observers, for example, watched the behaviour of viewers in 200 American households. As a result Lull makes an important distinction between uses of television which he describes as structural and relational.

- The *structural* uses are about answering particular needs such as the need for information and entertainment or even company when alone. Here there is a direct relationship between the viewer and the programming.
- The *rational* uses were much more to do with organising the life of the home and the relationships within it. People used television as a regular social ritual, the context for a group discussion, even a way of being alone. Here the relationship between viewer and programming is indirect.

It is the second set of uses that has become increasingly significant both for mainstream broadcast scheduling and for significant innovations like the Nintendo Wii. For the latter the relative crudity and clunkiness of the graphics and game play (in the face of the almost virtual reality of Xbox and PlayStation 3) has been traded for the human interaction across demographic barriers. In addition, whereas the home Karaoke machine never broke retail records, the game player franchises 'Singstar' and 'Lips', even 'Rock Band', are coining it. At the centre of all these developments are the family and the TV, a traditional bond which many theorists had predicted would end due to the range of media on offer. One theory which explained how this breakdown was inevitable is fragmentation.

'Fragmentation' argues that multi-channel TV and all the attendant technologies for personalising viewing would inevitably undermine the mass audience with serious consequences for most of us in the medium to long term. These consequences reach out beyond the media sphere and into wider society. They include:

- The extinction of the PSB tradition/strand and ultimately of high-quality television content. The undermining of the old terrestrial flagship brands (this was also forecast at the original deregulation in the 1980s, along with Italian housewives stripping on TV).
- The end of the mass TV audience sharing significant experiences 'live' (sporting events, royal weddings, etc.).
- All kinds of social ills resulting from the undermining of the family with each family member retreating to his or her own 'viewing station'.

Obviously this is an exaggeration of the more pessimistic readings but it does demonstrate the flaw in the notion that cultural change can be rationally plotted and predicted. It is precisely the irrationality of people and systems that makes the process so fascinating; this may be seen in the example of *The X Factor*.

Specimen questions provided by WJEC for Section B (Audience and Industry)

Explore the impact of digital technologies on your selected industry. [30]

The TV industry is an ideal focus for this question as you can consider the range of different ways of accessing TV programmes, how TVs are no longer used only to watch TV, the concept of convergence and theories of fragmentation.

The following section on the resilience of mass audience TV programmes suggests – perhaps counter-intuitively – that the impact of digital technologies hasn't been as great as predicted.

The X Factor and the mass TV audience

The mass popularity and family viewing which *The X Factor* inspired was in direct contradiction to the theory of fragmentation; in 2009 *The X Factor* built an

Figure 4.14 *The X Factor*: homely charm or mass manipulation?

audience over a dozen weeks that peaked in the 'live' final at 19 million. Everyone looked for ways of explaining this phenomenon. Some thought of *The X Factor* as a special text (or especially dangerous) and then either referred to its 'homely charm' or slipped back to models of mass manipulation, the hoodwinked audience, to explain its popularity. This analysis didn't get very far simply because the format is in fact quite simple: a jury consisting of two wise older men and two presentable younger women judge as a dozen champions of the British public (chosen by Destiny) almost literally (and in a positive way) sing for their lives (or at least for the right to trade theirs in for a better one). This is not a new idea: it's *Search for a Star*, *New Faces*, *Opportunity Knocks* (ask your (Grand)parents).

The key is about finding contexts in which people will want to use your product. Interactivity must mean more than exercising your right to phone in; the challenge is to get your audience members interacting with one another in response to and as a result of their experience of your product. The Wii, for example, persuaded family members of all ages to clumsily take part in a bowling competition without balls and without graphical sophistication. One reason for the success of the Wii was that its marketing cleverly took a myth about family life – that families do things together (when they don't) – and tapped into a mixture of desire/hope/fear/guilt on the part of people who wanted to live up to the imaginary ideal.

This interaction is now of course more accessible via the World Wide Web and, the cynic would say, exploitable. Certainly a franchise like the X Factor leaves no stone unturned in its quest for new ways to connect with its audience: text messages, blogs, websites, support programmes on ITV3. The point is that this is more than new places to market, it is more profoundly embracing the reality of convergence culture to create a new model of what might be partly called a trans-media text: though very much with its nucleus on the terra firma of the Saturday night early evening schedule. It's partly also about learning a lot from *Doctor Who* with its family audience appeal, spin-offs and multi-platform presence and less from *Big Brother* (niche target audience of teens/young adults). Ultimately these interactions, this new model, were as confirmed by the attacks on the programme (such as the internet campaign which made Rage Against the Machine the Christmas number one in 2009 rather than *The X Factor* winner) as by the 19 million who watched the live final. In fact all of this very much corroborates the argument that the internet has changed everything, that, as Ross and Nightingale suggest, "the information age is changing what it means to be an audience". At the same time though it stops short of quite accepting their more strident assertion, "Audiences are learning how to *be* the media, how to net-*work*". Henry Jenkins still seems to provide the more balanced view: "The inter active audience is more than a marketing concept and less than a semiotic democracy" (semiotic democracy is Fiske's term for the process by which everyone makes their own meanings).

Torchwood and *Peep Show*: convergence and trans-media storytelling

In simple terms, where television is succeeding it is negotiating convergence on its own terms, enlisting potential competitor media as significant collaborators. This has necessitated a reinterpretation of the art of scheduling in the face of the decline of the 'static' live audience. Scheduling was once almost entirely about fixing broadcasting experiences to our routines and keeping us tuned to a single channel with a varied diet of favourite genres. Now texts are more discretely packaged, usually commercially endorsed experiences which can be accessed in a number of different formats at the audience's request in what has been called a 'Martini Media' after Martini's famous advertising tagline: "Anytime, any place, anywhere." And yet, at the same time they are more open-ended than ever before, seeping across media platforms, trans-media experiences in infinitely different combinations and routines. This new scheduling is partly a campaign of marketing and distribution (support programmes and websites build up the brand, etc.), but more interestingly it is also offering possibilities for the textual experience to be more dynamic and open-ended. Henry Jenkins has coined the term 'trans-media storytelling' for this "new aesthetic that has emerged in response to media convergence". The important point is that while scheduling was always an 'art' of sorts, it is now considered as part of what Jana Bennett, Controller of BBC Television, called the "creative revolution every bit as ambitious as the technical one we've seen".

If you want a case study look no further than the revival of that old sci-fi chestnut *Dr Who*. In a detailed and readable essay '*Doctor Who* and the Convergence of Media' (2008), Neil Perryman provides an extensive survey of how the BBC's decision to bring back the cult series unwittingly created a blueprint for addressing the new trans-media landscape. At the centre of the project is a commitment to the creative process, the creation of a 'factory' of ideas based around script writer Russell T. Davies and producer Julie Gardner. However, more telling is BBC Director General Mark Thompson's admission that "There's a coherent plan in place for the whole audience relationship with the content almost from the start." Here is the new 'scheduling' at the heart of the creative process. The idea is to abandon the linear model in all respects so that this is not simply an extension out across platforms or into related products and to embrace the creative complexity enabled by the trans-media context: not spin-off but – back-around-and-through. Perryman writes of "extra-value content and narrative complexity . . . by deploying a series of evolving and challenging storytelling strategies across a wide range of media platforms". It could be argued that this new dispensation which foregrounds a kind of formal hybridity renders a traditional concept like 'genre' almost redundant. *Doctor Who* bears a factory mark rather more than a generic code and this may be not so much a matter of franchise as auteurship.

Certainly if you identify something like *Torchwood* Series 3 (*Children of Earth*) as a text it is easy to see the 'Who' signature, which is mostly synonymous with that of the chief writer (since he is the easiest 'auteur' fit). As such, while there are sci-fi generic aspects to *Children of Earth*, genre had become sidelined by issues of form and identity, although it was a surprise even to star actor John Barrowman that pitching *Children of Earth* into a prime BBC1 slot for five consecutive nights became the item's most significant statement. For here the realities of the 'on demand' world proved, as Mark Thompson predicted, to be "creatively inspiring and liberating". In the same way that advertisers have been forced to rethink, well everything, Russell Davies and his team attempted a spectacular and unprecedented coup. Experiments with the 'for five nights' had been attempted with a concept very like *24* where the emerging story was, for example, happening over the 'real time' of the five days. Heavyweight crime dramas like *Above Suspicion* and *Silent Witness* do something similar over two and three nights, though the focus here is on intensity and focus.

The planning behind *Torchwood* was a little more open and creative, and, it must be said, encouraged by a soundtrack record of success: who'd have ever thought that by 2009 *Doctor Who* would become an established part of the BBC's Christmas Day schedule? *Torchwood's* planning may have run along the following lines:

- Given we have six hours of TV to make,
- and we have an established residual audience who will access this however we package it,
- and we have a brand/auteur identity which might at least turn heads,
- where is the sense of the conventional option of BBC2 every Tuesday at 9 p.m. for six hours (or even upping the ante to BBC1)?

Instead what you get is six hours of old-fashioned 'Earth in Danger' narrative, complete with social comment, political debate, human interest, fantasy, comedy and ultimately tragedy. You get convincing special effects, genuinely frightening aliens and a powerfully implausible ending yet which is thematically consonant with the general humanist and collectivist message of the franchise. But above all you get six hours of prime-time 'family drama', a substantial sci-fi narrative, which you know is very unlikely to be consumed 'live' over five nights. This is the antithesis of the argument that PVRs have made all slots potentially prime since it plays on the symbolism of prime time while carrying little risk to the time-shift audience. *Children of Earth* thus becomes an advertisement for and endorsement of the creative factory while at the same time conducting a high-profile argument for quality and variety in mainstream TV.

Figure 4.15 Promoting *Torchwood*

One of the ways in which this has been reinforced, which has irked both media commentators and audience members alike, is the BBC's rather more explicit approach to self-promotion. Something very like the old radio play list (where producers decided which records would be played on BBC radio) appears to be operating when guests are chosen for chatshows and even news magazine programmes (e.g. *Morning BBC*). Stars are identified when they happen to be starring in forthcoming BBC programmes. Equally, as we have suggested, this is now built into the ways in which programmes converse with their audience.

Thus a hit show like *The Apprentice* offers straightforwardly a weekly one-hour report on hours of action which leaves us and 'Surrallon' to match words and actions in very much a courtroom style, though as a 'who-didn't-do it' since s/he who fails to dare, loses: and before we have time to fully digest Surrallon's verdict (and whether we agree) we are whisked off to BBC2 where a second panel (consisting of a cross-section of the funny, the famous and the business-savvy) subjects these judgements to a kind of lightweight judicial review. And if that's not finished, the wheel comes full circle on the following morning with the 'This week's loser' interview exclusive to Radio 5 live and including a phone-in. This is important because it returns us to real time and the realisation that reality TV is still 'made', which means 'recorded', 'edited' and neither 'pure' nor 'simple'.

The cult sitcom *Peep Show* continues these arguments about multiple formats and the notion of stylistic identity being individual rather than generic. Here is a show that has always attracted critical acclaim but for most of its six-year run has seen very unimpressive viewing figures, not many more than a million viewers until the latest run (2009). Although it has not always been a given, the show has persisted for a number of reasons which include the quality of the work itself, the positive critical reception and the sense that it is an investment in the developing profiles of Mitchell and Webb. A jump in audience figures for Series 6 (to 1.8 million) may suggest Channel 4's patience is paying off though the switch to an earlier time slot of 10 p.m. perhaps also suggests accessing a bigger teen audience. However, the other supporter of the programme has been the consistently high sales of series DVDs.

Although it has many of the trademarks of classic situation comedy including a traditional situation (an American version was unsurprisingly called *The Odd Couple*), *Peep Show* works around substantial series-long and trans-series narratives. A series is not just six encounters with our quirky friends but rather six chapters in an ongoing set of stories. The fact that the programme's stylistic signature is the use of point of view to allow us intimate access to what our favourite characters see reinforces the integrity of the show – as innovative and distinctive (it has also been claimed that this artiness prevented the show from finding a wider audience). The DVD 'box set' format (which in this case is a single, slim, coloured case per series) therefore perhaps better suits the *Peep Show* identity than any evening slot can, even with a catch-up on your PVR.

Todorov (1969) argued that "a world without a theory of genre was unthinkable since genre integrates the reader into the world of the characters and prepares us for a certain kind of reading". In other words, genre delineates the boundaries

Figure 4.16 *Peep Show*: traditional sitcom with trans-series narrative

of the possibilities of meaning, reducing complexity and enabling the text for us. In this context *Peep Show* seems hardly to have a generic identity at all since all of these functions appear to be delivered elsewhere, through identities that are formed in more specific individual contexts, of form and of style of performance. Todorov also pointed out that genres exist in historical contexts which allow their particular stories. It may be that the era of television genres is over or at least needs significant renegotiation.

References

Jenkins, H. (2003) 'Interactive Audiences', in V. Nightingale and K. Ross (eds) *Media and Audiences: New Perspectives*. Open University Press.

McLuhan, M. and McLuhan, E. (1992) *Laws of Media: The New Science*. University of Toronto Press.

Perryman, N. (2008) '*Doctor Who* and the Convergence of Media: A Case Study in Transmedia Storytelling', *Convergence*, 14 (1): 21–39.

Ross, K. and Nightingale, V. (2003) *Media and Audiences: New Perspectives*. Open University Press.

Specimen questions provided by WJEC for Section A (Text)

How do your chosen texts use genre conventions? [30] or perhaps a similar approach to a different concept: *How do your chosen texts use narrative conventions?* [30]

(source: http://www.wjec.co.uk/uploads/publications/6052.pdf)

These Text questions are as applicable to the TV case study as to the earlier example of film (they could also be applied to computer games).

This demonstrates one of the challenging areas of this exam: deciding which industry to use for which question. To make this decision (fairly quickly and under the added stress of exam conditions!) you need to consider the questions holistically, as clearly your decision about Section A (or B) will then mean that you cannot use that industry again for Section B (or A).

Consider what combination of questions and industries will best demonstrate your sophisticated understanding of media concepts and debates – perhaps a discussion of Texts (trans-media narratives) which analyses the very latest developments in narrative and genre in response to new technologies would do this.

PASSING MS3: MEDIA INVESTIGATION AND PRODUCTION

5

The components

■ The research investigation (1400 to 1800 words, 45 marks)
■ Production work (individual or group, 45 marks)
■ Evaluation (500 to 750 words, 10 marks)

Rationale: what are the aims of the coursework unit?

It is important to consider the aims of this unit before you start. This will help you to understand what is being assessed and therefore what is expected in a successful piece of coursework. It is a mistake to think that the coursework is predominantly 'practical work' with the written element as an add-on of lesser importance. In this coursework unit the written components (research and evaluation) are of equal value to the production work. One of the main aims of the unit is to integrate the two:

■ The research investigation lays the foundation for the production work.
■ The production work is a way of testing the ideas in the research.
■ Both the research and the production work demonstrate your understanding of Media Studies concepts.

These aims are clarified in the exam board assessment objectives; MS3 is assessed against three AOs (there are four across the A level as a whole) which state that students must be able to:

■ **AO2** Apply knowledge and understanding when analysing media products and processes, and when evaluating their own practical work, to show how meanings and responses are created. **[8.75%]**

- **AO3** Demonstrate the ability to plan and construct media products using appropriate technical and creative skills. **[11.25%]**
- **AO4** Demonstrate the ability to undertake, apply and present appropriate research. **[5%]**

The percentages show how these objectives are weighted in relation to the assignment. AO2 and AO4 relate primarily to the research investigation and evaluation, AO3 to the production work. There is some area of overlap though; for example, the ability to 'apply and present appropriate research' will be demonstrated through the production work itself as well as the written investigation.

Synoptic assessment

MS3 is a synoptic unit – it draws on all the knowledge and skills you have developed at AS and A2 including the key theoretical concepts, research skills and technical ability.

At MS3 you will demonstrate:

- research skills
- ability to use specialist media terminology
- technical and creative media skills.

You will also have the chance to:

- explore an area of the media which you have chosen and are particularly interested in
- work independently as well as part of a team.

In addition to considering the AOs, looking at the mark scheme is a useful way of preparing for a successful piece of coursework – it helps you to understand exactly what the examiner is looking for.

The mark scheme

Each of the three elements of the coursework has a separate mark scheme which directly relates to the AOs. Each mark scheme is divided into four levels (grades are never used in exam marking) with a range of marks applying to each level. For each level there is a marking descriptor, explaining what should be present in the work to achieve each level.

The mark scheme for production makes explicit reference to the link between research and production work showing how important it is to consider the two as integrated.

Level 4: 36–45

- Excellent ability to plan and construct media products.
- Sophisticated technical and creative skills.
- Sophisticated ability to use the research investigation to inform the product.

At the top of Level 3 (31–35) the requirement is for 'good ability' in these areas while the top Level 2 (18–21) asks for 'some' ability.

Quality of written communication

In each of the mark schemes there is also a reference to the 'quality of written communication'. While this is not an English course there is the recognition that ideas need to be expressed clearly with attention to structure and accuracy (e.g. dates, terminology, use of references).

To look at the mark schemes in full go to the exam board website – or ask your teacher.

The marking process

The marking of coursework is different to that of other assessed units as the completed work will be marked by your teacher. A sample of each centre's (school, college) work is then sent to an exam board moderator to check that the mark scheme has been followed correctly. Although your teacher can offer help and guidance throughout the coursework process, he or she won't be able to tell you what mark you have achieved – you will receive this with your final A level results.

Preparation stages

Before deciding what your area of investigation – and therefore your practical work – will be it is worth considering some of the restrictions on what you are able to do as well as what kind of approach will work best for you. Think about the following.

Your choice of production task will determine whether you work as part of a group or individually.

The exam board guidelines state:

> **Digital media (web sites) and print based productions (newspapers, magazines, advertising campaigns etc.) must be undertaken individually.**
>
> **Audio (radio) and audio-visual productions (TV, Film) may be undertaken either individually or in small groups of no more than 4 students.**

Therefore in choosing your production task you need to take into account:

- Whether you want to work in a group or individually.
- What production you did at AS – you cannot do the same media form for A2.
- Your existing creative and technical skills – and how you might successfully develop these skills.
- What particular areas of interest in the media do you have? Remember: your research investigation is directly linked to the production.

What production work did you do for the AS coursework?

- What did you enjoy about it? What was difficult or frustrating?
- Did you work in a group – if so, did you find that it suited you? How would you go about improving your performance as part of a team? The ability to work well in a small group is likely to be important throughout your academic and work experience so it is definitely worth considering this option.

Clearly, working independently or as part of a team requires different skills – all of which are important in your development as a student.

Individual research investigation and group work

The importance of communication within a group from the very beginning of the coursework is clear when you consider the need to allocate a different – but related – area of investigation for each member of the group. Each group member must produce an independent research investigation but, together with the rest of the group, it must create a detailed investigation into a particular area. This isn't as difficult as it sounds! For example, if the production work is going to be an extract from a reality TV show, then the research could be divided up as follows:

- An investigation into the genre conventions of reality TV.
- An investigation into the construction of narrative in reality TV.
- An investigation into the representation of masculinity in reality TV.
- An investigation into the representation of family in reality TV.

The individual nature of each research investigation will be further emphasised by the focus on different texts within the reality TV genre.

The research investigation: what is it?

The specification states that the research investigation must:

- Be text based (one or two texts).
- Have a clearly defined focus (be in depth rather than wide-ranging).

- Be structured around one of the following concepts: *Genre*, *Narrative* or *Representation*.

Choosing your topic area for the research investigation

Choosing an area for your research can be one of the hardest aspects of the project, but it should also be one of the most enjoyable. It is a chance to investigate an area which you are interested in; to set the agenda for your own studies.

- Is your focus going to be contemporary, an exploration of a text from the recent past or a historical example? There is no requirement for the text to be contemporary but you should consider how your investigation will link to your production.
- Can the text be defined as a media text? The definition will be through form, technology, platform, audience.
- Is it a text which is easily available for you to study?

There are a variety of ways to choose your text and area for investigation. The following examples illustrate different ways of developing your initial thoughts and testing your ideas within the context of the relevant media concepts.

Choosing through text

One way of approaching this project is to choose a media text with which you are familiar and interested in researching further. A mind map can be a useful framework for constructing an initial review of the text (see Figure 5.1)

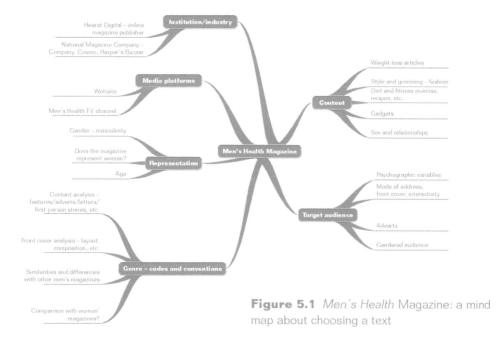

Figure 5.1 *Men's Health* Magazine: a mind map about choosing a text

Once you have completed outlining your initial areas you can then start to narrow down the research to conform to the requirements of the investigation. Study the mind map on *Men's Health* and, using a table, organise the different areas into the relevant concepts – genre, representation and narrative. It is immediately clear that genre and representation are the most applicable concepts here. There is an overlap between the two concepts which suggests that these are very rich areas to look at.

POSSIBLE RESEARCH INVESTIGATION TITLES

An investigation into the **representation** of masculinity in *Men's Health* magazine, with a particular focus on the December 2009 issue.

An investigation into the **genre conventions** of men's magazines (*Men's Health* and *GQ*).

Choosing through genre

A different way of approaching your selection would be to start with a genre that you're interested in (e.g. the TV crime drama) (Figure 5.2).

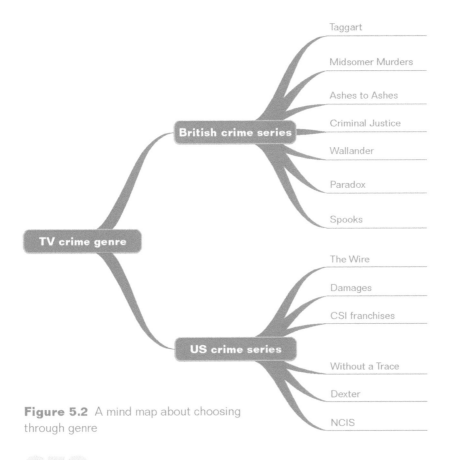

Figure 5.2 A mind map about choosing through genre

Once you have a range of possible texts, you can start to categorise them further. This will help you to narrow down your choice to one or two texts and decide how suitable a programme might be for your research as well as develop your ideas. This process could be done through a thought shower, a mind map or a table.

Form

Series	Serial/mini-series	Franchise	Hybrid genre
Taggart, The Wire Midsomer Murders, Dexter, Without a Trace NCIS, Spooks, CSI, Ashes to Ashes, Wallander	Damages, Criminal Justice, Paradox	Ashes to Ashes, CSI Miami, CSI New York	Paradox (crime/SF) Spooks (crime/spy thriller)

Subject

Police	Government agency	PI	Other
Taggart, The Wire, Midsomer Murders, Ashes to Ashes, Criminal Justice, Paradox, Wallander	Spooks, NCIS, Without a Trace, Dexter, CSI	None	The Wire, Criminal Justice (judicial system), Damages (lawyers)

Character focus

Central hero	Group	Pair	Other
Midsomer Murders, Wallander	Taggart, Spooks, NCIS, Without a Trace, CSI	Ashes to Ashes, Paradox	Dexter – anti-hero; The Wire – focus on different groups (police, drug dealers, gangsters, etc.) Damages – hero and villain roles unclear Criminal Justice – focus on police, lawyers, social worker

Figure 5.3 *Criminal Justice* (BBC) and *The Wire* (HBO): unconventional in form and content

Although this clearly isn't a scientific sample of the contemporary crime series, reflecting on your categories will raise some interesting points. In relation to the previous tables these would include:

- None of the programmes feature private investigators (something which used to be very popular). Following this up suggests some other examples: *The No.1 Ladies' Detective Agency* (BBC, series of films, none scheduled), *Mayo* (BBC, comedy/crime drama, 2006 to 2007), *Rosemary and Thyme* (ITV, gardening detectives, 2003 to 2007).
- Following on from this, *Harper's Island* (US, 2009, shown on BBC3) has an 'amateur' detective and is an interesting genre hybrid (thriller/slasher).
- A common characteristic of the genre seems to be a long-running series (often spawning franchises) centred on the police – or other officials who work in a group.

Programmes which seem unconventional are: *Criminal Justice, Damages, The Wire, Dexter* in broadcast form, structure and content.

Testing a proposed area: an investigation into the narrative structure of *Criminal Justice*

Structure area of investigation by selecting areas of the concept (narrative) which are relevant:

- *Criminal Justice* follows one crime and examines how it affects all those involved – the accused, victim, police, lawyers, social services.
- The plot is structured over a series of five episodes.
- Each series is self-contained but some of the same characters appear across series.

Therefore relevant areas would include open and closed narratives and how that constructs audience positioning.

Linked production: The credit sequence for a new TV crime series.

Suggested research titles:

- The **representation** of gender and identity in vampire TV series.
- The development of **genre conventions** in the vampire genre (TV and Film).

Linked production: The credit sequence or opening sequence for a new vampire TV series.

A research project into the recent popularity of films and TV series which feature vampires illustrates some of the different approaches to discussing the relationship between the media and identity. This type of analysis may be structured in the following ways:

- The representation of different identities: vampire texts are a rich source here because they tend to focus on themes around the family, nationality, gender and sexuality.
- The way in which identity is constructed through opposition to the 'other' (them); vampires are 'other' because they are non-human but are often used symbolically as a stand-in for other fears in a society at a particular time.
- They also show how the reaction to the 'other' has changed over time. Many vampire stories emphasise the possibility of moving between human and vampire, suggesting that the line between the two isn't that hard to cross.

The following case study covers a wider range of areas and texts than you would need to focus on in an investigation; it is intended to indicate some of the possible approaches to such a study.

Case study 5.1
SOME CONTEXT

Vampires in film and TV: the third wave (2008 to present)

A renewed interest in vampires in popular culture has been evident in recent years. These new entries have been notable in their subversion of some of the most familiar and apparently rigid rules of the genre, the shift in identification and sympathy to the non-human, the setting, which is contemporary

continued

or future societies rather than the past, and the more explicit treatment of vampire/human love affairs.

Recent examples include:

True Blood (US, HBO, 2008–)
The Vampire Diaries (US, CBS, 2009–)
Being Human (UK, BBC, 2009–)
Cirque du Freak: The Vampire's Assistant (US, Paul Weitz, 2009)
Twilight (US, Catherine Hardwicke, 2008) (and sequels)
Let the Right One In (Sweden, Tomas Alfredson, 2008)
Daybreakers (US, Michael Spierig, Peter Spierig, 2010)

Vampires in the media: the second wave (1980s and 1990s)

Clearly the current interest in vampires in popular culture exists within a context; they are close relations to the development in gothic horror – aimed primarily at a youth audience – in the late twentieth century. Films such as *The Lost Boys* (US, Joel Schumacher, 1987) and *Near Dark* (US, Kathryn Bigelow, 1987), the TV series *Buffy the Vampire Slayer* (US, 1997–2003) (based on a less successful film from 1992) established some of the themes, styles and characteristics evident in the more recent examples. These include the reinvention of genre rules, a contemporary small-town setting, concern with issues around the family, gender and sexuality. (In both *The Lost Boys* and *Near Dark* the male hero is attracted to a female vampire who has to be rescued and made human before they can be together. Buffy's love interest is Angel, a vampire, but one who has a soul and a conscience, making him at least part human.)

The themes of identity evident in these examples are structured around a system of oppositions:

- Law and order against criminality and anarchy.
- Nature and deviance.

These themes are then addressed through a narrative which centres on the family and teenage sexuality, using these as concepts to explore what is acceptable to society and what needs to be rejected. The fun and attraction of vampire films is that the border between the acceptable and unacceptable is constantly broken down – the vampires seeming to move between the two sides of the divide. The hero's family in these films is non-traditional in some way and vulnerable to attack from the vampire. In contrast the vampire 'family' is a secure and stable unit demonstrating traditional gender roles, such as the patriarch and the maternal woman. In contrast the vampires also represent chaos and anarchy, a threat to the civilised, law-abiding society, but this is part of their glamour and excitement, providing the temptation for the hero to turn into a vampire.

These seeming contradictions – where the 'other' is more attractive than the recognisable and reassuring – are usually resolved at the end of the film. The narrative is structured around the battle between human and vampire for the love of the female vampire; the human hero wins, the vampires are vanquished and the narrative conforms to the conventional heterosexual resolution. Therefore, despite the fact that the vampires are attractive and charismatic they are ultimately unacceptable to society (and the audience).

Count Dracula: the first wave (1890s)

The genre conventions we now recognise in vampire texts were established (drawing on myths and legends) in *Dracula* (1897), the gothic horror novel by Bram Stoker:

- The character of Dracula is 'foreign' and doesn't belong to a specific country – he is able to travel freely across borders.
- Dracula inspires terror and desire in his victims.
- Dracula attacks both male and female victims.
- He is 'undead'.
- He can only be killed by daylight or by a stake through the heart.
- Garlic and crucifixes are effective weapons against him.
- He has no reflection.
- Dracula must be 'invited in'.

The character of Dracula has been the focus of many attempts to explain the audience's fascination with this genre. Much of this work has examined the way in which he operates as a symbol for discussing various taboos and anxieties in society – these have tended to focus on issues of identity such as nationality and sexuality, with the vampire challenging accepted definitions and boundaries. In *Reading the Vampire* (1994) Ken Gelder describes it thus: "A vampire's function is to cross back and forth over boundaries which should otherwise be secure – between humans and animals, humans and God, man and woman." This analysis suggests that we like vampires so much because it allows us to explore different identities – perhaps even ones we feel uneasy about – but we can still come back to our conventional selves by the end of the film. The recognition of the boundaries

continued

between humans and vampires (us and them) is evident in the taglines for *Daybreakers*:

> **In 2019, The Most Precious Natural Resource . . . Is Us.**
> **The battle between immortality and humanity is on.**
> **The face of humanity has changed forever.**

And in the final line of the film: **We can change you back**.

All of this suggests a clear dividing line – if it is crossed then you must cross back to being human. In contrast, *Twilight* suggests a much less rigid divide between the two groups, emphasising instead the romantic possibilities of the two groups coming together.

> **When you can live forever what do you live for?**
>
> **Forever.Begins.Now.**   **Nothing will be the same.**

Figure 5.4 Human/non-human relationships: *True Blood* and *Twilight*

DRACULA AND NATIONAL IDENTITY

While the vampire is most commonly discussed in terms of sexuality, the idea that Dracula is a metaphor for issues of national identity is also common. The original novel uses the fear of an attack on national identity to create the horror of Dracula – he is a diverse figure, made up of many races, something which was seen as undesirable. Dracula's diversity signified confusion and instability, something which national identity seeks to overcome to create a powerful and stable society. Dracula's move to England from Eastern Europe had connotations of invasion and contamination.

ACTIVITY

Identity analysis

Take a contemporary vampire text and consider how it explores themes of identity.

Does it fit into any of the categories discussed above?

To help in constructing an analysis make notes on the following:

- Who is the audience intended to identify with – vampire or human? Both?
- Which rules of the genre are adhered to and which are broken?
- What examples of a family unit are there? Biological or constructed, vampire or human – what values do these different families represent?
- How are the vampires signified as 'other' than human? Twinkling? Sucking blood? What is the vampire's own-response to these non-human characteristics?
- What examples are there of national or ethnic identity in the text? Is there any link between being non-human and these identities?
- Is there a range of representations of sexuality and sexual relationships? List the different examples in your text.

Case study 5.2
CONSTRUCTION OF IDENTITY IN *TWILIGHT*

Gender identity

Twilight questions the conventional gender roles in vampire texts (with the exception of Buffy) by having a female central character that is drawn to the male vampire rather than the other way around. Bella Swan, despite her feminine name, is a tomboy who wears casual clothes which hide her body, is bookish and drives a truck (some viewers might recognise this character as very similar to the 'Final Girl' of the horror genre). While this representation of gender identity challenges the dominant feminine stereotype in some ways, Bella is still rescued by the male characters and is driven by love and emotion. There are other characters in the film that seem to cross the traditional borders of gender conventions, such as Eric, whose love of gossip and fashion is more usually coded as female.

National and ethnic identity

In *Twilight*, the town of Forks is a symbol for the US and as such it draws on a range of cultural signifiers, traditional and contemporary. Forks does exist but its representation on screen is not about realism. Forks on screen draws on a romanticised view of small-town America which seems to refer back to the past (or at least to films of the past) emphasising the community structure of home, high school, the diner, independent shops and the local sheriff. The town has an ethnic mix with American Asians and African Americans playing prominent roles. The town is divided though in some ways across ethnic lines with the Quielete reservation remaining a separate community. The conservative, nostalgic view of national identity symbolised by Forks is undercut by the ethnic diversity of the characters and of course by the two groups of vampires who are foreign to the town.

Sexuality and the other

Gay and straight sexuality is represented in *Twilight*, and Eric conforms to the popular Hollywood character of the gay best friend – a sympathetic character familiar from romcom and sitcom. In keeping with the conventions of this type of character, Eric doesn't have any on-screen relationships. Bella's female friends at school are all in different stages of heterosexual relationships. The experience of Bella's own parents who have separated works as a contrast to the 'true' vampire love which will last 'forever'. Bella and Edward's relationship is in many ways coded as heterosexual and the narrative stages are very similar to a conventional romantic plotline; the initial apparent dislike which changes after a dramatic event (he saves her from being crushed by a car), the happy interlude of a romantic dinner, confession of his secret, declaration of love, meeting the family, the union disrupted when happiness is almost snatched away, but she is saved, and they are united in an embrace at the high school prom. The normalising of the human, non-human affair has been read in different (sometimes contradictory) ways:

- It appeals to a young teen audience who want the emotion and drama of a fantasy romance but not the physical engagement.
- it's a signal that diverse cultures, sexualities, ethnicities are now integrated into the mainstream.
- The human/non-human love affair is a stand-in for other 'taboo' representations (at least in mainstream media), such as homosexuality.
- The character of Edward is coded to be read as 'queer' to some sections of the audience; that he has to lie to fit in, go against his natural urges to be accepted in society, that he 'comes out' to Bella, have all been used to read the vampire as a symbol of those individuals and groups not accepted by society.

3. Choosing through issue

It may be that you are interested in exploring a particular media issue or debate, perhaps something that you covered at AS and which you would like to research further. Here are some suggestions.

Representation of teenagers in the news:

- Look back at your AS work – how many different areas are relevant to this topic?

  - Definitions of representation.
  - Positive and negative images.
  - Analysis of news – print and broadcast, regional and local, conventions, layout, news values, etc.
  - Work on representations of particular groups – not necessarily teenagers, maybe fictional texts – which could serve as a framework for your investigation.

If you decide to develop your investigation from the starting point of an issue rather than a text, you will still need to make sure that your research is focused around one – or two – texts. For example, an investigation into the representation of teenage girls in the local press with specific reference to the *Argus Lite* (22 January 2010) and *Dagenham and Barking Examiner* (29 January 2010).

Sample case study

Suggested titles

1. An investigation into the use of **hybrid conventions** of film documentary with specific reference to *Man on Wire* (2008).
2. Construction of **narrative** in C4 short documentaries.
3. The **representation** of national identity in 3MW documentaries.

Linked production: Produce a documentary 'portrait' for the Channel 4 3MW series.

Initial research

Man on Wire (James Marsh, 2008)

Synopsis (taken from the official website)

On 7 August 1974, a young Frenchman, Philippe Petit, stepped out on to a wire illegally rigged between New York's Twin Towers, then the world's tallest buildings. After nearly an hour dancing on the wire he was arrested, taken for psychological evaluation, and brought to jail before he was finally released. Following six and a half years of dreaming of the Towers, Petit spent eight months in New York City planning the execution of the coup, a unique and magnificent spectacle that became known as the artistic crime of the century.

As a starting point, research relevant institutional information to provide a foundation for your investigation.

Institutional context: production, distribution and exhibition.

Source	Type of source	Information	Outcomes/next step
manonwire. com	Secondary research Official website	Production context: multiple production companies: Magnolia, Wall to Wall, Discovery, BBC, UK Film Council	Suggests low-budget, niche audience film. Co-production by TV and film companies typical of contemporary media production. Why did the Film Council award lottery money? Research distributors and producers – go to industry websites.
Imdb.com	Secondary research Media industry website	Magnolia pictures (US) is the distributor.	Magnolia distributes low-budget British and US features and documentary – often with a social agenda.
		BBC production through *Storyville* strand.	Go to *Storyville* website for information on other documentaries.
		Directed by James Marsh – previous films include hybrid documentaries such as *Wisconsin Death Trip, Burger and the King*.	Watch previous films (but both too old for a contemporary research investigation).
		Exhibition: 43 screens (UK). In US opened on two screens, building to 93 after Oscar win.	Limited exhibition will be evidence for type of audience. Oscar win characteristic of the number of awards received.
http:// www.bbc. co.uk/ bbcfour/ documen- taries/ storyville/	Secondary research Media industry website	*Storyville* is a series of documentaries about international people and events shown on BBC4.	*Man on Wire* funded through the licence fee (PSB). Many of the *Storyville* documentaries are portraits of individuals – famous and anonymous.

continued

Source	Type of source	Information	Outcomes/next step
			May be a useful comparison text.
http://www.ukfilmcouncil.org.uk/newcinemafund		Funded with money from the New Cinema Fund which aims to 'encourage unique ideas, innovative approaches and original voices'.	This definition would be a way to discuss the techniques used in the film.

3MW

3 Minute Wonders are a series of shorts from new directors who haven't yet made a film for broadcast TV. The films are often – but not always – documentaries and are shown four nights a week after the Channel 4 7 p.m. news. The films are connected by subject, but they also have to be able to stand alone and be understood in isolation.

There is an archive of films on the *3 Minute Wonder* website, which will give you a chance to research a range of examples: http://www.channel4.com/culture/microsites/0–9/3mw/index.html.

Typical of the types of documentaries made for *3MW* is the series *Nursing Britain*. Each of the four films follows the experiences of a foreign NHS worker either newly arrived or long established. Through the focus on an individual, these portraits also explore wider social and cultural issues such as Britain as a multicultural society or the future of the NHS. The series on the Aylesbury Estate in South London (on C4, July 2007, available on YouTube) constructed a portrait of estate life through the stories of different residents, while placing their experiences in the context of ten years of a Blair government.

The commissioning editor of the *3MW* series states:

> **I'm actively searching for directors with unique perspectives who want to tell stories in new, exciting, non-traditional ways. I'm interested in ideas that feel timely and connected to something happening in the outside world . . . . It's also**

> important that the trajectory of the films feels absolutely suited to the three minutes so the **form and structure of the film is crucial** to me. 🙶

Link to production: This reference to the content and style of the films is something you should take into account in your production. Research this by watching a range of 3MW films and note how they tell stories in 'new and exciting ways' – this might be to do with the form or perhaps a subject which hasn't been covered elsewhere. (Also note the similarity to the stated aims of the Film Council in funding films like *Man on Wire* referred to earlier.)

Relevant theoretical approaches:

- Genre
- Defining types of documentary
- Representation and realism.

What is a documentary?

Whichever theoretical area you choose to investigate you will need to develop a definition of the term 'documentary'. Defining the documentary has become increasingly complicated with the development of new styles of documentary and hybrid forms (e.g. documentary drama, reality TV), but there are still some characteristics that we expect from a text in order for it to be defined as a documentary. It will be:

- Non-fiction
- About the real (historical, political, cultural events) world
- Informative, educational
- Based on observation rather than intervention
- Unstaged
- Filmed in a particular style (e.g. interviews, voice-over, handheld camera).

Even these few characteristics are likely to provoke questions and debate as you continue your study.

DOCUMENTARY STYLE AND REALISM

One of the important areas to analyse is that of realism and documentary form. This is central to defining the documentary and therefore will be essential whether your main focus is **genre** (realism is one of the genre

continued

conventions of documentary), **representation** (how do documentaries represent the real world?) or **narrative** (how do documentaries use realist techniques to shape the real world into a story for the audience?).

Read the following quote about the relationship between realism and the real world:

> " Realism is a construction, therefore it is impossible to achieve a perfect match between events in the real world and the text that represents them. "

(Kilborn and Izod, 1997)

Figure 5.5 A scene from *Man on Wire*: documentary realism

This suggests that:

- Realism is a style of filmmaking – just as Hollywood narrative and *film noir* are styles.
- Realism involves a series of choices on the part of the filmmaker (it is a construction).
- Documentaries can never directly reflect reality (it is impossible to achieve a perfect match).

SECONDARY RESEARCH: DOCUMENTARY REALISM

Develop your secondary research by following up the Kilborn and Izod quote opposite. Their book *An Introduction to Television Documentary – Confronting Reality* provides an overview of the key definitions and debates in the area. Begin by selecting the most relevant sections, chapters, pages, etc. (e.g. Part 1, Chapter 2 *How Real Can You Get? Realism and Documentary*).

Link to production: These questions of realism will have a practical application in your own documentary production; it is worth reflecting on how you would go about tackling the challenge of representing the real world on film. As a documentary-maker, ask yourself the following questions:

- To what extent can film (fiction or non-fiction) reflect the real world?
- How would you try to capture the real world on film? What techniques would you use?
- What would be some of the obstacles to showing the real world?
- What are some of the differences between the real world as you experience it and the real world as shown on film?
- Which films have you seen (fiction or non-fiction) which you think represent reality accurately? What were the techniques they used?

Once we start to consider documentaries in this way we can analyse the role of the documentary-maker. If they aren't just reflecting reality, then they must be shaping it somehow – perhaps to manipulate the way in which the audience responds to the film. In this way documentaries share many characteristics with fiction films.

OBJECTIVITY AND SUBJECTIVITY

Can a documentary (or documentary-maker) ever be objective? There is often the assumption that a documentary must 'show both sides of the story' but if a documentary is a construction, can it ever be objective? Do you think objectivity is even something which documentary-makers should aim for? When making your own documentary consider how the following affects objectivity: choice of subject, the use of editing, what is left in and what is excluded.

DEFINING MODES OF DOCUMENTARY

The term 'documentary' covers a variety of different styles of filmmaking, subject matter, aims and exhibition. There have been some attempts in academic study to categorise different documentaries into groups. This is

continued

Figure 5.6 Michael Moore: never attempting to be objective

a similar approach to grouping fiction films into genres but here the groups are referred to as documentary 'modes'. Many documentaries will feature conventions from more than one mode (rather like hybrid genres) and there are overlaps across the different modes.

Expository mode

- Voice-over, addresses the audience directly.
- The voice-over may either be a 'voice of God' commentator (heard but not seen) or a 'voice of authority' (seen and heard – usually an expert in the relevant field).
- Images are used to illustrate (or sometimes counterpoint) the voice-over.
- Editing is used for continuity, to link together images which support the argument put forward in the voice-over.
- Assembles a variety of footage, interviews, stills, archive material to support the argument.
- Attempts to persuade the audience of a particular point of view, often by appealing to logic and the idea of a commonsense response.

Observational mode

- Location shooting – handheld cameras.
- Long takes dominate.

- Synchronous (direct) sound recording.
- No voice-over (in its purest form).
- No interviews.
- Documentary-maker's presence is hidden.
- Subjects pretend they are not being filmed.

Participatory (also referred to as interactive)

- Documentary-maker (and crew) interacts with the subject.
- Interviews dominate but tend to be informal – literally 'on-the-run' questioning.
- Use of archive material – stills, news footage, newspaper headlines, letters, etc.
- Location shooting – handheld camera.
- Long takes dominate.
- Synchronous (direct) sound recording.
- Voice-over – usually by the documentary-maker.
- Documentary-maker is visible to the audience – intervenes and participates in the action.

Reflexive documentary

- Borrows techniques from fiction film for an emotional, subjective response.
- Emphasises the expressive nature of film; anti-realist techniques (e.g. re-enactments, expressive lighting, dramatic music).
- Voice-over (when present) is likely to be questioning and uncertain – rather than authoritative.
- Reliance on suggestion rather than fact.

Performative mode

- Documentary-maker (and crew) interacts with the subject.
- Documentary-maker comments on the process of making the documentary.
- The documentary is often shaped into the narrative of an investigation or search – to which there may be no satisfactory conclusion.
- Addresses the audience in an emotional and direct way.
- Subject matter often to do with identity (gender, sexuality) rather than with 'factual' subjects.

continued

Initially these groups may seem difficult to apply because of the number of conventions, but there are clear patterns which emerge across the groups:

- Which conventions appear more than once across groups?
- Which modes seem most similar to each other?

Another way of using the modes is to think about the role or position of the documentary-maker and therefore the role of the audience.

Group A: Expository, observational

These modes attempt to hide the role of the filmmaker and emphasises the filmmaker's interpretation of the world.

Group B: Participatory, reflexive, performative

These modes foreground the role of the filmmaker and shift the emphasis to the way in which the audience interprets the documentary.

ACTIVITY

Can you list some examples of documentaries which fit into each group?

SECONDARY RESEARCH: BILL NICHOLS AND MODES OF DOCUMENTARY

Bill Nichols is one of the key theorists in the study of documentary and identified the modes of documentary representation which have since been debated, argued over and added to. In *Representing Reality* (1991) Nichols identified four dominant groups in documentary: expository, observational, interactive and reflexive. In *Blurred Boundaries* (1994) this was expanded to include poetic as an early form (1920s) and performative as a recent development in documentary style.

Nichols' work is sometimes attacked for being rigid and prescriptive. He does, however, emphasise that the modes tend to be combined and altered in individual films and that older categories do not disappear with the introduction of new modes.

Why do new modes of representation within documentary emerge? Nichols identifies the modes as developing chronologically and in reaction to the limitations of the previous mode.

In studying the development of new modes it is apparent that there are a range of contextual factors which affect this development – new technology, institutions and audience. Rather than initially defining them through techniques and conventions, it is helpful to introduce the concept of different modes of representation in terms of understanding the role of the documentary-maker.

Link to production: As a documentary-maker will you appear on screen or remain behind the camera?

If you do appear on screen there are a variety of different approaches you can use. You could be an interviewer or a 'presenter' of factual information or you might develop a persona in a similar way to Nick Broomfield or Michael Moore. Whatever role you choose should be appropriate to the type of documentary you're making; it should develop from the aim of your documentary.

Remember that if you do appear on screen you will also need to carry out another identifiable role such as editing, camera operator, etc. for assessment.

PRIMARY RESEARCH: COMPARING DIFFERENT ROLES AND MODES

To analyse the different functions available to documentary-makers look at a range of contrasting documentaries. Some suggestions:

- *The World's . . . and Me* (available to watch at http://www.channel4. com/programmes/the-worlds-and-me). Channel 4 TV series in which comedian Mark Dolan visits 'extraordinary' children – strongest, smallest, cleverest, etc.
- *The Red Lion*. Part of Channel 4's long-running *Cutting Edge* series of documentaries, *The Red Lion* is a documentary by the respected documentary-maker Sue Bourne who examines British pub culture by visiting over 600 Red Lion pubs (available to watch at http://www. channel4.com/programmes/the-red-lion).
- *Être et Avoir*. Documentary which follows a single class school in rural France for a year; this uses many of the techniques of observational documentary – particularly hiding the presence of the documentary-maker (available on DVD, or an extensive selection of clips are on YouTube).

continued

For each documentary consider:

- What is the role of the documentary-maker?
- Is the audience aware of their presence? If so, how?
- Do you think the role of the documentary-maker fits the subject matter?
- Do different documentary styles attract different types of audience?
- Which of the documentaries you have watched seems more or less mediated?

Mediation refers to the way in which documentary-makers record and represent the real world on film. The analysis of these techniques illustrates the different ways documentary is constructed – rather than being a direct recording of reality. Analysing these techniques in existing documentaries will also help you to consider your own approach to documentary-making. When constructing an analysis of the techniques it can be helpful to use a table with prompts.

PRIMARY RESEARCH

Title of documentary, director, year: *Man on Wire* (James Marsh, 2008). Sequence for analysis: Opening/pre-credit sequence (approximately 8 minutes)

Mediation techniques	Identification/ description	Function/effect
Types of shots Static or mobile? Handheld camera? Long takes?	1. Emphasis on mid-shots of people and close-ups of objects.	1. Hides the identity of the actors in the reconstruction – makes it easier for the viewer to think it's Philippe. Close-ups on objects emphasise the meticulous planning of the stunt.
	2. Some camera movement but slow and smooth – zooms and pans, not handheld.	2. Fluid camera movement creates the impression that the viewer is there – looking around the room, etc.
	3. Variety of shot lengths, changes in tempo of editing.	3. The increase in tempo creates tension and suspense – similar to a fiction film technique.

Mediation techniques	Identification/ description	Function/effect
Sound List the different types of sound – diegetic and non-diegetic.	4. Soundtrack (Michael Nyman).	4. Music is electronic, insistent, repetition of a theme adds to the tension of the sequence (use of Nyman for soundtrack also signals the film as 'alternative' 'artistic' because of the other films in which his music has been used).
	5. Sound effects – hammering nails into the coffin, etc.	5. Sound effects intensify Philippe's memory of the event – placing the viewer at the scene.
	6. Richard Nixon press conference: 'I'm not a crook'.	6. Nixon's defence makes the viewer consider whether Philippe is a criminal or not.
Interviews Who is interviewed? How are the interviews conducted? What information do they provide?	7. Philippe, interview responses also used as voice-over.	7. The main interviewee is the subject of the film – the 'man on wire'. Therefore we know he survived the walk between the Towers (takes away some of the suspense?), getting a firsthand account of the event (a version of it).
	8. Jean-Louis, Jean-François, Annie (group members and ex-girlfriend). David aka Donald, Alan aka Albert (sometime group members).	8. Other views of Philippe and his plan come from his close (ex?) friends which will provide a more complete picture. Already tensions are apparent through reference to arguments. Use of aliases reinforces heist genre. All the interviewees use emotional and subjective language: 'We're going to get caught', 'We're not going to die', 'Could no

continued

Mediation techniques	Identification/ description	Function/effect
		longer go on living'. Creates immediacy – firsthand knowledge.
	9. All interviews conducted with subjects seated, minimal *mise-en-scène*.	9. Minimal *mise-en-scène* gives little indication of the interviewees' status, current situation, etc., making us focus on their past experiences.
Archive material What different type of film footage/ material is used? Is it pre-existing ('found') or made especially for the documentary? –	10. Black-and-white reconstruction of preparations for the walk.	10. Use of black and white identifies this as something happening in the past. Iconography is reminiscent of a heist movie which provides tension for the viewer and makes the characters seem like outlaws (suggests the documentary-maker's view).
	11. Silent film pastiche of Philippe's early life.	11. The use of an irising effect links this to a silent film but also suggests it is Philippe's memory of an event (rather than objective). The style of filmmaking presents Philippe as a magician – someone extraordinary (how he sees himself?).
	12. Archive footage of the construction of the Twin Towers. Photos of Philippe as a boy.	12. The footage of the construction of the Twin Towers is shown in split screen with the photos of Philippe in the other half this firmly links the two: they seem to come into existence together.
Documentary -maker	13. Documentary-maker doesn't appear, we don't hear the	13. Because the documentary-maker

Mediation techniques	Identification/ description	Function/effect
Do they appear on screen? If so, describe their persona. Is the audience aware of the documentary-maker in any other way?	questions asked of the interviewees (if it's the documentary-maker asking them?). 14. Aware of the documentary-maker in the extreme mediation of different film styles.	(James Marsh) doesn't appear on screen it means the viewer can concentrate on Philippe – there isn't a competing presence. 14. The film language itself is foregrounded – aware of *Man on Wire* as a film made by a director – not a direct reflection of reality.

As this table suggests, *Man on Wire* is extreme in the use of mediation techniques; there is almost no observational or expository style documentary-making in it. The reasons for this may range from stylistic and artistic to practical:

■ The viewer knows that Philippe survived his walk; therefore the suspense and tension is constructed through the conventions of a crime film or heist.
■ There is almost no footage of the walk itself – the documentary-maker has to find other ways of creating a sense of awe in the viewer.
■ Much of the reconstruction draws on a theatrical style which fits with Philippe's persona as a showman.
■ The constant mix of diverse styles also seems to reflect Philippe's endless energy.

Link to production: Although it is unlikely that the subject of your documentary will have done anything as unique as Philippe in *Man on Wire*, there are elements of the documentary which will be applicable to planning your own style.

■ Think about representing the personality and characteristics of your subject through the style of filmmaking.
■ If you have interviews in your documentary, consider the *mise-en-scène* – do you want to provide clues to the audience about the interviewee or keep a blank background?

continued

- Remember that although this is a documentary you can still use techniques associated with fiction films – if it's justified. Here the opening of the documentary withholds information from the viewer to create a disorientating but gripping start.

RESEARCH AND PRODUCTION

Brief for production: Produce a 3MW documentary which creates a **portrait of an individual or group** within a wider **social, cultural or geographical** context.

You need to do this in three minutes.

SECONDARY RESEARCH AND PRACTICAL SKILLS

In preparation for your work consider studying some of the many books which are now available on documentary-making. These provide practical suggestions and guidance on how to produce a successful documentary. Some suggestions:

Directing the Documentary by Michael Rabiger (Focal Press 2004).
The Shut Up and Shoot Documentary Guide: *A Down and Dirty DV Production* by Anthony Artis (Focal Press 2007).

There are also some very useful websites which provide professional and amateur help and experience. One which should be of particular use to you is the 4Docs website: http://www.channel4.com/culture/microsites/F/fourdocs/video/video3.html.

The site includes a **wiki** which gives tips on getting funding, the legal issues relevant to documentary, what equipment to use and the latest online developments. The basis of the wiki is information provided by 4Docs, but a wiki is a collaborative website and therefore includes contributions from its users to create an up-to-date resource. There is also a **blog** on the site which gives details of documentary competitions and festivals as well as highlighting new documentary releases and TV screenings.

PRIMARY RESEARCH AND PRODUCTION

In preparation for constructing your own film watch the 3MW film *Pockets* (available at 4Docs).

Pockets takes a simple, clearly focused idea – what people have in their pockets – and presents it in a striking, uncluttered way. The film seems to work because it:

- Uses an everyday experience to which most people can relate.
- Chooses a variety of people in terms of age, gender, ethnicity, appearance, etc.
- Links form and content: using extreme close-ups of objects and faces, bringing the foreground into focus while the background is less clear, using extra lighting to focus on the subject matter.
- Leaves some things unsaid; rather than explaining everything for the audience (sometimes people explain the meaning behind their objects; sometimes the audience is left to think about what significance they might have).
- Uses non-diegetic sound sparingly.

Link to production: *Pockets* provides an excellent example of how attention to detail in framing, composition and editing is vital to creating a successful film – particularly when working in 'miniature' (three minutes). It also shows the importance of a strong, interesting idea.

ACTIVITY

How might you apply the approaches in *Pockets* to your own film?

The production: successful group work and individual skills

Working as part of a successful group requires practice and the development of particular skills – it is a good idea to take some time at the start of the coursework process to discuss how the team will work. The following are some tips to help your team work together well – and therefore produce a successful production.

Getting started

1. Does everyone in the group know each other? Make sure that everyone knows each other's names at least!
2. Everyone needs to discuss and clarify the goals of the group's work. Go around the group and hear everyone's ideas (before discussing them) or encourage different ideas by brainstorming. This will help you to see any problems which might arise later in the production – it also helps everyone to feel part of the group.

Organising the work

3. Allocate responsibility for different parts of the project to different individuals (for further information on clearly definable roles see below).
4. Develop a timeline, including who will do what, by when. Include time at the end of the production for final checks, review, presentation, etc. – this always takes longer than you anticipate! At the end of each session the team should review and agree what work they expect to complete during the following session.
5. At the beginning of each session decide what you expect to have accomplished by the end of the session.

Monitoring progress

During the production process it's a good idea to review how the group is working – and hopefully solve any problems before they become disastrous!

■ Are all members accomplishing the work expected of them? Is there anything that group members can do to help those experiencing difficulties?
■ Are there disagreements or difficulties within the group that need to be addressed? (Is someone dominating? Is someone left out?)
■ Is outside help needed to solve any problems?
■ Is everyone enjoying the work?

(*Source: Tips for Group Work* adapted from Derek Bok Center for Teaching and Learning, Harvard University, 1997)

You can also benefit by taking a reflective approach and asking yourself some questions about working in a group:

■ Where do you fit in? What is your role in groups?
■ Do you cooperate with others, lead, follow, contribute, guide, advise or just watch?
■ Should you take a more active role? Should you contribute more?
■ Have you a dominant personality? If so – should you encourage others to contribute?

Group work and individual contributions

The exam board states:

> ❝ Students working in groups must all have a **clearly defined production role** which allows them to demonstrate a **significant** and **definable contribution** to the production. ❞

You can do this by assigning different parts of the production to different members of the group (e.g. being responsible for all the decisions and completion of a particular scene). An alternative approach – and one which is closer to professional practice – would be to define the different roles needed to produce the coursework and to assign one to each member of the group.

Possible roles:

- Camera operator
- Sound design/recording
- Editing.

Each group member should take primary responsibility for a role, but everyone should experience the different technical and creative aspects. You also need to consider the relative contribution of each role:

- Is there scope for the person responsible for sound to make a major contribution?
- Perhaps the role of camera operator could be shared (each person would need to be responsible for a specific part of the filming).

Skills for individual work

If you have decided to work on one of the individual production tasks, then you also need to consider how you can work most effectively:

- Draw up a timeline or timetable which includes your deadlines and the amount of time you will have to work on the project.
- Be realistic about the amount of time you will have – do you have time in class? Do you need access to specialist equipment or are there aspects you can work on at home?
- Will you need training to use software programs, etc.?
- Working individually doesn't mean that you have to work in isolation – discuss your ideas with your teacher or other members of the class.
- Perhaps the students working on individual projects could form a group to provide feedback and evaluate ideas.

Moving from AS to A2: production skills

With any media work that you do, it is always worth asking the question why you are doing it. Just as you adopt a questioning attitude to theoretical perspectives, so you should be prepared to question the value of undertaking media production. After all, no one would seriously think that A2 Media Studies production work is intended to train you for a job in the industry. So it is well worth asking before you embark on your media production: Why am I doing this? Why does someone else (i.e. the exam board) want me to do this? What am I trying to achieve? How is it different from what I did at AS?

Recap of learning at AS

Here are four things you might have discovered from your AS production work:

- Production is time consuming.
- Production is equipment intensive.
- Production relies on the cooperation of other people.
- If production can go wrong production will go wrong.

So one thing you might think about A2 is that being forewarned is to be forearmed.

Spend a few minutes looking back at your experience of AS production. Based on the results of this contemplation, make a list identifying:

- What went well?
- Want went not so well?
- What was a total disaster?

Dig out your AS work if you still have it. Don't look only at the product but also consider all the research and pre-production that you amassed. Looking through it all, decide:

- What is good.
- What is OK.
- What is totally embarrassing.

Look back at the list of four things you might have learned about production from your AS work. Is there anything you can add to the list?

Having looked back at your AS experience, it is a good idea to look forward and think about how you will go about building on this experience.

Developing production skills

You will see that production is a substantial piece of work that will influence your final grade significantly. Remember that production is work that you have control over, not like an unseen exam question. In general terms the reward you get for it will be proportional to the work you put into it.

Let us review some of the key elements that you will have learned in the production process. A book of this sort is not a good place for us to look in detail at production techniques but does lend itself to an opportunity to tease out the key principles that underpin good production work. If you need help on some more format-specific production skills, you should go to our website, www.routledge.com/textbooks/a2mediastudies, which will offer the best and most up-to-date information to help you with your production skills. There you will find some useful advice on the more technical aspects of productions for television and radio, newspapers and magazines, and new media.

In addition, a simple web search will open up to you quite an array of sites that offer help and support on technical issues, such as using Photoshop. There are a number of 'how-to' videos on YouTube which offer both basic and more sophisticated guidance.

Production skills at AS are likely to have introduced you to at least a couple of production formats. This is a good starting point to consider where to go from there. Logically, if you have built up a level of expertise in handling a technology, you are likely to want to stick with it and try to develop further. On the other hand, if your review of AS production served only to remind you of what a nightmare it all was, there may be an argument for cutting your losses and trying something new. Remember too that your production skills are by no means limited to classroom learning. If you use production skills in other contexts, such as taking photos, writing scripts, reviews or features, or even social networking, then use them. The overriding argument that should drive you on is about choosing a technology or technologies appropriate to what you are attempting to do.

What am I trying to achieve? What will final product look like? What impact do I want it to have on my audience? Imagine your best audience reaction.

PLANNING

The key to effective production work, whether you are a media professional or an A2 student, lies in planning. Time invested in preparing for your production will be time well spent – although the planning is not assessed it is a vital stage in producing successful production work. Production is often a complex logistical operation. This is where your experience of working at AS should really be of benefit. You will have realised that careful planning in the initial stages not only ensures a good outcome, but can also save a significant amount of time and energy along the way.

One of the most important aspects of the planning stage is to think through exactly who the target audience for your production is.

ACTIVITY

Assemble a small focus group that is representative of your audience. Ideally it would be helpful if you can go back to this group at different points in the production process and get their feedback on what you have come up with. This may involve you in going outside of your school or college to gain access to this group of people.

Figure 5.7 *Saga* Magazine, a magazine successfully targeted at a niche audience: September 2009

One example of a media product aimed at a particular audience is the 'grey' magazines aimed specifically at the over-sixties. Such magazines can be difficult to find since they tend not to be on newsagents' shelves but are ordered specially – either by a newsagent for known customers or directly by the readers themselves on a subscription basis. However, if you were to look at these magazines you would find that they make certain presumptions about the over-sixties, which may prompt you to think about the (possibly enormous) market of over-sixties who may not feel they are appropriately catered for by these magazines.

Equally, research into magazines aimed at teenage girls may suggest that all these magazines are in fact very similar. It would be acceptable to produce a magazine which conformed to these conventions, but it may be an interesting challenge to produce a magazine for this audience that is totally different from all the others already available. It is not for us to suggest what the contents of such a teenage girl magazine might be but simply to suggest that you examine that area.

You may find it worth your while to interview your family and friends about their media consumption and ask them to suggest ways in which they feel they are not being catered for by existing media products.

The subject material of your production is inevitably linked with its target audience and so must obviously appeal to its intended audience and be in an appropriate medium for this audience. It must also be possible to produce the material within the constraints of the medium that you have decided to employ. For instance, you are unlikely to be able to make a video about a wartime submarine since your ability to create realistic sets and costumes will be severely limited in a school/ college context. However, the possibilities offered by a radio play are almost endless.

You also have to be realistic about the time, money and energy that you have. Do not be over-ambitious – be realistic. For example, if you have decided to target 40-year-old sci-fi film enthusiasts, then it is fundamentally unrealistic to decide to make a fiction film, largely because you are unlikely to have the equipment and budget necessary to do so. But if you think around the problem, then you might:

- make a television or radio magazine programme that is about sci-fi films;
- make a trailer/advertising campaign for a new sci-fi film;
- make a parody of a sci-fi film of the 1950s (though note that parody/pastiche is actually a sophisticated skill).

The production process can be usefully broken down into three stages:

- planning
- production
- post-production.

PLANNING

Having made all the decisions about the nature of your product, you now enter the phase that is absolutely necessary to all media products. In the real world it is a rare individual who is allowed a completely free rein to go out and do whatever s/he sees fit at the time 'because it feels right'. Nowadays, whatever the product, an enormous amount of work goes into the planning stage.

If you are making a video, then what you should *not* do is just go out and start filming. You will need to produce a script and an accompanying shotlist so that you have a basic idea of what the final product will look like. You will also need to prepare careful plans of what will be shot, when and where, who in the group will be needed, when people will be available and what will be needed (props, costumes, equipment). While this may not necessarily all be true of a documentary, even then there are only a few documentary-makers who simply go out with a camera and see what happens. They are much more likely to have decided in the first place who they want to interview, where, when, what they want to ask them, and also (if the truth be told) what sort of light they want to show them in.

This preparation work may not be the most exciting part of the production process – and there will always be members of the group who just want to get on and do it

– but at the end of the day all your planning will save you a great deal of time, and also prevent you from making a lot of mistakes. It should mean that the final product is delivered on time – which of course in the real media world is incredibly important.

PRODUCTION

There are two very important primary stages to the production process. Perhaps the most important is that of familiarisation with the technology available to you, to remind yourself exactly what the equipment you are using is capable of doing for you.

When you feel comfortable again with the equipment, when you know its capabilities and your own limitations, when everyone has agreed on their tasks, when everyone knows what they are doing and when everyone feels confident and prepared . . . then you can begin!

Here are some other tips to bear in mind while working on your production:

1. Keep everything. That front cover might not have seemed right at the time but you may change your mind after you have tried and failed to improve on it. Equally, all the video material you create may come in useful when editing. Shoot, watch and log it all, every day if possible.
2. Bear in mind at all times that it is your ideas, and your attempts to get your ideas into concrete form, that matter. You are not professionals working full-time on the job. You will be rewarded for making a genuine attempt at something, even though it may seem to you to be a failure.
3. Never lose sight of the *planning*. You will almost certainly be working within a genre – keep in mind at all times the conventions of that genre and its likely audience. Your audience needs to be entertained and challenged, otherwise your product has failed.
4. Even though you might be striving for originality, the chances of achieving it are pretty slight. For instance, if you are working within a particular magazine genre and want to create a product that is totally original (and has the potential to be a fantastic financial success), you should always bear in mind that there are people employed in the media world who are paid huge sums of money each year to try to dream up similar ideas. And they rarely succeed either. It is a good idea to be as ambitious as possible, but that ambition needs to be tempered with a dose of reality.

POST-PRODUCTION

Many candidates simply produce an artefact and leave it at that. It is very important that you consider the presentation of your product very carefully. There is little point in working very hard on your video production and then delivering the finished product in a shabby, unmarked DVD case. The same is often true of a radio production. Similarly, do not present a magazine that is unkempt, badly bound or a second-generation copy that is hard to read.

The evaluation

The evaluation is the final part of the project and is an opportunity to reflect on the coursework experience. The evaluation must demonstrate the link between the research and the production; it is a chance to show how your production work was informed by the research.

The specification states that:

- The evaluation must be individually produced.
- The evaluation **must** explore how the production has been informed by the research undertaken.
- The word count is 500–750 words.
- There is flexibility in presentation. Using bullet points and images as well as focused paragraphs is encouraged.

You can choose to present your evaluation in one of a variety of forms:

- An essay – the use of bullet points, subheadings and images is encouraged.
- A digital presentation with slide notes (such as PowerPoint).
- A blog.

Choosing which format to use is likely to depend on your audience (and personal preference):

- Are you going to present your evaluation to the class after the screening of your film?
- Is your work going to be available to watch on the college intranet?

Writing the evaluation should be a matter of reviewing the processes which led you to create your practical work. In the sample case study the highlighted links between the research and the creative process would provide the basis for the evaluation:

- What typical documentary conventions are evident in your film? Have you subverted these conventions in any way?
- How have you used realist techniques in your documentary?
- Does your documentary conform to a particular mode? Did you set out to produce a hybrid or pure documentary style?
- What is the role of the documentary-maker in your film?

For each of these areas provide analysis of specific examples from the texts studied as part of your research and your own film, showing how your creative decisions were based on your research investigation into documentary. The evaluation is about reflecting on the integration of research and production – not an account of the ups and downs of group work.

You could conclude your evaluation by considering whether there were areas of your research which are not represented in your production; how might these areas be addressed?

Resources

Broadcast documentary

Pockets (James Lee, 2008)

The World's Most . . . and Me (C4, 2009)

The Red Lion (Sue Bourne, C4, 2009)

Film documentary

Man on Wire (James Marsh, 2008)

Être et Avoir (Nicholas Philibert, 2004)

Websites

www.routledge.com/textbooks/a2mediastudies

3MW: http://www.channel4.com/culture/microsites/0-9/3mw/index.html

Four Docs: http://www.4docs.org.uk/

Storyville: http://www.bbc.co.uk/bbcfour/documentaries/storyville/. Homepage of BBC's international documentary strand includes interviews, articles on Storyville documentaries, and links to available programmes on iplayer.

Books

The following are specialist, academic sources:

Cousins, M. and Macdonald, K. (eds) (2005) *Imagining Reality*. Faber.

Kilborn, R. and Izod, J. (1997) *An Introduction To Television Documentary – Confronting Reality*. Manchester University Press.

Nichols, B. (1991) *Representing Reality*. Indiana University Press.

—— (1994) *Blurred Boundaries*. Indiana University Press.

—— (2002) *Introduction to Documentary*. Indiana University Press.

Overviews and summaries of debates around documentaries may be found in a range of Media and Film Studies textbooks:

Artis, A. (2007) *The Shut Up and Shoot Documentary Guide: A Down and Dirty DV Production*. Focal Press.
Casey Benyahia, S. *et al.* (2009) *A2 Film Studies: The Essential Introduction* (2nd edn). Routledge.
Cook, P. (ed.) (2008) *The Cinema Book* (3rd edn). British Film Institute.
Nelmes, J. (ed.) (2007) *An Introduction to Film Studies* (3rd edn). Routledge.
Rabiger, M. (2004) *Directing the Documentary*. Focal Press.

Vampire genre

Gelder, K. (1994) *Reading the Vampire*. Routledge.

EPILOGUE: THAT'S IT! WHAT NOW?

> **Education is not the filling of a pail, but the lighting of a fire.**
>
> (W. B. Yeats)

If we could be excused here for using a cliché, it is said that all good things must come to an end and we certainly hope that you will be regarding your experiences as a media student as at least good if not exciting, inspiring and perhaps even life-changing. However, after you sit your final examination, that will in effect be it and your time as a GCE student will be over. All that will remain will be waiting for the results and taking the next steps in your life. Prior to looking a little more closely at what these steps might be and how your A level in Media Studies might fit into your plans, just take a moment or so to consider why you chose to study Media in the first place.

Perhaps you had a certain aspiration for the future, a desire to work as a journalist, a film director, TV presenter or in a media-related area such as graphic design, advertising, public relations or publishing. Maybe you entered this subject with an open (or blank) mind as to what you wished to do in the future and chose media because it complemented your other GCE choices well either for similarity or for balance, because you saw it as an opportunity to learn new skills or maybe you even chose the subject because you thought it looked like fun. Whatever the reason, you ended up choosing this subject and, whichever direction you take in the future, it is worth pausing for a moment to consider what you have actually done in this subject over the past two years, or even longer if you studied the subject at GCSE level too.

In choosing Media Studies, you will have experienced a subject which combines practical and creative skills with analytical and conceptual skills. In your two practical units at AS and A2 level, you will have been tested on your ability to produce media texts which are creative, imaginative and original and, while they may have lacked that professional finish, they needed to be recognisable as potential media texts. In working on this area, you will have learned new practical skills or improved those you already had in areas such as desk-top publishing, filming, digital video editing, photography, script writing, web design and audio recording.

The examined assessments have required you to analyse, to consider many points of view and perspectives – many of which you may not have agreed with, to research and apply your findings, to be autonomous and to refer to relevant theories, and to think quickly; for example, how did you feel in Module 1 when the examination board sent you an unseen media text and asked you to analyse it? Many students panic and yet you had to recall all that information about media language, audiences, representations and industry as well as widen your answer to incorporate your own examples and then write it all down under exam conditions over three questions in two-and-a-half hours. This, by any standards, is no mean feat and your having experienced this will make you a stronger and more rounded student for doing so.

Furthermore, Module 4 may hardly be said to be for the faint-hearted. In all, you need detailed knowledge of at least nine media texts drawn from three different media types. You need to be able to approach this information from three quite different approaches (text, audience and industry) and, as with most exams, enter the exam hall with very little idea about exactly what the exam board are going to ask you, and again three answers under exam conditions in two-and-a-half hours is far from a breeze.

By now no doubt you have at least one eye on the future. University is an ever-popular choice for post-A level students, especially in media-related areas, one of the fastest growing in higher education. Naturally, if a media area is your preference for higher education, then you will have been well prepared for it through your GCE study but even if you are embarking upon a course in an unrelated area, the skills you have learned to use on this course will stand you in very good stead in other subjects.

It is a harsh reality that media careers are notoriously difficult to enter even with a degree, and that persistence, hard work and luck are required in addition to your studies. The good news is that as in education, the creative and media sector is growing in industry too but there is lots of competition for media-related posts such as media sales, advertising, journalism and marketing and, in areas such as film crew work, photography, animation and design, the workforce often comprises freelance operatives, and work is temporary and uncertain. In any creative industry, it is a good idea to build up a portfolio of your own work; your practical tasks completed in your Media Studies course can be included in this together with any other work you may have completed on an amateur or hobby basis. Most film and TV directors, for example, have built up an impressive array of amateur films often by simply using a home video camera, and journalists write in their spare time anything from articles for fanzines and hospital or school newspapers to articles about current affairs, sports or culture which are sent off to local and national newspapers in the hope of having them published. Nevertheless, your qualification in A level Media Studies is a big step in the right direction and has taught you many valuable skills about the media world and about how media texts are constructed.

Sadly, you will not see a job advertisement like the one below. While Media Studies and courses which follow on from it at university can be a step in the right direction, you will need persistence, hard work and perhaps even an element of luck if you want to be a top film director, or even a low-budget one.

WANTED
FILM DIRECTOR
Salary Circa $20 million

(+profit percentage, car, pension)

It's time to call "Action!" on your new career. Paramount Pictures are looking for a young and enthusiastic film director for their next film project. The successful candidate will be a good time keeper, have a commanding presence, be willing to work long hours and be creative.

APPLICANTS WITHOUT AN A LEVEL IN
MEDIA STUDIES NEED NOT APPLY.

Experience of practical work at GCE A level essential.

Please apply in writing to:
Paramount Pictures
Hollywood
California
USA
(No time wasters)

If Media Studies as a subject can be categorised at all, then surely it is a subject which requires you to be both analytical and creative, to produce your own work and to comment upon the work of others, to agree and to disagree, to find balance and to criticise, to be autonomous and to respect the established perspectives and theories offered by writers and professional exponents of media, and to learn new ways of seeing the world and looking at things in a new and challenging way. So to go back to Yeats' quote at the beginning of this chapter, from a schooling point of view and in terms of preparing you for an examination let us be frank: you need to do what is needed to pass and so all textbooks are designed to help fill your pail.

However, since you have been studying the media with all of its debates, theories, perspectives, analyses, creativity, imagination and relevance to the modern world, we hope that, more than that, we have also seen your fire well and truly lit.

GLOSSARY

360-degree content producing news across all platforms.

Alternative representations a representation that is different from the dominant representation, often with different values from the dominant ideology and invariably made by non-mainstream media companies.

Anchoring when a caption is placed in an open text to anchor meaning.

Base in Marxist terminology, the base refers to the economic core upon which a society is organised. It is the central means by which wealth is created and distributed among the people within that society.

Bourgeoisie the Marxist name for those who own or control the means of production or services; the middle classes.

Bricolage the dictionary usefully defines it as "a construction made of whatever materials are at hand; something created from a variety of available things", which is precisely how postmodernists use it, though the constructions are of meaning. *Bricoleurs* (French) are tinkers, people who travel around collecting other people's unwanted possessions.

Capitalism the economic system in which a society is focused upon the pursuit of capital (wealth). In Britain and other Western countries, capitalism may be said to be at the heart of the economic base. The main criticism is that it does not seek to create wealth for all people. For there to be wealthy people, others have to remain poor. Therefore critics of capitalism argue that while it is good at creating wealth, the unavoidable consequence of capitalism is inequality: the rich get richer and the poor get poorer. As capitalism has spread across the world, this inequality is no longer confined to within a country but is seen on a global scale.

Cinematography the use of the camera in filmmaking. This includes the shots used and the camera movements.

Citizen journalism means that ordinary people as well as professional journalists are creating the news.

Closed and open texts a text with only one possible meaning is said to be a closed text whereas a more ambiguous text with more than one possible interpretation is an open text. An open text may also be called *polysemic*, literally meaning many signs.

Deconstruction studying a media text by 'taking it apart' into its constituent elements and explaining each element.

Democracy power belongs to all of the people.

Distribution the distributor is an organisation which mediates between the producer and exhibitor to make the text available for consumption by an audience; for example, in film the distributor is the link between a film producer and the exhibitor (cinema, DVD, TV), who ensures that the film is seen by the widest audience possible. In media the term 'distribution' also refers to the *marketing* and advertising of media texts.

Dominant ideology a set of values that reflects and reinforces the values of those in power.

Dominant representation the representation that comes to dominate the media; it is repeated in the media over time.

Editing for some people, editing simply refers to removing sections that are not needed but in truth there is much more of a contribution to the overall feel of the film from editing. It refers to placing the shots in a sequence that will be understandable to the audience and also the length of the shots. As a result, the job of the editor is to ensure the correct pacing for a sequence: fast and with quick cuts for a chase sequence, for example, or slower and with fades for a dream sequence.

False consciousness a term which suggests that the working classes are not fully aware of the exploitation they endure at the hands of the ruling class. It is regarded as a reason why those who are exploited do not rise up and rebel against the ruling elite.

Film sound often overlooked compared to the more visual elements but crucial to creating the atmosphere for a film. Generally, sound may be divided into two sections. *Diegetic sound* refers to that sound which both the audience and the characters in the film can hear; it includes dialogue and sounds made by objects in the scene such as a gunshot, a car engine or a character striking a match. *Non-diegetic sound* refers to that which just the audience can hear and it includes narration or voice-over and incidental music.

Freedom of expression everyone has a right to express their own views, but often within certain laws or regulations.

Genre the French word which simply means 'type', used to categorise media texts such as films into recognisable groups.

Ideal type of reader an absolutely typical and average member of the target audience. Newspapers tend to present their content aimed at this idealised person and so all the articles, despite being produced by a number of different contributors and on a variety of topics, have the same mode of address and reflect the ideology, interests and perspectives of the ideal type of reader.

Juxtaposition placing two contrasting elements next to one another in order to increase the impact of each (e.g. darkness seems to be darker when it is placed next to brightness and, in a film, a sudden increase in volume makes it seem much louder due to the contrast).

Mediation when the media comes between the audience and the original source; it mediates.

Mise-en-scène another French term which literally translated means 'put in the scene'. It refers to the control the director and the set decorators have over the visual elements of the film. In films set in the contemporary world, this is much more of a straightforward task than setting a film in Roman Britain when costume, transport and general everyday objects must all reflect the era in which the film is set. Lighting can also play an integral part in the *mise-en-scène* as mood and atmosphere are created by the use of appropriate lighting.

Mode of address the language and style in which a media product is presented so that it appeals directly to its intended audience. For example, red-top popular newspapers adopt a chatty and informal mode of address to appeal to their readers.

Preferred reading the most likely interpretation of an open text.

Production the production stage refers to the developers or producers of a media text (e.g. Hollywood as the producer of blockbusters, the BBC as the producer of TV news programmes).

Proletariat the name Marx gave to those who work the means of production and provide the services offered in a society; the working classes.

Public service broadcaster a media organisation which is funded directly by the public and has a duty to provide a service. All sections of the public (both majority and minority audiences) must be addressed and the organisation is non-profit in its nature. The BBC, funded by the public through the licence fee, is such an organisation. The lack of advertisements on the BBC is a direct result of its non-profit creed.

Repertoire of generic elements/generic features the features we normally associate with media texts that belong to a certain genre which a text *can* demonstrate but which in some cases may not. For example, space is a feature of some science fiction films but there are many sci-fi texts which do not have space as a feature. However, some generic features are more prescriptive; for example, it is hard to envisage a western film which does not feature cowboys and which is not set in the western and southern states of the USA in the 1870s or 1880s.

Semiotics the study of signs and their meanings. First used by Ferdinand de Saussure in his Course in General Linguistics at the University of Geneva

(1906–11), semiotics is an important part of Media Studies as it is a device by which meanings are attached to the signs we see in media texts.

Self-representation when a group represent themselves in the media.

Stereotype a simple, generalised and exaggerated representation. A few characteristics, usually negative, are presumed to belong to the whole group.

Superstructure the name Marxists give to the institutions which exist in a society other than those associated with the economy, which would be part of the base. These institutions include religions, the law, education, the political system and the media. Marxists believe not only that these institutions are shaped by the economic base but also that the superstructure helps to legitimise the base and ensure its future as the economic system of that society.

User-generated content media content shown by the mainstream media that is produced by the users or audience.

BIBLIOGRAPHY

Abercrombie, N. (1996) *Television and Society*. Polity Press.

Artis, A. (2007) *The Shut Up and Shoot Documentary Guide: A Down and Dirty DV Production*. Focal Press.

Auslander, P. (1999) *Liveness: Performance in a Mediatized Culture*. Routledge.

Barker, M. and Petley, J. (eds) *Ill Effects: The Media/Violence Debate*. Routledge.

Barrett, P. (2006) 'White Thumbs, Black Bodies: Race, violence and neoliberal fantasies in *Grand Theft Auto: San Andreas*', *The Review of Education, Pedagogy and Cultural Studies*, 28: 95–119.

Barthes, R. (1977) 'Rhetoric of the Image', in R. Barthes, *Image, Music, Text*, ed. and trans. S. Heath. Hill and Wang.

Barthes, R. (1997) 'Semiology and the Urban', in N. Leach, (ed.) *Rethinking Architecture*. Routledge.

Beavis, C. (1998) Computer Games: Youth culture, resistant readers and consuming passions (accessed at http://www.aare.edu.au/98pap/bea98139.htm).

Benyahia, S.C., Gaffney, F. and White, J. (2009) *A2 Film Studies: The Essential Introduction* (2nd edn). Routledge.

Berger, J. (1972) *Ways of Seeing*. Penguin.

Blumer, J. and Katz, E. (1975) *The Uses of Mass Communication: Current Perspectives on Gratification Research*. Sage.

Bordwell, D. and Thompson, K. (2006) 'Narrative as a Formal System', in *Film Art: An Introduction* (6th edn). McGraw Hill.

Branston, G. with Stafford, R. (2010) *The Media Student's Book* (5th edn). Routledge.

Butler, J. (1990) *Gender Trouble: Feminism and the Subversion of Identity*. Routledge.

Chomsky, N. (1988) *Manufacturing Consent: The Political Economy of the Mass Media*. Pantheon Books.

Chomsky, N. (2004) *Hegemony and Survival: America's Quest for Global Dominance*. Penguin Books.

Clover, C. (1992) *Men, Women and Chainsaws: Gender in the Modern Horror Film*. Princeton University Press.

Cohen, S. (2002) *Folk Devils and Moral Panics: The Creation of Mods and Rockers*. Routledge.

Cook, P. (ed.) (2008) *The Cinema Book* (3rd edn). BFI Publishing.

Cousins, M. and Macdonald, K. (eds) (2005) *Imagining Reality*. Faber.

Derry, C. (1977) *Dark Dreams: A Psychological History of the Modern Horror Film*. A. S. Barnes & Co.

Doty, A. (1995) 'There's Something Queer Here', in C.K. Creekmur and A. Doty (eds) *Out in Culture: Gay, Lesbian and Queer Essays on Popular Culture*. Duke University Press.

Doty, A. (1998) 'Queer Theory', in J. Hill and P. Church Gibson (eds) *The Oxford Guide to Film Studies*. Oxford University Press.

Dyer, R. (1977) 'Entertainment and Utopia', *Movie*, 24.

Dyer, R. (1993) *The Matter of Images: Essays on Representation*. Routledge.

Dyer, R. (2002) *Only Entertainment*. Routledge.

Fiske, J. (1987) *Television Culture*. Methuen.

Fiske, J. (1989) *Reading the Popular*. Routledge.

Freidan, B. (2010) *The Feminine Mystique*. Penguin Classics (originally published 1963).

Galtung, J. and Ruge, M. (1965) 'The Structure of Foreign News: The presentation of the Congo, Cuba and Cyprus crises in four foreign newspapers', *Journal of International Peace Research*, 1: 64–90.

Gauntlett, D. (2008) *Media, Gender and Identity*. Routledge.

Gee, J. (2003) *What Video Games Have to Teach Us about Learning and Literacy*. Palgrave Macmillan.

Gelder, K. (1994) *Reading the Vampire*. Routledge.

Geraghty, C. (1991) *Women and Soap Opera*. Policy Press.

Giddens, A. (1993) *Sociology*. Polity Press.

Giddens, A. (1999) *Runaway World: How Globalization is Reshaping Our Lives*. Profile.

Gramsci, A. (1971) *Selections from the Prision Notebook*, ed. and trans. Q. Hoare and G. Nowell Smith. Lawrence and Wishart.

Graner-Ray, S. (2003) *Gender Inclusive Game Design: Expanding The Market*. Charles River Media.

Gray, A. (1992) *Video Playtime*. Routledge.

Greer, G. (1970) *The Female Eunuch*. MacGibbon & Kee.

Gross, L. (1989) 'Out Of The Mainstream: Sexual minorities and the mass media', in E. Seiter *et al.* (eds) *Remote Control: Television, Audiences And Cultural Power*. Routledge.

Hall, S. (1997) *Representation: Cultural Representations and Signifying Practices*. Sage.

Halloran, J. (1971) *The Effects of Television*, Panther.

Harcup, T. and O'Neill, D. (2001) 'What is News? Galtung and Ruge revisited', in P. Rayner, P. Wall and S. Kruger (2003) *Media Studies: The Essential Resource*. Routledge.

Hartley, J. (1982) *Understanding News*, Routledge.

Herman, E. and Chomsky, N. (1988) *Manufacturing Consent: The Political Economy of The Mass Media*. Pantheon Books.

Hobson, D. (1982) *Crossroads: The Drama of a Soap Opera*. Methuen.

Jenkins, H. (2003) 'Interactive Audiences', in V. Nightingale and K. Ross (eds) *Media and Audiences: New Perspectives*. Open University Press.

Johnson-Eilola (1997) 'Living on the Surface: Learning in the age of global communication networks', in I. Snyder (ed.) *Page to Screen: Taking Literacy into the Electronic Era*. Allen & Unwin.

Kendall, A. and McDougall, J. (2009) 'Just Gaming: On being *differently* literate', *Eludamos. Journal for Computer Game Culture*, 3 (2): 245–60.

Kilborn, R. and Izod, J. (1997) *An Introduction To Television Documentary – Confronting Reality*. Manchester University Press.

Lake Crane, J. (1994) *Terror in Everyday Life: Singular Moments in the History of the Horror Film*. Sage.

Lazard, L. (2009) ' "You'll Like This – It's Feminist!" Representations of strong women in horrror fiction', *Feminism and Psychology*, 19 (1). Sage.

Levy, A. (2005) *Female Chauvinist Pigs: Women and the Rise of Raunch Culture*. Pocket Books.

Luke, C. (ed.) (1996) *Feminisms and Pedagogies of Everyday Life*. State University of New York Press.

Lyotard, J.F. [1979] (1984) *The Postmodern Condition*. Manchester University Press.

McCombs, M. and Shaw, D. (1972) 'The Agenda-setting Function of Mass Media', *Public Opinion Quarterly* 36 (summer): 176–87.

McKee, R. (1997) Classic Five Part Narrative taken from McKee's story seminar at Northern Alberta Institute of Technology.

McLuhan, M. (1964) *Understanding Media*. Routledge.

McLuhan, M. and McLuhan, E. (1992) *Laws of Media: The New Science*. University of Toronto Press.

McRobbie, A. (1991) *Feminism and Youth Culture: From Jackie to Just 17*. Macmillan.

McRobbie, A. (2008) *The Aftermath of Feminism: Gender, Culture and Social Change*. Sage.

Medhurst, A. (1998) 'Tracing desires: sexuality and media texts', in A. Briggs and P. Cobley (eds) *The Media: An Introduction*. Longman.

Morley, D. (1980) *The Nationwide Audience*. BFI Publishing.

Morley, D. (1986) *Family Television*. Comedia.

Mulvey, L. [1975] (2003) 'Visual pleasure and narrative cimena', in W. Brooker and D. Jermyn (eds) *The Audience Studies Reader*. Routledge.

Nelmes, J. (ed.) (2007) *An Introduction to Film Studies* (3rd edn). Routledge.

Nichols, B. (1991) *Representing Reality*. Indiana University Press.

Nichols, B. (1994) *Blurred Boundaries*. Indiana University Press.

Nichols, B. (2002) *Introduction to Documentary*. Indiana University Press.

Packard, V. [1957] (1979) *The Hidden Persuaders*. Penguin.

Papadopoulos, L. (2010) *Sexualisation of Young People Review* (accessed at http://www.homeoffice.gov.uk/documents/Sexualisation-young-people.pdf).

Perkins, T. (1997) 'Rethinking Stereotypes', in M. Barrett *et al.* (eds) *Ideology and Cultural Production*. Croom Helm.

Perryman, N. (2008) '*Doctor Who* and the Convergence of Media: A case study in transmedia storytelling', *Convergence*, 14 (1): 21–39.

Petley, J. (1999) 'The Regulation of Media Content', in J. Stokes and A. Reading (eds) *The Media in Britain: Current Debates and Developments*. Macmillan.

Poole, E. (2000) 'Media representations and British Muslims', *Dialogue Magazine*.

Postman, N. (1985) *Amusing Ourselves to Death*. Methuen.

Storey, J. (ed.) (1998) *Cultural Theory and Popular Culture: An Introduction*. University of Georgia Press.

Rabiger, M. (2004) *Directing the Documentary*. Focal Press.

Radway, J. (1984) *Reading the Romance: Women, Patriarchy and Popular Literature*. Verso.

Reah, D. (2002) *The Language of Newspapers* (2nd edn). Routledge.

Ross, K. (2000) 'Whose image? TV criticism and black minority viewers', in S. Cottle (ed.) *Ethnic Minorities and the Media*. Open University Press.

Ross, K. and Nightingale, V. (2003) *Media and Audiences: New Perspectives*. Open University Press.

Said, E. (1978) *Orientalism*. Pantheon Books.

Schatz, T. (1981) *Hollywood Genres; Formulas, Film Making and The Studio System*. McGraw-Hill.

Sefton-Green, J. (1998) 'Introduction: Being young in the digital age', in J. Sefton-Green (ed.) *Digital Diversions: Youth Culture in the Age of Multimedia*. UCL Press.

Stacey, J. (1994) *Star Gazing: Hollywood Cinema and Female Spectatorship*. Routledge.

Tilley, A. (1991) 'Narrative', in D. Lusted (ed.) *The Media Studies Book: A Guide for Teachers*. Routledge.

Todorov, T. (1969) *Grammaire du Décameron*. Mouton.

Tunstall, J. (1983) *The Media in Britain*. Constable.

Williams, K. (2003) *Understanding Media Theory*. Arnold.

Williams, R. [1974] (1989) 'Drama in a Dramatised Society', in R. Williams, *On Television*. Routledge.

Williams, R. (1977) *Marxism and Literature*. Oxford University Press.

Winship, J. (1987) *Inside Women's Magazines*. Pandora.

Wolf, N. (1991) *The Beauty Myth: How Images of Beauty Are Used Against Women*. Anchor Press.

Woodward, K. (1997) 'Concepts of identity and difference', in K. Woodward (ed.) *Identity and Difference*. Sage.

Wright Mills, C. (2000) [1956] *The Power Elite*. Oxford University Press.

Useful online resources

Race, Representation and the Media Report (www.channel4.com).
www.guardian.co.uk
www.mediaed.org
www.heromachine2.
www.youtube.com
www.asa.org.uk
www.zeeuk.com
www.manchester.gov.uk
www.nwda.co.uk
www.asiansoundradio.co.uk
www.unityradio.fm
www.manchestereveningnews.co.uk
www.manchestermule.co.uk
www.salfordstar.com
www.screenonline.org
www.youtube.com/shows
http://www.homeoffice.gov.uk/documents/Sexualisation-young-people.pdf
www.vgfreedom.blogspot.com
www.lacan.com/zizekchro1.htm
www.indymedia.org.uk
www.theory.org.uk
http://www.pressgazette.co.uk/section.asp?navcode=161
http://www.abc.org.uk/
http://www.newspapersoc.org.uk/
www.pcc.org.uk

INDEX

Note: page numbers in italics denote figures where they are separated from their textual reference

Communication, Cultural and Media Studies

The Key Concepts

Third Edition

This book provides a topical and authoritative guide to Communication, Cultural and Media Studies, ideal for students of Advanced Subsidiary or Advanced Level courses. It brings together in an accessible form some of the most important concepts that you will need, and shows how they have been – or might be – used. This third edition of the classic text *Key Concepts in Communication and Cultural Studies* forms an up-to-date, multi-disciplinary explanation and assessment of the key concepts and new terms that you will encounter in your studies, from 'anti-globalisation', to 'reality TV', from 'celebrity' to 'tech-wreck'.

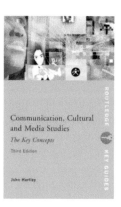

This new edition includes:

- Over 70 new entries
- Coverage of recent developments in the field
- Coverage of interactive media and the 'new economy'
- An extensive bibliography to aid further study

John Hartley is Professor and Dean of the Creative Industries Faculty at Queensland University of Technology, Australia. He is author of many books and articles on television, journalism and cultural studies. His most recent books are: *Popular Reality* (1996), *Uses of Television* (1999), *The Indigenous Public Sphere*, with Alan McKee (2000), *American Cultural Studies: A Reader*, edited with Roberta E. Pearson (2000) and *A Short History of Cultural Studies* (2003).

ISBN 978–0–415–26889–9 (paperback)
ISBN 978–0–203–44993–6 (e-book)

Available at all good bookshops
For ordering and further information please visit
www.routledge.com

Communication Studies: The Essential Resource

Edited by Andrew Beck, Peter Bennett and Peter Wall

This book brings together a huge range of material including academic articles, film scripts and interplanetary messages adrift on space probes with supporting commentary to clarify their importance to the field. *Communication Studies: The Essential Resource* is a collection of essays and texts for all those studying communication at university and pre-university level.

Individual sections address:

- texts and meanings in communication
- themes in personal communication
- communication practice
- culture, communication and context
- debates and controversies in communication.

Edited by the same teachers and examiners who brought us *AS Communication Studies: The Essential Introduction*, this volume will help communications students to engage with the subject successfully. Its key features include:

- suggested further activities at the end of each chapter
- a glossary of key terms
- a comprehensive bibliography with web resources.

ISBN13: 978–0–415–28792–0 (hbk)
ISBN13: 978–0–415–28793–7 (pbk)

Available at all good bookshops
For ordering and further information please visit:
www.routledge.com

Film: The Essential Study Guide

Edited by Ruth Doughty and Deborah Shaw

Providing a key resource to new students, *Film: The Essential Study Guide* introduces all the skills needed to succeed on a film studies course.

This succinct, accessible guide covers key topics such as:

- Using the library
- Online research and resources
- Viewing skills
- How to watch and study foreign language films
- Essay writing
- Presentation skills
- Referencing and plagiarism
- Practical filmmaking

Including exercises and examples, *Film: The Essential Study Guide* helps film students understand how study skills are applicable to their learning and gives them the tools to flourish in their degree.

ISBN13: 978–0–415–43700–4 (pbk)
ISBN 3: 978–0–203–00292–6 (ebk)

Available at all good bookshops
For ordering and further information please visit:
www.routledge.com